Practical Models for Technical Communication

Development Edition

by Shannon Kelley

with additional contributions by Shobana Breeden,
Chris Cottrell, Liaken Hadley, Adam Karnes,
Stephanie Lenox, Brian Mosher,
Magdalen Powers, and Catherine Shride

Practical Models for Technical Communication
ISBN: 978-1-943536-59-7
Development Edition 0.9 (Fall 2019)
© 2019, Chemeketa Community College. All rights reserved.

Special Thanks!
This textbook is being developed with a grant from John and Bobbie Clyde.
Their generous gift supports the involvement of Chemeketa faculty in this project.

Chemeketa Press
Chemeketa Press is a nonprofit publishing endeavor at Chemeketa Community College. Working together with faculty, staff, and students, we develop and publish affordable and effective alternatives to commercial textbooks. All proceeds from the sale of this book will be used to develop new textbooks. For more information, please visit chemeketapress.org.

Publisher: David Hallett
Director: Steve Richardson
Managing Editor: Brian Mosher
Instructional Editor: Stephanie Lenox
Manuscript Support: Stephanie Lenox, Nadia Isom, Taylor Wynia
Design Editor: Ronald Cox IV
Interior Design: Ronald Cox IV, Leo Martinez, Brandi Harbison, Tiana Miller, Brice Spreadbury, Shaun Jaquez, Matt Sanchez
Cover Design: Ronald Cox IV

Acknowledgments appear on page 331 and constitute an extension of the copyright page.

Printed in the United States of America.

Contents

Introduction vii
    To Students vii
    To Faculty viii

Chapter 1: Technical Communication Fundamentals 1
    Why Technical Communication Matters 2
    Technical Communication Defined 3
    The Problem-Solution Framework 5
    Purposeful Communication 7
    Characteristics of Technical Communication 8
    Creating User-Friendly Content 15
    Conclusion 25

Chapter 2: Technical Communication Ethics 27
    Why Ethics Matter 28
    Ethics Defined 29
    Ethics at Work 33
    Distorted or Misleading Information 37
    Visual Misrepresentation 44
    Using Information Ethically 46
    Conclusion 50

Chapter 3: Design and Collaboration 51
    Why Design Matters 52
    Principles of Document Design 55
    Working with Others 73
    Conclusion 76

Chapter 4: Multimodal and Multimedia Communication 77
    Why Multimodal and Multimedia Communication Matter 78
    Multimodal Communication at Work 81
    Rhetorical Awareness and Digital Literacy 84
    Output Options 86
    Conclusion 93

Chapter 5: Research Methods for Technical Communication ... 95
- Why Research Matters ... 96
- Steps for Research ... 99
- Primary and Secondary Research ... 106
- Using Sources Effectively ... 110
- Citing Sources ... 113
- Intellectual Property ... 117
- Advanced Research ... 120
- Conclusion ... 122

Chapter 6: Job Materials ... 123
- Why Job Materials Matter ... 124
- Organize Your Materials ... 127
- Steps for Creating Job Materials ... 133
- Cover Letters ... 135
- Characteristics of Effective Job Materials ... 140
- Job Materials Best Practices ... 145
- Ethical Considerations ... 149
- Putting It All Together ... 150
- Conclusion ... 154

Chapter 7: Workplace Communication ... 155
- Why Workplace Communication Matters ... 156
- Types of Workplace Communication ... 158
- Communicating Professionally ... 171
- Checklist for Business Etiquette ... 176
- Conclusion ... 177

Chapter 8: Technical Definitions and Descriptions ... 179
- Why Definitions and Descriptions Matter ... 180
- Creating Definitions and Descriptions ... 181
- Parenthetical Definitions ... 185
- Sentence Definitions ... 187
- Extended Definitions ... 189
- Descriptions ... 191
- The Known-New Contract ... 195
- Legal and Ethical Implications ... 196
- Conclusion ... 196

Chapter 9: Instructions and Procedures 197
Why Instructions and Procedures Matter 198
Instructions 202
Procedures 209
Usability Testing 215
Legal and Ethical Concerns 220
Conclusion 222

Chapter 10: Proposals and Short Reports 223
Why Proposals and Short Reports Matter 224
Proposals Defined 224
Types of Proposals 229
Typical Elements of a Proposal 230
Short Reports Defined 235
Steps for Writing Proposals and Short Reports 240
Principles for Proposals and Short Reports 242
Conclusion 244

Chapter 11: Formal Reports 245
Why Formal Reports Matter 246
Types of Formal Reports 248
The Steps of a Formal Report 251
Writing the Formal Report 258
Checklist for Revision 268
Conclusion 297

Chapter 12: Make Technical Communication Work for You 299
Bridging the Gap 300
Applying Your Skills 301
Meet the Professionals 307
Tips for Success 312
Conclusion 313

Glossary Index 315

Acknowledgments 331

About Development Editions

Chemeketa Press uses a software development model to publish textbooks that are more affordable and more effective than commercial textbooks. This means that we first publish books like this textbook when they are fully functional and mostly finished, like an early release of a new software program. We then work with the faculty and students who are using the development edition — you, for example — to make improvements, correct errors, and thus prepare the book for its final publication in about a year. Because this is still a work in progress, we've reduced the price to you by 20 percent.

You can join Chemeketa Press in its mission to make textbooks affordable again by helping us finish this textbook. Do you have any suggestions for how we can make this book more effective for you and others? Have you found any errors within chapters? If so, let us know. You can either tell your professor, who will tell us, or you can contact us directly at collegepress@chemeketa.edu. Thanks for your help!

Introduction

To Students

This book began with feedback from students in technical communication courses. They wanted a book with better visuals, organization, and models. They wanted a book that was easy to navigate and streamlined for their needs. They wanted a useful and practical book with a price tag that didn't make them break out in a cold sweat. At every step of the way, the instructors who contributed to this book had you in mind.

Our goal for this book was to avoid writing *about* technical communication. We wanted the book to be a model *for* technical communication. A textbook is, in fact, a technical document. To be effective, the book needs to demonstrate all the principles it teaches. We practiced what we preached when writing this book—communicating concepts with clarity, precision, and conciseness requires multiple drafts and revisions.

This is where you come in. We invite you to approach this development edition as a term-length usability study. In usability testing, the developers of a product evaluate its performance by observing how the target audience use the product. This textbook is designed to provide you with solid tools, useful models, interesting scenarios, and a vocabulary of technical terms that will allow you to communicate effectively as part of a fast-paced, global workforce.

To get the most out of this book, you must first read the pages assigned by your instructor. After you've done that, take a step back and consider how the book, chapter, or section you just read works as an example of technical communication. Like any text, you should approach this book with a curious and critical mind. If a model we provide helps you understand a concept, let your instructor know. If we fail to follow our own rules, let your instructor know. You are part of our development team now. Your collaboration is vital to the success of this project.

How to Read This Book

Instructions are a familiar type of technical document that we explore in this textbook. Instructions guide a user through a process. They must be specific, so some of the steps might seem obvious, like step 1. But their purpose is to make the process possible and even easy for anyone to do. In this section are some instructions to help you get the most out of this book. Welcome to the future of technical communication.

Instructions

1. Take the book in your hand and open it to the assigned chapter.
2. Turn off all devices of distraction.
3. Before reading, scan the headings, bold terms, and marginal notes.
4. Note the placement of figures, tables, and charts.
5. Note how long the chapter is.
6. Skim the abstract and the first sentence of each paragraph.
7. Return to the beginning and start reading.
8. Pause periodically to ask yourself, *How can I use this idea right now?*
9. Record terms and questions that you want to remember for later.

To Faculty

The development edition of *Practical Models for Technical Communication* is the result of countless hours of faculty and student input. Faculty on the development team visited classes, surveyed students, and analyzed the content of all the leading technical communication textbooks. The result is a textbook that is tailored to your students and your classroom. Thank you for using this book and for being a part of its development. Below is a summary of the book's important features.

Key Features

- **Looking Ahead**—Every chapter opens with a table of contents in miniature. This section offers a quick overview of the chapter to assist in your preparation for class.
- **Abstract**—The abstracts at the beginning of each chapter demonstrate concise, specific writing that sums up the chapter. Use this pedagogical element as a classroom exercise to reinforce this essential technical skill. Discuss it, revise it, make it better.
- **Bold Terms and Glossary**—When important terms are first introduced, they are always accompanied by a sentence definition. This book has an entire chapter on technical descriptions and definitions, but each bold term can be treated as a mini-lesson in writing effective definitions. The glossary at the end collects all the definitions for easy reference.
- **Instructional Captions**—The captions are designed to reinforce the visual information provided by the figures. Rather than restating what the student is looking at, the captions provide bite-sized supplemental information about the concept to enhance understanding.

- **Case Studies** — Throughout the book, you'll find case studies that can serve as a conversation starter in the classroom. These compact scenarios show how individuals interact with technical communication principles in the workplace and beyond.
- **Extended Technical Scenarios** — In each chapter, students will follow a character who must create a technical document. As with any good story, each character encounters challenges, and their drafts serve as a starting place for students to begin seeing themselves as technical communicators.
- **Traffic Signals** — Models of technical documents are accompanied by traffic signals that indicate how finished the document is. A red light indicates a document that is at the beginning stages or insufficient. The hope is that you'll stop at these models to examine why they aren't working. Models with a yellow light show a work in progress. Models with a green light are final versions that are ready to go out into the world.
- **Annotated Models** — Marginal notes accompany every model to identify places where the document is working or needs work. The notes encourage your students to interact critically with the documents and understand specific examples of the chapter's concepts.
- **Figures, Tables, and Charts** — Whenever possible, this book aims to translate concepts into visuals to support the text.
- **Problem-Solution Framework** — The Problem-Solution Framework provides a conceptual model for students and instructors to think about the goals of technical communication. This model embraces the importance of purpose, audience, and message and adds to it by emphasizing how technical communicators are hired to solve problems.
- **Marginal Notes** — The notes in the margins reveal the connections within the text by pointing to other chapters where a concept is discussed in greater depth. They also reveal connections beyond the text to provide insight.

How You Can Help

The development team would like to build resources that align with this textbook. If you have a classroom activity, student model, assignment, or syllabus that works with this text, please share it with us. We hope to use these resources (with your permission) to create a toolbox for future instructors who use this textbook. Please feel free to contact us at collegepress@chemeketa.edu.

Chapter 1
Technical Communication Fundamentals

Abstract: Welcome to technical communication. Each chapter begins with an abstract that models concise writing and prepares you for the content to come. As you'll learn in this book, technical communication is a journey from problem to solution. The technical communicator must use and arrange clear, concise, precise, and accurate information to create successful, user-friendly documents. Different media, such as images or videos, often help make this information understandable. The key is to know the material's purpose and its audience (user) and choose the best form for the message. If users can solve their problems or accomplish their goals using content you create, they win, you win, and your employer wins. This chapter also introduces you to the Problem-Solution Framework that will guide your choices as you become a more proficient technical communicator.

Looking Ahead

1. Why Technical Communication Matters

2. Technical Communication Defined

3. The Problem-Solution Framework

4. Purposeful Communication

5. Characteristics of Technical Communication

6. Creating User-Friendly Content

Why Technical Communication Matters

Have you ever tried to explain to someone how to tie their shoes? It's much harder than it seems. You've been tying your own shoes since you were a kid so that now you can do it without thinking. In order to show someone else how to do it, however, you have to take what has become an automatic action and break it down into small steps in a specific order. This process takes mental dexterity. You have to imagine yourself in that person's shoes, literally. You have to recall the frustrating knots you created when you first started. If you do your job well, you build up someone's confidence and prevent them from tripping over their untied laces.

This is your goal in technical communication. With time and practice you can develop the skills you need to make a complex topic sound simple. That's why you're reading this book. In the pages that follow, you will learn how technical communication is similar to the shoe-tying situation above. The ability to explain with clarity is crucial on the job, whether you work for a government think tank, an engineering firm, or a preschool. What's more, you can apply these skills at any stage in your professional development.

Students sometimes dread a course in technical communication because they worry that the word *technical* implies learning complicated and boring material. Some may avoid or postpone the course, assuming that the skills aren't necessary for them. Some may believe they can't be successful because they're not a *writer*. This textbook aims to show you that technical communication isn't hyper-specialized, impractical, or intimidating. Rather, it is valuable and doable. Perhaps the example of another student's experience will convince you.

Maribel was a typical student at Acme Community College (ACC) working toward an associate's degree and, ultimately, a bachelor's in engineering from a four-year college. During her time at ACC, she begrudgingly took a required

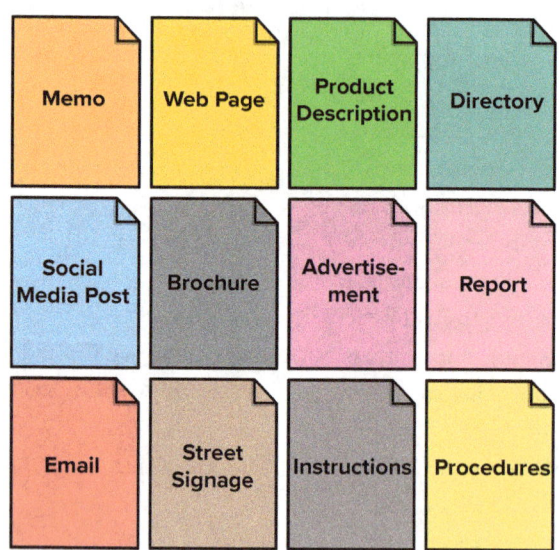

Figure 1. Technical documents take many different forms. The common denominator in technical communication is the creation of content to meet a specific need and produce a desired result for the end user.

course in technical communication. She assumed that the class would be all about creating long, tedious documents, such as instructions for how to set up a wireless printer.

However, Maribel's course taught her that technical communication is about translating complex ideas into language that most people can understand. She'd originally thought that as an engineer she wouldn't need to worry about writing. However, she soon discovered the real task of technical communication is to help people solve problems, and isn't that what they pay engineers to do?

Now, as a full-time engineer, Maribel thinks about helping others understand and solve problems in everything she writes, from simple company emails to high-stakes presentations or plans for new bridges. She now knows she uses technical communication every day, even while teaching her daughter to tie her shoes. This text exists to guide you in a similar process of discovery.

Technical Communication Defined

Technical communication involves generating content about practical information in a field that requires clarity, precision, and accuracy. A technical communicator creates a purposeful message for a specific audience. This can take many forms as you can see in figure 1.

Although written content is one method used by technical communicators, it's not the only one. You'll notice that technical communication is also about formatting, layout, and visual design, not just words on a page. As a result, this book uses the phrase "technical communication" instead of "technical writing." This textbook introduces you to the diversity of approaches to technical communication and a range of communication skills that will be useful in any profession.

Technical documents—the content generated by technical communicators—surround you. For example, a bus stop contains specific information relevant to users of public transportation. Riders need to sort through arrival and departure times quickly and efficiently so they don't miss their bus. Effective design organizes the information, such as what bus stops where, at what time, and where it's headed. When a document like this fails to do its job, the consequences are real.

Consider where and how technical documents intersect with your life. You'll begin to see examples everywhere. Store directories, the washing label

Depending on your field, a **technical document** may have a different name: deliverable, product, report, text, etc.

sewn inside your shirt, heating instructions for a microwave dinner—these are technical documents, too. As simple as these examples sound, they didn't just happen. Someone thought about you when they designed the mall kiosk to help you get to that weird shop that sells pickle-flavored lip balm. The icons on your shirt's label tell you at a glance how to wash your favorite shirt so it lasts longer. Dinner is saved—as well as your delicate taste buds—with instructions that tell you to let the microwaved mashed potatoes sit for five minutes before shoveling them into your mouth.

Technical communicators make information useable and accessible, and this is a valuable skill you can apply to a wide range of occupations. When you learn how to communicate in clear, clean, and crisp sentences, you have an advantage over people who may have technical expertise but cannot explain what they do to a general audience.

Technical communicators are a diverse group. Look around and you'll see several majors represented in your classroom. You might have classmates studying computer science, engineering, business, education, medicine, or human services. Technical communicators could be teachers who provide student reports for extra instructional assistance, nurses who write detailed patient summaries during shift changes to ensure continuity of care, or engineers who create product or process schemas.

Technical communication is about communicating the most direct and effective path toward a solution. Employers and organizations tackle issues, and they need people with advanced communication skills who can translate ideas into plain English. As a technical communicator, your task is to create content that meets specific needs and advances the mission of your employer or client.

This book teaches you how to solve technical problems by focusing on the following concepts in your writing:

- The audience's attributes (called a *user* in this book)
- The purpose of the document
- The message that will resolve the problem

Wherever you might be headed after this, you are responsible for using the tools described in this book to make someone's life easier and, sometimes, safer. Effective technical communication involves creativity, discipline, and resourcefulness. Your job is to anticipate roadblocks and clear the path for users.

The Problem-Solution Framework

In an ideal world, technical communicators wouldn't be necessary. Instead, everyone would work through their daily tasks without encountering problems. That ideal world doesn't exist, unfortunately. Individuals often encounter obstacles—complex technical problems—that prevent them from completing tasks. Most users need outside help to move beyond the obstacle.

This is where a technical communicator comes in. Technical communicators can use the **Problem-Solution Framework** to develop a solution in the form of a technical document. When technical communicators consider purpose and audience, they craft a solution in the form of a message (figure 2).

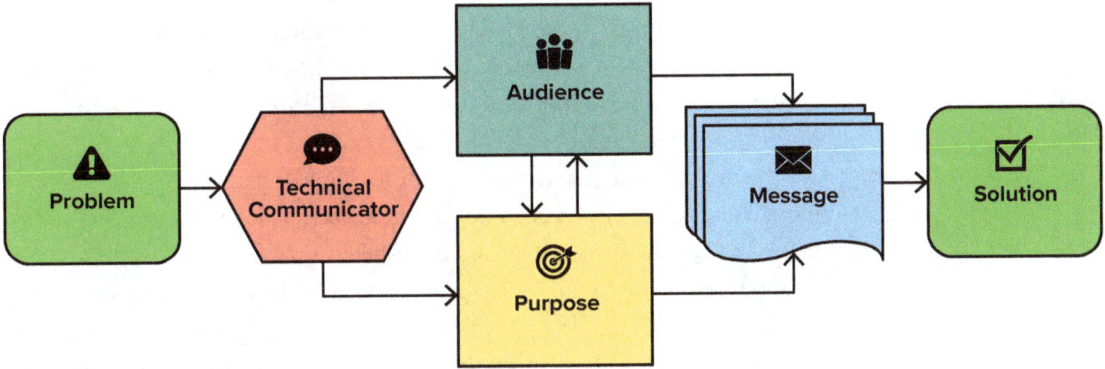

Figure 2. The Problem-Solution Framework allows the technical communicator to think through an assignment, including the task's purpose, audience, and message, before creating a technical document.

Purpose

Your **purpose** in any technical document is to guide the user to a successful solution. Purpose is the reason for the document's existence and guides all the choices involved in the document's completion. The way you write the document, its length, its style—all components—need to relate back to the purpose.

Audience

The intended users of the document are the **audience**. The way you communicate will vary from one document to the next because of differences in audience. You don't guide a professional coder in the same way you do a first-time computer user, for example.

Message

What you communicate—the language and visuals of a text—forms the **message**. The document's message results from your consideration of the document's purpose and audience. Within this message, you can usually find a call to action, which could be as simple as "please review and respond by noon tomorrow" or as involved as "this report recommends the replacement of all office chairs with ergonomic models to prevent employee injury."

The Framework in Context

One simple way to visualize the Problem-Solution Framework is to think of a three-legged stool (figure 3). The solution is a stool that's strong enough to support a user. The three legs of the stool are the elements of purpose, audience, and message. Without all three legs—all three elements—the stool can't support weight and will collapse.

Here is another way to think about it. Suppose you need a shelf for your room. You stack books on every horizontal surface, which displaces your roommate. To keep the peace, you buy a bookshelf from a furniture distributor that sells inexpensive products—inexpensive because the customers assemble the furniture themselves. If you've ever tried to put together a table, or shelf, or whatever, on your own with just the instructions, you know how vulnerable you are. You are at the mercy of the technical communicator.

Let's hope the person making the instructions has kept the Problem-Solution Framework in mind. They know your purpose—to assemble the much-needed shelf without throwing pieces of it at your roommate in frustration. They know about you, the audience—an intelligent but otherwise average person who is not a builder of furniture or even the least bit handy. They know that the instructions (the message) must be simple, clear, and detailed enough to take you step by step through building a shelf that will sit level and hold your collection of sci-fi novels and vegan cookbooks.

You'll encounter the Problem-Solution Framework in future chapters. For now, familiarize yourself with how a technical communicator moves a user from problem to solution.

Figure 3. This stool is another way to think about the Problem-Solution Framework. The document's purpose, audience, and message all work together to support the solution.

Purposeful Communication

More now than ever, the ways we access and use information are constantly and rapidly changing. Technical communicators must adapt quickly to the expectations and reading habits of their audiences. For example, when was the last time you read a web page from beginning to end? When you got your new phone, did you sit down to read the user's manual? How do you find what you need on an online schedule compared with a printed schedule? Think about those questions for a minute. Consider the implications for the design of those documents.

Using versus Reading Documents

In this textbook, technical documents refer to any mode of communication, whether online or in print, designed to meet a specific need. This means a video, a web page, or a résumé are all considered documents, and it's important to think critically about how you *use* them.

Using documents might be a new concept for you. You're likely more familiar with reading them. Why does this distinction matter?

The difference between *using* and *reading* shows how today's audience interacts with documents. For centuries, print media—books, newspapers, and letters—represented the primary way to give and get information. Now, thanks to Google and social media and celebrity cat memes, we live in an age of information overload. We don't interact with content simply as readers. Instead, we look for ways to use content, and we want it to be quick, easy, and attractive. We doubt you've read your phone's manual, but if you did, it would likely be because you've encountered a problem. This is where all technical communication begins.

Designing for Use

Because of this emphasis on using over reading, technical documents don't focus on text alone, and sometimes not at all. IKEA furniture instructions, for example, present a series of images that show users how to assemble their products. In this way, IKEA communicates a multistep process to their international audience. Customers in Denmark use the same documents as customers in Austria and complete the assembly using just the images.

The technical communicators who create documents such as these have power to influence the user's experience, so the stakes are high. But you've got this. Ever since you first learned how to tie your shoes or read, you've been sorting out what's important from what's not. You make snap judgments about the usefulness of a document without thinking about it. Your eye scans for headings, bold text, menus, images, video play buttons, and so forth. You are an information *user*.

You are a designer of information, too. Think about the directions you gave to your house for your cousin's graduation party. You explained how to get there turn by turn and included street names. Visitors in the past have complained about being unable to see your house number, so you provided another landmark to guide people to your party. Most arrived as planned and close to on time. Your experience as both a user and designer of information means that you already have significant knowledge about technical communication, although you might not have recognized it as such.

Characteristics of Technical Communication

You might wonder what makes technical communication different from other forms of communication. Many students assume that technical communication is unique and find it surprising when they see that technical communication shares characteristics with other forms of communication. Many of the concepts you've studied in other writing or composition courses carry over to technical communication.

What makes technical communication different is the emphasis on communicating technically complex or practical information. You can see this difference most clearly when you compare technical writing with creative writing (figure 4).

Three attributes that distinguish technical communication are its emphasis on multiple modes and media, its focus on the user, and its concern with the needs of the audience. When technical communicators craft their messages, they keep these concerns in mind.

Chapter 1: Technical Communication Fundamentals

Creative Writing

From Jack London's "To Build a Fire"

Focuses on the main character

Uses descriptive language

Uses imagery and metaphor

Selects words to create a scene or feeling

Varies sentence length and complexity

[He gathered] dry firewood--sticks and twigs principally, but also larger portions of seasoned branches and fine, dry, last-year's grasses. He threw down several large pieces on top of the snow. This served for a foundation and prevented the young flame from drowning itself in the snow it otherwise would melt. The flame he got by touching a match to a small shred of birch-bark that he took from his pocket. This burned even more readily than paper. Placing it on the foundation, he fed the young flame with wisps of dry grass and with the tiniest dry twigs. . . . Gradually, as the flame grew stronger, he increased the size of the twigs with which he fed it. . . . He worked methodically, even collecting an armful of the larger branches to be used later when the fire gathered strength.

Technical Writing

How to Build a Fire in the Snow

Focuses on the end user (implied "you")

Uses directive language

Uses specific and precise details

Uses active voice to show action

Uses sentences that are direct and simple

1. Gather at least 3 armfuls of dry sticks, twigs, and grasses. They should range in size from under an inch in diameter (kindling) to 3 inches or larger (logs).
2. Lay 3 or 4 of the logs on the ground to form a base to protect the early flames from being extinguished by the wet ground.
3. Lay 2 or 3 handfuls of the kindling on and around the logs.
4. Use a flint or match to strike a flame and hold it to the smallest kindling.
5. Add wood gradually, increasing the size of the sticks as the fire grows in strength until it reaches the desired size.
6. Add wood to the fire when it begins to decrease.

Figure 4. Examine this comparison of creative writing and technical writing. Consider the context and purpose of each type of writing. How do the audience's expectations differ for each? When and where might someone encounter each selection?

Multimodal and Multimedia

Technical communicators must weigh the needs of the audience, the technical content, and the form that the content will take. Today's users prefer interactive documents presented in a variety of forms. Lack of choice frustrates users who are accustomed to accessing information in multiple ways. Two terms that can help us think about this distinction are mode and medium.

- **Mode** refers to how a user will interact with content.
- **Medium** relates to the delivery or storage of information, in other words, how information gets to the user.

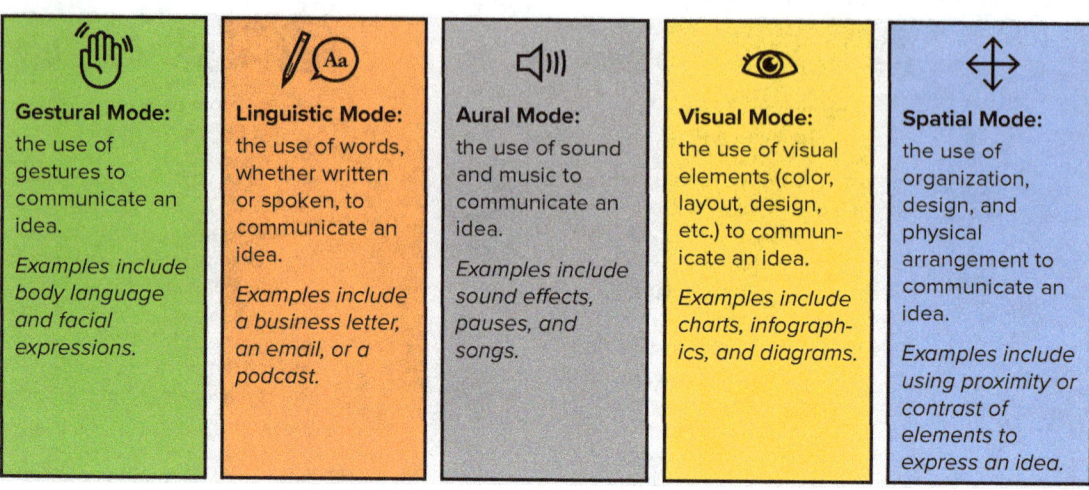

Figure 5. *Technical communication is multimodal. You may not use all these modes all of the time, but it's important to make conscious choices about which mode or combination of modes best convey your ideas.*

See **Chapter 4** for an extended exploration of multimodal communication.

Different modes of communication include linguistic (words), aural (sounds), visual (images), spatial (arrangement), and gestural (movement) (figure 5). A document with more than one of these modes uses multimodal communication. While most YouTube videos involve all five modes, a hearing-impaired person interacts differently with the video than a hearing person does.

This textbook is a medium. A PowerPoint presentation is a medium. A podcast is a medium. **Media** is the plural form of medium, so **multimedia communication** is when a technical communicator makes use of more than one method of delivery. Think of a web page that has more than one of these media in one place. That's a good example of multimedia.

User-Focused

Consider for a moment the essays, reports, and research papers you've written for other courses. Did you think about your audience? Many students—if they think about their audience at all—focus on what the teacher has stated about the assignment (how many pages, the topic, and other required elements). This is a common view of documents produced for school. You write to satisfy the requirements rather than to satisfy a user.

Now, contrast that with text messages you've sent or posts you've put up on social media. Who was the intended audience? For that text message, it was your friend, right? You wrote those words for a specific person. And with the social media post? You know your followers will see it. Maybe there are even a few followers you are hoping won't see it (such as your parents or employer). For both messages, you used language and images to capture your audience's attention.

In this book, we refer to the audience for technical communication as **users**, people who use your document to accomplish something. Once you enter the workforce, however, you will have another audience to consider—the client.

Clients are people who pay you for work. They hire technical communicators to create content for them. You're not just writing for the end user—the people who come to the website and see the blog post you've written or the patients waiting in the doctor's office who pick up the pamphlet you designed. No, you are also writing to meet the needs of a client, someone who pays you or who offers you experience in the form of an internship. Because they are paying you in cash or experience, clients expect you to do what they ask. It's challenging to balance these demands, but that's what you need to do if you want to keep your job. It requires you to have knowledge of the product, the process, the users, and the client.

Look at the following case study to consider what can happen when the user's experience is not considered.

User-Focused Content: A Case Study

In her second year at Acme Community College, Maribel began looking at four-year universities. She found a school in southern California that looked like a good fit. So Maribel scheduled a tour of the campus, purchased a flight into the Orange County airport, and rented a car with Speedy Car Rental. When her flight landed, Maribel pulled up the rental confirmation on her phone and followed the instructions to "Ground Transportation."

At Ground Transportation, she saw a sign for "Rental Cars" with an arrow pointing to the left and for "Shuttles" pointing to the right (figure 6). The sign was clear. The only problem was that Speedy Car Rental was not listed.

She checked her email from Speedy again but found no further instructions. After asking at the Cheap-O-Cars counter, Maribel

Figure 6. Where in the world is Speedy Car Rental?

dragged her suitcase back to the "Shuttles" location and asked for help again.

"Excuse me, where do I catch the shuttle to Speedy Car Rental?"

The attendant pointed to a florescent pink sign that read, "Shuttles every fifteen minutes."

Maribel waited for thirty minutes. Shuttles came and went, but none for Speedy Car Rental. Then she noticed a bulletin board with several papers pinned to it. One torn sheet of white paper announced that "Speedy Car Rental has arranged to partner with Holiday Hotel shuttle." After travelling all day and searching all over for simple information, Maribel was fuming.

Right on schedule, the Holiday Hotel shuttle arrived. But, as she lugged her suitcase up the steps of the bus, she couldn't help wondering what else could go wrong.

- How many instances of technical communication can you identify in this scenario?
- Which failed the user? Why?
- What human factors in this scenario affected how information was communicated and received?
- What environmental conditions contributed to these failed modes of communication?
- What could have been done to make these technical documents more user-friendly?

Need-Driven

To create content for specific users, you need to understand their needs. If you miss the mark here, your product will fail no matter how professional it appears. This idea — that you have to know your audience's needs — is essential in technical communication. You'll encounter this concept many more times before you finish this textbook.

How do you get a solid idea of your audience and their needs? First, stop and take a careful look at who your users might be. Get detailed. The more you understand their experiences, the more likely you are to meet their needs. You may need to step outside your comfort zone and get to know more about their culture, demographic, and desires.

Avoid the temptation to say you're writing for a general audience. For example, a writer contacts a book editor to assist with his second book after poor sales of his first book. The first question the editor asks is, "Who is your intended audience?"

"Everyone," the writer replies. "Everyone should read this book." This could be true, but most successful books target a particular type of reader who wants a particular reading experience. Useful technical communication focuses on a specific user as well. To be successful, you need to be intentional and systematic in understanding what that person wants and needs. One way to do this is to create a user profile.

Creating a User Profile

Unless you are producing content for a group of people you already know well, you will need to conduct research to understand your audience. A **user profile** collects information about your potential audience assembled through interviews, surveys, reports, or conversations with your client. In other words, a user profile requires you to conduct primary research. These firsthand accounts can help you determine the user's **demographics**, which are the unique characteristics of your target audience (figure 7).

To access a useful resource for **demographic data** about populations within the United States, visit www.usa.gov/statistics.

Demographic Categories	Questions to get to know your user better
Age	How old is your typical user? What is the general age range? Do you have a multigenerational audience?
Education	How experienced are they? What level of schooling have they completed?
Gender	Which genders are you aiming at? And are you excluding any genders?
Income	How much money do your users make?
Interests	What hobbies and interests do your users share?
Language	What is their native language? How many languages do they speak?
Location	Where in the world are they? Big city? Small town? Out in the country? Desert? Mountains? Oceanside? Developed or developing nation?
Mode of Travel	What kind of car do they drive? Do they use public transportation? Ride a bike? Walk?
Nationality	Are your users primarily from a specific country?
Politics	How do they align with various political frameworks or concepts?

Figure 7. Use these categories and questions to develop a user profile.

The more you define your typical users, the more you can anticipate their needs. This includes the ways they might use your content, the potential pitfalls, and the level of detail and explanation you need to include.

Each document has unique needs based on the problem it is solving. The specifics of this problem determine the content and design of the document. You should tailor the presentation of a document to the needs of your particular audience. Consider the following scenario to see how this concept plays out.

Need-Driven Content: A Case Study

A recipe is a technical document that solves the problem of how to make a certain dish. The content focuses on ingredients, preparation instructions, safety warnings, and alternatives or troubleshooting tips. The design focuses on presenting this content in a way that makes it easy to follow. Compare these two approaches for a soufflé recipe to see how content and design should work together.

Example 1:
A nicely risen soufflé can be impressive, and I think you can do it once you get the hang of it. If you want a cheesy soufflé, you can add Swiss cheese and even some chives to the sauce mix (butter, egg yolks, flour, milk, salt, and pepper) once they're all mixed and cooked together, but before you put it in the oven, which must already be at temperature. Don't fold the whites in all at once. Do it in two batches. Make sure they're stiff, but don't let them get dry. Make sure you prepare the dish so the soufflé doesn't stick. When it sticks, it's almost as frustrating as when it doesn't rise. Timing is also very important. You want it to come out of the oven right as you want to serve it.

Example 2:

Soufflé

2 tbsp butter

2 tbsp all-purpose flour

½ tsp salt

pepper, as desired

¾ cup milk

4 eggs & 2 egg whites

¼ tsp cream of tartar

Preheat oven to 375F.

Melt butter in a saucepan over low heat and add flour, salt, and pepper.

Cook and stir until smooth.

Add milk.

Keep stirring for approximately 20 minutes until smooth and thick.

- In what ways is the content different? What about the design?
- What additions contribute to the readability of the second recipe?
- In both, what assumptions does the recipe make about its user's cooking experience?

Creating User-Friendly Content

Content refers to anything you communicate through your document, including text, image, video, or audio. While many examples of technical content do an adequate job of conveying ideas, the best forms of technical communication present information in ways that are easy to understand. This does not mean "dumbing down" information for your user. The responsibility for creating user-friendly content is yours. Do not make your user work to understand you.

When you write clearly, you show respect for your user's time and attention. You can improve technical documents' usability by making content clear, concise, precise, accurate, and both scannable and skimmable. The following sections will explore these ideas in more detail.

Be Clear

Users come to you, or a document you created, with a goal in mind. They want to accomplish a task, learn something new, or fix a problem. **Clarity** means creating understandable content through your words, sentences, and organization so users can take action. When a document is clear, the reader gets what they need with as little effort as possible. When a document isn't clear, the reader may give up in frustration.

Specialized terminology—something you'll encounter frequently in technical communication—can be a source of frustration for a general audience. Experts often develop their own language when they talk to each other. However, when you're creating content for users, you need to keep in mind what they know and what they need to know. Just like in the shoe-tying example at the beginning of the chapter, experts must break down their knowledge into smaller, incremental steps that a novice can follow. Take note of the difference in usability between the two examples on the next pages (figure 8).

Clear writing also means presenting content in a logical sequence. An organized sentence presents information in the order the user needs it. Sentences written in active voice tend to be clearer because they state directly who is doing what. For instance, take a second look at the final paragraphs in figure 8. The first letter reads, "For your review, an itemized list of labor and materials is attached." A more direct and active version can be found in the second letter: "Please review the itemized list of labor and materials I've attached." Clear organization begins at the sentence level and extends throughout the entire document.

Practical Models for Technical Communication

Most users won't read every word in a technical document, which is why clear organization is a must. Headings, subheadings, numbers, bullets, and verbal organizers help users track the information and find what they need. Take a look at the two versions of this flyer to see how simple changes can clarify your message, even if you don't change a word (figure 9).

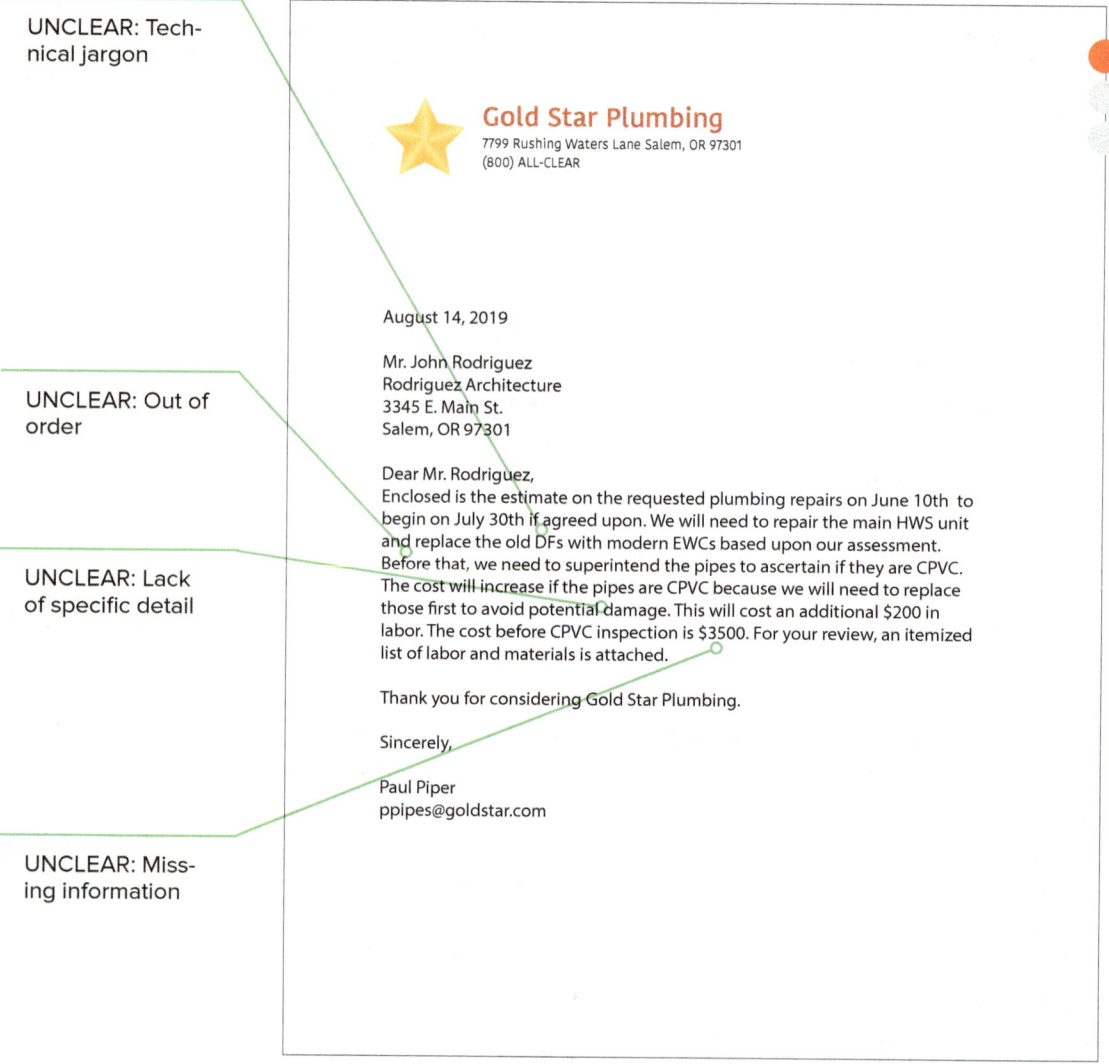

Figure 8. Your first drafts of any technical document are likely to need some revision. Notice the way the second letter takes a step back and considers the audience and how to organize information in a way that will be easy to read and understand.

Chapter 1: Technical Communication Fundamentals

Gold Star Plumbing
7799 Rushing Waters Lane Salem, OR 97301
(800) ALL-CLEAR

August 14, 2019

Mr. John Rodriguez
Rodriguez Architecture
3345 E. Main St.
Salem, OR 97301

Dear Mr. Rodriguez,

Per your June 10th request, I have completed the estimate for the building's plumbing repairs. We would like to begin on July 30th, with your approval.

We first need to make sure that the pipes are not chlorinated polyvinyl chloride (CPVC). These are known to break easily and could cause significant water damage. They would need to be replaced prior to the other repairs. Once completed, we will repair the main water heater and replace the old drinking fountains with new electrical ones.

The total cost including the pipe inspection is $3700. If we need to replace the pipes, it will be an additional $500, for a total of $4200. Please review the itemized list of labor and materials I've attached, and let me know if you have any questions or concerns.

Thank you for considering Gold Star Plumbing.

Sincerely,

Paul Piper
ppipes@goldstar.com

CLEAR: Verbal organizers help with sequencing of information.

SIMPLE: The technical term remains but the letter now explains what it means.

SIMPLE: Mr. Rodriguez is an architect, not a plumber, so this language is more understandable.

CLEAR: The numbers add up now. The next step is plainly spelled out.

Practical Models for Technical Communication

> Verbal organizers help break up the text.

> Dense paragraphs lower readability. No one really wants to read a paragraph that looks like this.

Tips for Buying a New Car

Buying a new car does not have to be stressful. It can even be a worthwhile experience with a little preparation. Here are a few tips to make car shopping simple.

First, do a bit of homework on your finances before you head to the dealership. Answer the following questions: How much is your old car worth as a trade-in? Visit the Kelley Blue Book website to see how much you can reasonably expect for your vehicle. How much can you afford monthly? Consider how much you are willing and able to finance and for how long. The length of the loan means more interest. Check with your bank or credit union to see what types of loans they have available so that you can compare it to what the dealer's creditors offer. Do you have a down payment? Remember that some dealers have "no money down" offers, others don't. How much are you able to pay for car insurance? Keep in mind that buying a new vehicle will most likely increase your premiums. The more the vehicle is worth, the higher the cost to insure it.

Next, consider your current needs. Answer the following questions: What is the vehicle primary purpose? Think about who and what you will be hauling around — just yourself, kids, other adults, work materials, groceries. How often will you drive it and for how far? Consider gas mileage and whether the car with be a daily driver or weekend fun. What is your style? Make a list of the features you want in a car and how these coincide with your needs. You may like the look of a sporty sedan but need a minivan. What are your options? Do some legwork to find vehicles that meet your needs and offer you a style that you enjoy. Within these, which ones have the best customer and safety ratings? Which ones work within your budget?

Finally, know that the dealer is there to make money – the salesperson is not your friend. If you visit the car lot armed with knowledge you are less likely to drive away with something you regret. Be patient with the process and shop around until you find a dealer that can meet your needs.

Figure 9. In the first example, no effort has been made to enhance the document's appearance. In the second version on the next page, the use of headings, subheadings, bold text, and bullets make the content easier to read.

TIPS FOR BUYING A NEW CAR

Buying a new car does not have to be stressful. It can even be a worthwhile experience with a little preparation. Here are a few tips to make car shopping simple.

Know before You Go - $$$

First, do a bit of homework on your finances before you head to the dealership. Answer the following questions:

- **How much is your old car worth as a trade-in?** Visit the Kelley Blue Book website to see how much you can reasonably expect for your vehicle.
- **How much can you afford monthly?** Consider how much you are willing and able to finance and for how long. The length of the loan means more interest. Check with your bank or credit union to see what types of loans they have available so that you can compare it to what the dealer's creditors offer.
- **Do you have a down payment?** Remember that some dealers have "no money down" offers, others don't.
- **How much are you able to pay for car insurance?** Keep in mind that buying a new vehicle will most likely increase your premiums. The more the vehicle is worth, the higher the cost to insure it.

Know before You Go – Make and Model

Next, consider your current needs. Answer the following questions:

- **What is the vehicle's primary purpose?** Think about who and what you will be hauling around — just yourself, kids, other adults, work materials, groceries.
- **How often will you drive it and for how far?** Consider gas mileage and whether the car with be a daily driver or weekend fun.
- **What is your style?** Make a list of the features you want in a car and how these coincide with your needs. You may like the look of a sporty sedan but need a minivan.
- **What are your options?** Do some legwork to find vehicles that meet your needs and offer you a style that you enjoy. Within these, which ones have the best customer and safety ratings? Which ones work within your budget?

Know before You Go – The Dealer

Finally, know that the dealer is there to make money – the salesperson is not your friend. If you visit the car lot armed with knowledge you are less likely to drive away with something you regret. Be patient with the process and shop around until you find a dealer that can meet your needs.

Headings grab people's attention and let them know what the document or section is about.

Subheadings categorize information, increase readability, and allow readers to find what they need easily.

Bullets break up the monotony of reading and single out important items.

Notice the consistent organization. Questions are in bold followed by sentences of similar length and form.

Be Concise

Conciseness means that your document has enough detail and information without unnecessary content. For example, your first draft of an email to your boss might look like this: "The first widget worked better than the second one because it was faster and easier to use." There's nothing wrong about this sentence, but consider your audience. If your boss receives over two hundred emails a day, wouldn't she prefer something more to the point? Your second draft gets you there: "The first widget outperformed the second."

The first time you describe a process or give instructions you might use more words than necessary. That's normal. Make a game out of hunting for every opportunity to trim your sentences, even by a word or two. With time, you can cultivate a habit of concise writing, or at least rewriting for conciseness.

New writers sometimes over-explain or use more words than necessary to describe a concept. The same can be true of writers who are familiar with a

Wordy	Concise
A majority of writers struggle to write **in a way that is** concise.	Most writers struggle to write concisely.
In many cases, writers **are in a position to** solve the problem by eliminating fillers.	Often writers can solve the problem by eliminating fillers.
Another common cause of wordiness is **the use of redundant, repetitive, and recurring** phrases.	Additionally, redundancy causes wordiness.
Perhaps it could be hedging and **the tendency to utilize very** unnecessary qualifiers **that** also contribute to wordiness.	Hedging and unnecessary qualifiers also contribute to wordiness.
The meaning of hedging **is when** a writer **attempts to mitigate a potential loss and safeguard his or her statements with exceptions that allow for unstated contingencies or for a withdrawal from commitment.**	Insecure writers hedge to avoid direct statement. (The wordy example contains so many fillers that a complete rewrite is necessary.)

Figure 10. Study how these sentences move from wordy to concise. The phrases or words **tend** to result in less efficient writing.

topic—they might struggle to decide what is necessary for the audience. The examples in figure 10 translate wordy sentences into more concise versions. Look again, and you'll notice that it's the tiny words that often set up a writer for wordiness: *of, in, it, is, that, to*. These are some of the most common words in the English language. You need these words to hold a sentence together. Too many of them, however, can overwhelm the words that carry information and overburden your user.

Technical communication gets to the point. When your content is concise, it means that you have removed **redundancy**, the unnecessary repetition of words, phrases, or ideas. It also means that you've cut out anything unrelated or irrelevant, no matter how clever it feels to you. Think of your sentences like a simple machine. Avoid additional parts that don't help to move it forward.

Be Precise

To make your content precise means to focus it like a laser. This idea applies to the overall organization of your documents, paragraphs, and sentences, but precision is most evident at the word level. When you express your meaning through laser-focused words that meet your audience's needs, you achieve **precision**.

You can make your writing precise by using the ladder of abstraction, a concept developed by English professor S.I. Hayakawa in his book *Language in Thought and Action*. Picture a ladder with words on four levels. At the bottom level are words that are specific, tangible, or concrete. As you move up the ladder, the words become less specific, more general, and more abstract. Precision often involves using language that is more concrete and specific, as you see in the words on the first level of the ladder of abstraction (figure 11).

A thesaurus can also be a great way to find the exact word. A thesaurus is a reference guide that contains a list of synonyms (words with similar meanings) for common words. Microsoft

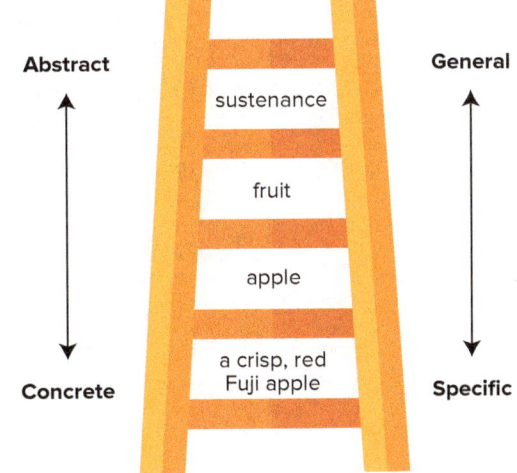

Figure 11. Precision in writing requires words that we can see clearly and recognize. The ladder of abstraction is one way to think about how you can move from general to specific language.

Word has a simplified thesaurus. Most online dictionaries also have a thesaurus component. You can also find print thesauruses, which makes great reference tools.

A thesaurus must be used with caution, though. New writers often select random words from the thesaurus to make their writing sound more intelligent. This practice decreases your clarity and precision. Writer Stephen King warns against the use of a thesaurus because "any word you have to hunt for in a thesaurus is the wrong word." The best word, in his opinion, is the word you already know and the word you know your audience knows.

Consider the different meanings for each of these synonyms for "old":

- Obsolete
- Vintage
- Old-fashioned
- Neolithic
- Classic

If you are talking about a piece of software, calling it "obsolete" would imply that it is no longer in use and has lost its value. Calling it "vintage" means it may have accrued value for collectors and is still being used in some fashion. Either of these words is more precise than the word "old."

While native and non-native speakers of English know thousands of words, a person's daily use of the language is a fraction of that total. Rather than looking in the thesaurus for fancy words, search for the familiar word that conveys precisely what you want to say.

Be Accurate

While precision deals with using the most appropriate content for the situation, accuracy refers to using content based on verifiable information. **Accuracy** means that a document is free of error. Keeping a document accurate requires that you avoid making assumptions or telling yourself that it's "close enough." This means you need to research any gaps in your knowledge before you try to instruct, inform, or persuade someone to do something. As you aim for accuracy, make sure you have a clear distinction between facts, inferences, and judgments.

Facts

Facts are verifiable. When you write a college paper or a researched report, you provide documentation of your sources so your audience (your teacher) can check that your information is factual. In many technical fields, facts are data. **Data** are the bits of information—typically numbers—a communicator uses to support a larger idea.

A single data set needs context and explanation to be factual in a useful sense. For example, try to make meaning out of this data: the National Highway Traffic Safety Administration (NHTSA) states that there were 34,439 fatal crashes in 2016. This piece of data is interesting, but it needs more context to be useful. Is that number an increase or decrease from years prior? What is the distribution of these fatal crashes? Are fatalities more common in certain states than others?

Inferences

Inferences are conclusions based on data. When you make an inference from the available facts, you make meaning of the data. You need more than one data set to reach any reasonable conclusions, otherwise you risk making false statements. In many technical fields, it's expensive or dangerous to make recommendations based on insufficient data.

As you saw in the previous example, the 2016 statistic about fatal auto crashes can't support an accurate inference. The fact merely exists. If you add another fact to the first one, you can begin to make connections that lead to a reasonable inference. For example, of the 34,439 fatal crashes in 2016, 10,111 were caused by speeding. What do these facts, side by side, tell you?

Judgments

When you form an opinion based on facts, inferences, and values, you express a **judgment** in the form of a recommended course of action. As a technical communicator, you need to share judgments that are accurate and ethical.

Based on the fatal crash data on speeding, you could make a judgment that "if fewer people drove above legal speed limits, fewer crashes might occur, so people should not speed in their cars." This would be a reasonable and accurate judgment, given this data.

Be Scannable and Skimmable

Scanning means to look for a specific piece of information in a document. If you need to call your doctor, you might scan the doctor's website for different ways to contact the office. Or you might search for the return policy on a receipt for a sweater that didn't fit right. In both cases, you know the information is available—you just need to find its specific location.

Skimming is different. **Skimming** means you look for the general or main ideas of a document. Readers do this to get a sense of the overall organization or key ideas in a document. Newspaper headlines are a great example. If you skimmed a newspaper and read only the headlines you would have a general idea of that day's news. You can use this tactic with scholarly articles and studies, which can be long and dense. If you scan the abstract, introduction, and discussion, you can get a sense of what the study covers and whether it applies to your research.

Take a moment to notice how your eyes move across this screenshot of a web page in figure 12. The visual elements on this page allow your eyes to scan for useful information. Your eye will most likely land first in the top left-hand corner of the page because that is where our eyes have been trained to

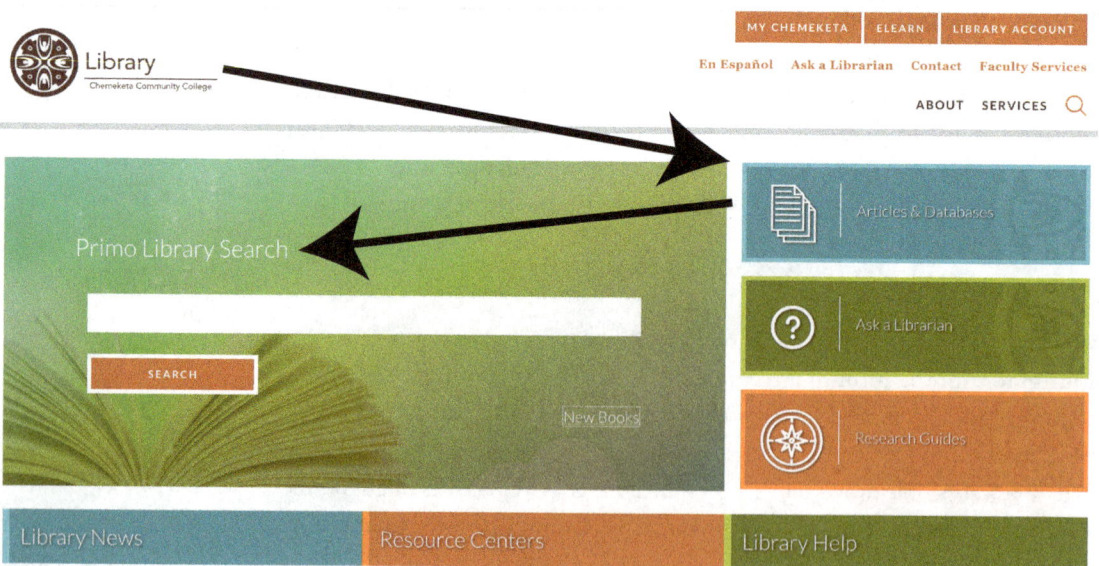

Figure 12. Web pages are designed to be scanned. The directional lines show how the structure of the page helps you find what you need. The principles of design will be discussed in more detail in Chapter 3.

go ever since we learned how to read. Where does your eye go next? The icons on the right draw the user to the most frequently accessed information on the site. And next? Your eye bounces to the search bar where you can begin looking for materials for your next report.

In the Information Age, audiences expect to be able to scan and skim content. Consider the way a potential employer reviews a résumé, for instance. Your use of headings, subheadings, bullet points, lists, bold, italics, and white space can help direct the employer's eye to important information that will set you apart as an applicant. This concept connects basic design with your content. Effective design allows the user's eye to move over the page and grasp the major points without sustained effort. It is a new form of literacy. Your ability to write and design content for this method of reading is a must.

See **Chapter 6** for more about effective design of job materials.

Conclusion

If you started this text feeling intimidated, we hope you see all the ways that you've already been creating and using technical communication. Technical documents need not be complicated or tedious. Maybe you can identify with Maribel, the student who went from being wary of technical writing to finding it challenging and rewarding.

Equipped with an introductory knowledge of technical communication, you're ready to look in more detail at the specific considerations that effective communicators weigh in all compositions, such as design, collaboration, or research. The next chapter considers ethical communication. In it you'll learn how to keep your technical communication professional, honest, and accessible to all users.

Chapter 2
Technical Communication Ethics

Abstract: The creation of technical content involves choices. As a communicator, you make rhetorical decisions and design choices. You also make choices about what to include, what to exclude, and how to transfer that information to your user. Sometimes these choices have consequences. Every expert encounters the ethical dilemmas of his or her industry. When needs conflict—between your employer and your user or between your workload and your deadline or between your company and its customers—that's when you need to think clearly about where you stand. Most professions have a code of ethics, and this chapter introduces you to a code for technical communicators. These guiding principles will help you avoid distorting information (whether intentionally or unintentionally) and ensure that you respect yourself and the work of others.

Looking Ahead

1. Why Ethics Matter
2. Ethics Defined
3. Ethics at Work
4. Distorted or Misleading Information
5. Using Information Ethically

Why Ethics Matter

As a student and developing professional, your understanding of technical communication ethics is crucial. Ethical communication requires that you be responsible and reliable in what and how you communicate. Making the right choice isn't always easy—social pressures, stress, and time constraints can tempt people to cut corners. Because of this, it's important to remember that technical communicators are expected to provide audiences with the correct tools to make informed choices.

For example, a project lead needs an honest progress report to know whether a project is on track. If your report avoids telling the ugly truth that the project is over budget and behind schedule, you may spare the lead's feelings but ultimately risk their job or yours. Whatever the message, the audience must trust the quality of the communication and the technical communicator's honesty. Besides, the long-term consequences for unethical choices aren't worth the short-term gain. To better understand how ethics work in a professional setting, let's take a look at the decisions of one employee.

Recent graduate Kamaal now works in the student advising department for a small college. Kamaal spends part of his time creating technical documents to help students learn about career planning. He's behind in producing a document on the current job market. While researching online, he finds the exact information he needs. Kamaal considers copying the information, presenting it as his own, and submitting the document for approval to his boss. This seems like a great way to save some time. Besides, who's really going to notice?

Kamaal knows that copying information without acknowledgment is considered intellectual theft. It's a convenient solution, and it's unlikely anyone would notice. But what if Kamaal's boss decides to fact-check his data and finds the original document online? Kamaal didn't stay home from countless parties to study for his degree only to throw it all away with an unethical decision. Instead, he finds the original document, uses the information there to build his own document, and provides a reference list using Chicago style, which is what his boss expects.

Kamaal saw an "easy way out," but instead he exercised professionalism by doing the extra work and fulfilling the expectations of his boss. An ethical communicator is just that: a person who is professional in all communication. If Kamaal had made the unethical choice and got caught, he could have lost the trust of his boss or his job. Even if he didn't get caught, the choice to plagiarize is not harmless. If the original information was inaccurate or outdated, the end user—in this case, students—could have made serious missteps in their career planning based on what they read in Kamaal's document.

Ethics Defined

Ethics can be described as a system of principles or morals that determine the actions of an individual or a group. Ethical questions are not easily answered. They are rarely yes-no questions. Most of the time, ethical questions ask about what *should* be done and need to account for complex factors. For example, should you report a potential safety issue in the car your team is engineering or wait for road tests so the project comes in on time and within budget? What do you do when your good friend purposefully leaves information out of a progress report to make sure your team looks good to the boss? What might be the consequences for each choice?

Ethical questions provoke conversation, reflection, and debate. Your answers to these questions reveal what you value and how you want to act in the world. Entire courses are devoted to the study of ethics and can usually be found in philosophy departments. This chapter considers the overlap between ethics and professional conduct as it relates to technical communication.

Readers and users of technical documents need to trust that the information provided to them is true and reliable. You are responsible for creating accurate documents. The words you choose matter. The information you include or leave out matters. Personal ethics are just that, personal. But they form the foundation for most conversations about professional ethics. This chapter provides some ways to think and talk about this complex topic.

Ethics and the Problem-Solution Framework

Remember the Problem-Solution Framework from the first chapter? Let's review that model as you consider ethics in technical communication (figure 1). Once again, the challenge facing technical communicators is to provide a solution that moves users beyond a problem to task completion. The solution is a message in the form of a technical document. This message is always based on purpose and audience.

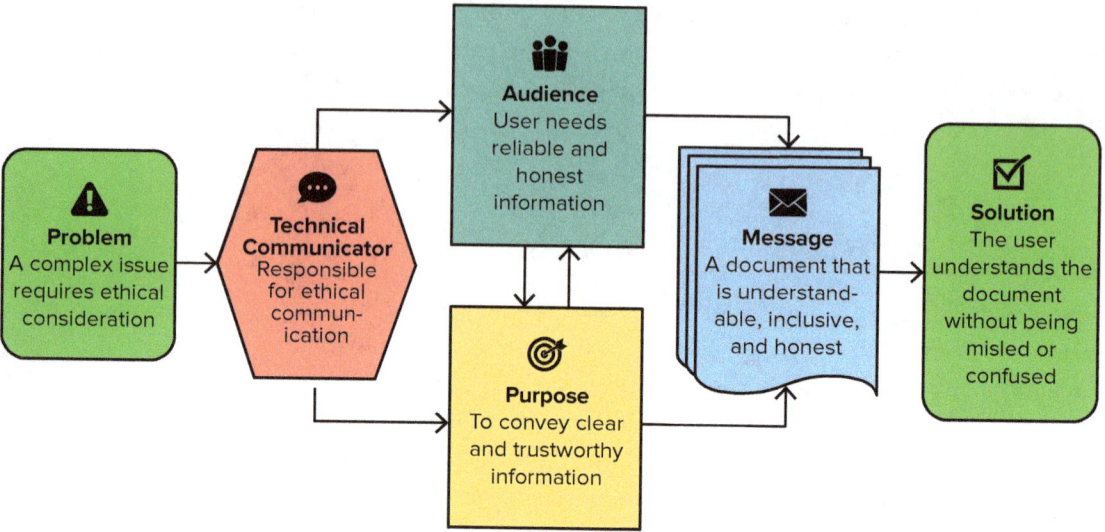

Figure 1. The Problem-Solution Framework can be applied to ethical problems as well as to technical problems.

In ethical areas, the user's problem is the need for communication that honors expectations of honesty and appropriateness. Certainly users wish that all communication was ethical, but sadly, it isn't. A reliable technical communicator solves this problem by honoring user expectations and creating ethical documents. This chapter highlights the unethical modes of communication that some communicators engage in, how to avoid these methods, and the best practices that communicators should follow instead.

The purpose of an ethical document is to communicate clearly and simply. Unethical communication impedes this purpose by including elements that confuse or mislead. Often users notice unethical communication and question the reliability of the document as a result. Even when users don't notice unethical communication—such as in a case of plagiarism—they may take action under false assumptions. In either case, unethical elements can undermine a technical document's purpose.

Unethical communication impacts the audience by failing to provide the end user with reliable information. Exclusionary language can prevent certain audience members from gaining full access to a document. Distorted information can mislead users, possibly with drastic results. Whether due to an oversight or a shortcut, unethical communication prevents users from their desired outcome.

The solution at the end of the framework results from properly weighing the ethical needs of purpose, audience, and message. In a sense, you solve the problem of ethics by not making a problem in the first place. Keep your documents beyond even a hint of ethical impropriety by communicating accurately, accessibly, and honestly.

Your Ethical Stance

Another way of thinking about the meaning of ethics is to consider your own ethical orientation. Ultimately, ethics relate to the choices you make and how they affect others.

At some point in your life, you have probably explored your morals and principles in depth, or you may not have given them much thought. Take this opportunity to consider who you are at this point in your life, how you want to contribute to your chosen field, and how you want to show up in the professional world (figure 2). Let's look at some considerations that can help you figure out where you stand ethically.

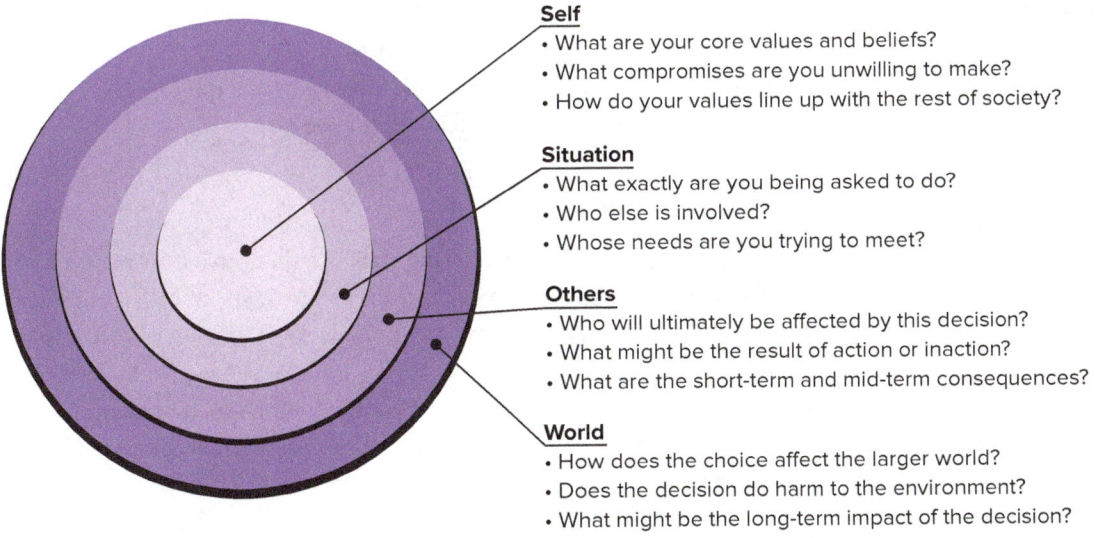

Figure 2. When it comes to ethics, start at the center with your personal values and move outward to reflect on the various questions involved in making a responsible decision.

Self

Chances are, you were taught a certain way to view the world. Sometimes this lines up with what your parents or guardians had in mind for you, but sometimes it doesn't. At a certain point, it's natural to question those ideologies to see if they are true for you. This is the point where you start to frame your own code of ethics and find the lines you don't want to cross.

Situation

This is where the particulars of the situation come into play. Professional ethics depend on the culture of your workplace. For example, what's permissible in the private sector (non-government jobs) may be frowned upon, or even grounds for dismissal, in a government workplace. Looking at the larger context, which includes both the short-term and long-term possibilities, is an important part of ethical decision-making.

Others

Think clearly about the potential impact of your decision on your professional relationships. Behind every technical document is a human being. You have an obligation to the users of documents you create. You are accountable to your employer and client. And you have a responsibility to yourself. How you balance these needs defines your approach to communication. Many of you may create content for global audiences, which requires an even greater awareness of how your choices affect other people.

World

Ethical decisions involve considering not just the impact on people, but also the world at large. Technical communicators, specifically those who work in the fields of science and technology, must consider both human and nonhuman factors in making ethical decisions. It would be irresponsible and unethical to ignore scholarly research about environmental issues affecting humans like overpopulation, waste disposal, and climate change to name a few.

Ethics at Work

Professional ethics often involve the legal obligations you have to your employer. Everything you create while you're being paid is an extension of the company or organization you work for. Each company will have its own standards and expectations, and you should familiarize yourself with them before you begin a new project. These standards can generally be found in your company's code of conduct.

Imagine a recent graduate moves home and starts working for a large but struggling textile company that employs many of the people in her community. She finds out the company is not using the sustainable practices they advertise because the updated equipment requires significant investment. If they were to use these sustainable practices, it could increase their overhead dramatically for years with no guarantee of success. As a result, they might have to let go of some employees. Meanwhile, the advertising has shown some increase in sales.

Should the recent graduate blow the whistle and risk people losing their jobs? Imagine if that same employer asked her to skew some data on a public report to downplay the financial situation of the company. This is a bad situation that may have serious legal consequences. What would you do in her place? In some cases, there is no easy answer. You might lose your job if you don't do what you're asked. Other people might lose their jobs if you bring attention to the topic.

Ethical behavior, including ethical technical communication, involves not just telling the truth and providing accurate information, but telling the truth and providing information so that a reasonable audience can make an informed decision. It also means that you act to prevent actual harm, with set criteria for what types and degrees of harm are more serious than others. For example, financial damage to your company outweighs your own frustration or convenience. As a guideline, ask yourself what would happen if your action (or non-action) became public. If your response could impact your job security or professional reputation—or just cause embarrassment—the action is likely unethical.

But it's not enough to just trust your gut. Experts need to confront ethical dilemmas directly by thinking about the different possible outcomes and how these outcomes affect various groups of people. How much should you say? To whom? And when? As you look at the examples in this chapter, consider how you might react in a professional situation.

Client and User Conflicts

One of the first places you may encounter an ethical conflict is when your client's needs conflict with your user's needs. It can be tempting to go for the easiest solution—often the solution that pleases your employer (or client) the most. After all, they're the ones paying for the work. A good point to remember is that solutions that appear easy are rarely so. What's convenient for you or your client is not automatically best for everyone involved.

Consider the following example. You've been hired to create a brochure advertising a new drug. The document is a type of pamphlet that will likely be picked up and glanced through in physician waiting rooms. Your client, a pharmaceutical company, has specific needs. They want the drug to be attractive to a wide audience. They want to sell their product. They want this drug to be a success and possibly be the one that *makes* the company. They want you to present it in a way that will entice people to ask their doctor to prescribe it to them. In no uncertain terms, they've communicated that they want you to focus on the benefits of the drug and minimize the drawbacks.

On the other side, you have the users. They have needs as well. They want to know if the drug can help them and what side effects it might have. They want to know if it will interact with other medications or conditions. They want to know if it's safe. If there are risks involved, they want to know that the potential benefits outweigh those risks.

Your decision in this situation can be an actual matter of life and death. If you don't give a realistic portrayal of the drug and its interactions, people who encounter your pamphlet may get misinformation that could affect them in serious ways. You're not the only one responsible, of course. There are doctors, FDA regulations on prescription drug ads, and your company's legal team. But your role in creating this information is critical. Being a professional means knowing where you stand and where you draw the line.

Ethics in Action

The Society for Technical Communication (STC) is a professional organization that has identified six ethical principles for its members: legality, honesty, confidentiality, quality, fairness, and professionalism ("Ethical Principles"). STC's board of directors adopted these principles in 1998, and they form the standard for professional activity and accountability in the field.

You can use these principles to begin talking about the kind of technical communicator you want to be and how you make decisions when the right answer is not clear. Let's take a closer look at these principles in context by examining how freelance technical communicator Julia navigates multiple professional environments and demands. As a freelancer, she must determine fair prices for contract work, pay attention to legal and contractual obligations, recognize when to keep information confidential, and weigh her personal values when encountering conflicts of interest.

View the complete code of ethics for technical communicators at www.stc.org.

The Big Six for Technical Communicators

Look at how the six principles of legality, honesty, confidentiality, quality, fairness, and professionalism have been defined and how Julia applies each one to her contract work. Find the complete code of ethics on the Society for Technical Communication's website. Compare the two versions and answer the questions below.

Legality

- Follow laws and regulations.
- Fulfill contractual terms.
- *Example*: Julia's contract job states she must produce or revise three pamphlets using data from a marketing research company. Legally, she can't use copyrighted material—this must be original work.
- *Example*: Julia has the opportunity to sign a substantial contract. The contract states that the person they hire must be an experienced writer and graphic designer. Julia is both. It also states that the person must be a trained photographer. While Julia considers herself a capable photographer, she is not professionally trained. It would be unethical to present herself as something she is not.

Honesty

- Be honest and accurate.
- Avoid ambiguity.
- Be clear, coherent, and concise.
- Get permission to use other's work and provide attribution.
- Aim to meet the needs of users and clients.
- Do not misuse the time or resources of clients or employers.

- *Example*: Julia is tasked with promoting the field of robotics and wants pamphlets for interested students. She researches the career to avoid misinforming students, estimates costs to produce the pamphlets (including work hours), and seeks permission to use attractive photographs owned by a third party before making the proposal to her boss.

Confidentiality

- Get consent to share business-sensitive information.
- Obtain releases from clients and employers.
- *Example*: Julia contracts with medical companies. A client suggests Julia ask for patient information so she can research patient reactions to a drug she has been asked to market. Julia knows she can't have this conversation with the doctor's office because it's a violation of the Health Insurance Portability and Accountability Act of 1996 (HIPAA).

Quality

- Do your best work.
- Negotiate fairly.
- Meet deadlines.
- *Example*: A client contacts Julia about designing promotional materials for a local gym. She and the client agree to have promotional materials on the front desk in three weeks. Julia estimates six hours of initial work and three to five revision hours. She has a design background but limited experience, so she researches fair prices and finds the average rate for experienced designers is about $75 an hour, while someone with her experience charges around $30. Julia provides an estimate of $330 (using the high end of hours she thinks the project will take). She provides documentation on how she reached her estimate, but then she finishes before deadline and under budget.

Fairness

- Respect the diversity of all.
- Align business interest with the public good.
- Avoid conflicts of interest.
- Disclose conflicts to those involved.
- *Example*: Julia's work impressed gym customers, resulting in new clients. She's approached by a business that supports policies at odds with the volunteer organization where she helps at-risk youth find education and job opportunities. Although she might make some extra money, she politely declines the work, citing the conflict between the business and her volunteer work.

Professionalism

- Provide constructive feedback to colleagues.
- Request constructive feedback for self-improvement.
- Help others who want to become technical communicators.
- Get involved in the technical communication community.
- *Example*: Julia makes sure to get an early draft or two to her employer or her clients for feedback because she knows it shows professionalism and the early feedback she receives will save everyone time and money.

Discussion:

- Think about this list and your career or particular field of study. Can you think of an example for each of these principles in your field?
- Can you explain to someone why each of these principles is important in your field?
- How would you adapt these principles to apply to your field of study? What would you add?

Distorted or Misleading Information

In technical communication, visuals are another area where unethical choices can lead to distorted or misleading information. Game designers Leticia and Jason, who you will meet in later chapters, created this chart to make it appear as though the release of their video game, *Alpacas of Doom!*, greatly reduced the number of alpaca attacks (figure 3). At a glance, you can see the number drastically drop immediately after the release of *Alpacas of Doom!*

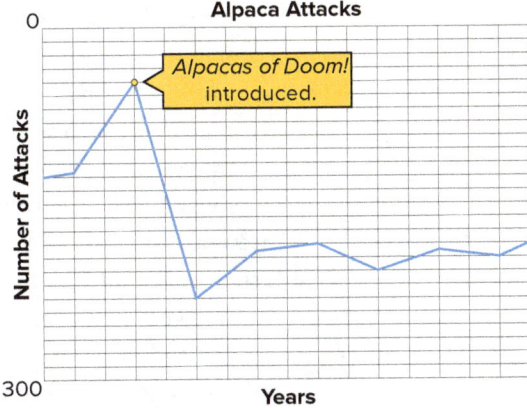

Look again. What does the chart really say? Leticia and Jason jokingly want the user to believe we are finally safe from vicious alpaca attacks, but they know the data says otherwise. Graphs typically arrange numbers from smaller to larger, so unless someone is reading closely, they might conclude that alpaca attacks decreased after the release of the game. In reality, the number of attacks increased. This visual information takes advantage of the user's expectation for how a graph is supposed to work.

Figure 3. *The graph's design invites a misreading of the data by inverting the numbers on the vertical axis ("Numbers of Attacks") from larger to smaller, rather than the typical arrangement of smaller to larger.*

Misrepresenting information is no joke. At best, it's guaranteed to make your audience hostile and leave too much interpretation in the hands of the user. At worst, misrepresentation or distortion will lead to faulty decision-making and could result in litigation, injury, or worse.

Take a moment to think of why distorted or misleading information might happen. Sometimes miscommunication results from not fully understanding the material. Maybe the writer wants to spare someone's feelings or wants to avoid blame or negative consequences by leaving out details or exaggerating results. A combination of laziness, distraction, lack of experience, competing interests, or any number of human flaws could lead someone to mislead their audience.

Whether or not miscommunication is intentional, misleading or distorted information can lead to serious problems. As a professional, you must set high standards for your work. In this section, we show types of distorted and confusing language so you can recognize these instances and avoid them in your writing. We also provide tips on how to make it right, so you can create technical documents that are accurate, effective, and ethical.

Ambiguity

Ambiguity is when you present multiple meanings at once. This can be done unintentionally (and should be corrected) but can also be intentional. Ambiguity weakens the effectiveness of technical communication and should be avoided. Intentional ambiguity, or **obfuscation**, is unethical because the communicator deliberately seeks to mislead readers.

Consider the following statement: "An employee has filed at least one complaint about a supervisor every month for the past year." This statement is ambiguous because it could be understood as multiple employees have filed complaints about a supervisor or one employee has filed complaints about several supervisors. Each scenario differs significantly. Depending on circumstances, complaints from a single employee might be evaluated differently than complaints from multiple employees.

Avoiding ambiguity isn't hard if you determine what's important about the message you're sending. In technical communication, you always lead with important information and follow with relevant additional details. Whether starting a paragraph or writing a sentence, the same principle is true.

Take the above example. Let's say this is *one* employee filing complaints and the audience is internal (nobody outside the company is expected to read this report). There is no reason to leave out names in this instance: "Michael Herrera has filed at least one complaint about his supervisor, Dana Samson, every month for the past year." This message becomes important (and damning) evidence about the professional relationship between two people along with a severe failure by the company to deal with the situation.

Relevant information that follows this opening sentence should include details about the nature of the complaints and an explanation of why this issue has continued for a year without being addressed.

Remember that ambiguity is avoided by leading with important information, using active sentences, and making sure your intentions are correct when crafting communication. Below are examples of specific kinds of ambiguity you might encounter in technical communication.

Euphemism

Euphemisms are words that replace other words to soften the impact of the real definition. Many euphemisms in the English language cluster around taboo subjects, such as death, sex, and bodily functions. For instance, rather than say that someone died, you might say one of the following:

- Harold passed away.
- Fido is in a better place now.

These euphemisms for death attempt to make it sound less frightening. Using more "polite" language to smooth social interactions when dealing with difficult concepts is the most commonly accepted use of euphemism. It provides distance and lessens the blow. Unfortunately, euphemisms can create distance that allows for, or even encourages, irresponsibility. Think about how many ways you can fire employees without taking responsibility:

- The department was downsized.
- Departmental reallocation of resources requires externalizing personnel proportionally.

Bad actors use euphemisms to hide reality, create a legal "interpretive" space, or to provide room for active denial later:

- Enhanced interrogation techniques (torture)
- Collateral damage (civilian death, injury, or property damage during military action)
- Ethnic cleansing (genocide)

In his bit about euphemism, comedian George Carlin quips: "The more syllables a euphemism has, the further divorced from reality it is." You can use his one-liner to determine when you are writing euphemistically. Is the sentence filling up with syllables? Are your sentences active or passive? Do others know what you mean?

Fix the problems created by euphemism by having an honest conversation with yourself. If you are trying to soften language by using euphemism, explore your intentions. Will the user benefit from this language, or is the benefit only on your end? If the latter, the choice is probably not ethical.

For example, let's look at this 2018 statement from GM motors: "Market conditions require that five North American assembly and propulsion plants will be unallocated product by the end of 2019." This is confusing language that is wide open to a variety of interpretation. An honest, clearer message would read, "Due to the popularity of SUV Crossovers, production plants that aren't equipped to build these vehicles will close by the end of 2019."

Bruce Barry, a professor at the Owen Graduate School of Management at Vanderbilt University, suggests GM used "euphemistic language in order to potentially avoid their responsibilities under either the law or their collective bargaining agreements." The word "unallocated" doesn't mean "shut down" or "close," which may save GM from paying severance or offering new jobs (and training) to their fired workers.

One trait about euphemism to bear in mind is that the true meaning of the euphemism eventually catches up, and the phrase will become uncomfortable again.

Circumlocution

Circumlocution is the act of burying the message in an overabundance of words. This can happen at the sentence or paragraph level, when the writer overstuffs their document with useless words that tire out readers or with language that circles the subject without landing. This tactic can also indicate the communicator is not knowledgeable on the subject but trying to appear knowledgeable by increasing word count.

It can also happen on a larger scale. For example, you might see this in court cases when one side is required to surrender evidence and they turn over boxes and boxes filled with documents so that the opposition must sift through all the debris. Circumlocution is often combined with jargon to "sound good." Double obfuscation. Yikes.

Politicians are well practiced in the use of excessive detail. Here's an example of a politician's response to being asked about federal aid for education from the book *Fallacies Arising from Ambiguity* by Douglas Walton:

> I firmly believe that every citizen is entitled to the best possible education. In fact, it is my unalterable conviction that it is the solemn obligation of each generation to endow its youth with the knowledge of the noble achievements of the human species and to make these endowments equally without regard to race, creed, sex, color, or region. I also hold that the burden of providing these rights and privileges should be equitably allotted among those most capable of assuming the burden.

Notice how the speaker avoids committing to an actual answer. Instead, he pumps his audience full of feel-good words that obfuscate the unpopular part of the policy. Try reading this out loud and you'll really hear it. This tactic is effective because the politician not only distracts his audience from the question, but he also gets them nodding along. Let's look at the same passage edited for clarity:

> I believe every citizen is equally entitled to the same high-quality education, it's the responsibility of the present generation to provide this education to the future generations, and we should pay a percentage of tax dollars into education according to our overall wealth.

While arguably not as pretty, the message is clearer: everyone gets the same quality education and wealthier people put more money into the fund that makes equal education possible.

Exclusive Language

Presenting information ethically means considering differences in culture and whether the language in the document is discriminatory. Discriminatory language is often subtle and based on the communicator's assumptions (like assuming the audience is male or that everyone in the audience is able-bodied). In addition to ethical considerations, discriminatory language in technical documents can have serious legal consequences. Responsible technical communicators need to present information in a way that will be understood by a wide range of users, regardless of their background. This means checking documents for language that could be confusing or offensive to readers and using design that accounts for the possibility of visual impairment.

Offensive References

Most cultures find specific words and gestures offensive depending on how they are delivered. In the US, the middle finger is typically hostile. In other cultures, giving a thumbs-up is viewed as offensive, which might come as a surprise to people living in the US who associate the thumbs-up with a job well done or an indication that you're ready to proceed. This cultural difference could be pertinent to a technical document.

Graphics and photos in documents that are created in the US sometimes feature a thumbs-up as a means of communicating approval or success. Clearly, "success" isn't how this image would be interpreted by a user from one of the cultures that view the thumbs-up as a rude gesture. For similar reasons, a company based in India won't use a swastika in images meant for an international audience, even though the symbol has religious meaning in Eurasian cultures. They know the symbol is firmly connected with Nazism in Europe and the US—there's no severing that connection.

It's also important to recognize that symbols, language, or gestures can change meaning over time. Words that are offensive to the average audience today might have been how you described a good mood one hundred years ago.

Technical communicators must be careful to review their content and ensure that it is suitable for users regardless of their cultural background. This requires research, awareness, and responsibility. Some of the work involves self-awareness—often our more casually offensive language is a product of bias or ignorance. For example, assuming only men are part of the audience when women are an estimated 51 percent of the US population or presenting materials that make certain minorities look unsavory or undesirable is not only unethical, it shows poor taste and separation from reality. Those are three traits that don't work well in technical communication fields.

Fix offensive references by researching international cultures for differences from your own culture, reviewing demographic realities, and identifying the biases that may interfere with effective communication.

Idioms

Idioms are phrases that have specific cultural meaning and that can't be understood simply by translating the individual words in the phrase. "Learn the ropes" is an example of an idiom. Unless a user has encountered this idiom before, that user probably won't understand that "learn the ropes" means that someone is developing basic skills in an area. Idioms are particular to a language but also regionally diverse. "Knock on wood" doesn't make sense to English speakers outside the US as a wish for good luck because they're more likely to "touch wood." This is the kind of phrase that you might add without realizing that some users won't understand it.

Fixing idioms isn't rocket science. In fact, it's a piece of cake. You just remember that phrases you use casually don't mean the same thing to an audience using your document one hundred miles away from where you wrote it. Let's try that again: fixing idioms isn't complicated. In fact, it's an easy task.

Jargon

Jargon is specialized language used by people within a field to communicate concepts anyone in the same profession will understand. A good example might be how two surgeons discuss a procedure with one another. They use specific medical terms to impart important information quickly so the patient survives. If you think about your own professional experiences, you have probably used jargon to communicate with your coworkers—either a shortcut word that everyone at work understands, or a term that only applies to that specific workplace.

Right now, you are learning vocabulary words in your classrooms that are the jargon you're expected to know and understand in your post-college profession. Jargon becomes problematic when technical communicators either forget that a general audience is unfamiliar with the term or use the unknown term against the audience.

When jargon is intentionally used with an audience who won't understand it, without providing clear definitions, the author's motive is questionable at best. Be on the lookout for words *designed* to halt understanding. A writer who doesn't want the audience to understand is up to no good.

There are many reasons writers might be intentionally unclear: to hide a lack of information, to disguise or downplay the actual situation, to speak directly to people "in the know" and keep everyone else in the dark, or to persuade the user to do something they want. If you've ever felt pressured into signing a contract you couldn't understand, you have experienced the power of jargon.

On the other hand, many writers are accidentally unclear. Every writer does this, especially in early drafts. Maybe you rushed and didn't review what you'd written. Maybe you thought you were clear but couldn't see the writing from the user's perspective. This is not an ethical problem. It's more an issue of taking your time, reading through your work, and getting second opinions. Still, the outcome is identical to intentional obfuscation: lack of clarity halts understanding, which is never the goal of ethical technical communicators.

Visual Misrepresentation

See **Chapter 3** for more on visual design.

Images are a common form of information that can be misleading, as you saw earlier with the graph about alpaca attacks. Before you create a graph or insert clip art into a report, think about how your audience will interpret it. Here's another visual example of information distortion (figure 4).

The person who created this chart may not have intended to distort or misrepresent the information. But, as a professional, you need to provide information in a way that allows your user to draw reasonable conclusions. A student looking at this chart might assume Professor C is a better teacher or an easy grader. But what if the difference is that Professor A is part-time and Professor C is full-time? There's no way to know for sure how this information should be interpreted. Leaving out this information is not just sloppy. It can lead to real consequences.

Depending on how you crop a picture, for example, you can misrepresent the subject. If the cropped image makes the house look as though it is surrounded by trees, but there are actually high voltage power lines beyond the border of the crop, you may be presenting the house, but not its context. The image in figure 5 has been cropped, edited, and brightened to enhance the house's visual appeal. Manipulating an image can be problematic if doing so creates false or unrealistic expectations.

Other ways to distort information involve the document itself. One of the most common culprits is the three-dimensional pie chart (see figure 6). Compare Item A with Item C. How different are they in size? It's hard to tell in this chart, isn't it? But

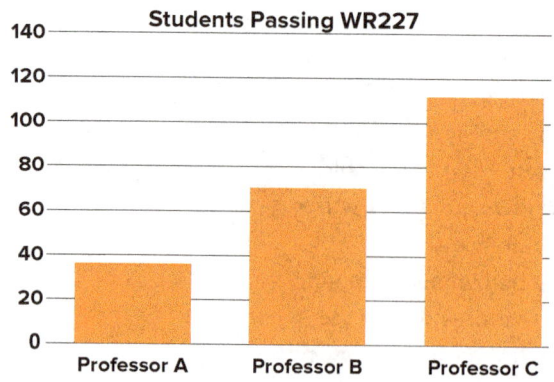

Figure 4. What problems do you see with this graph? What are some assumptions your user might make based on what they see in this chart? What could make this chart more useful and reliable? What are some possible ethical dilemmas that could arise here?

Chapter 2: Technical Communication Ethics   45

Figure 5. It's the same house but it isn't the same image or the same information. The choice of what to show and what not to show is an ethical one.

in the flat chart, it is clear that Item A is *more than twice the size* of Item C. Now, look at Items D and B. They're both the same percentage, but the chart's three-dimensionality distorts visual understanding of the ratios, so Item D looks much larger than B. It looks like it is over 50 percent of the graph. The whole idea in a pie chart is to demonstrate how a whole is divided into parts. The three-dimensional graph may look sleek, but it doesn't give a clear representation of the data.

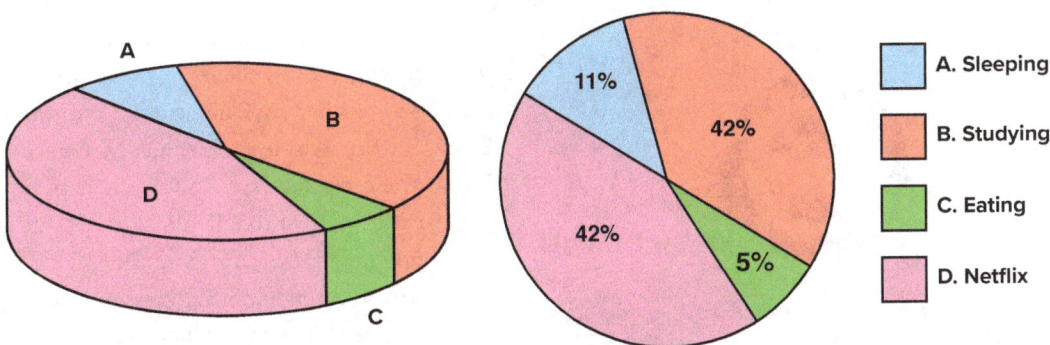

Figure 6. The three-dimensional version of this pie chart lacks important information to help the user interpret its data.

Using Information Ethically

Many of the projects you'll encounter professionally and as a student require the use of existing material. In fact, any time you perform research for a project, whether it's locating information or including others' points of view, you'll likely need to reference source material that you didn't create. When this happens, you'll need to be aware of the restrictions on using source material. This relates to ethics because how you acknowledge the work of others can have personal and professional consequences.

There are two major concerns for anyone who uses material they didn't create: copyright and citations. **Copyright** is the legal protection that exists for people who own their content. They have legal control over how that content gets used. Any use of that content by someone who isn't the owner is subject to the law, which requires them to get permission from the owner *before* they use the content. **Citations** are the academic convention that gives credit to the owner of content and also provides an ethical way to use content that may or may not be under copyright.

In professional settings, you need permission from the content's owner to use their copyrighted work. In academic settings, you don't need permission from the owner to use content because of something called educational fair use, but you always need to use citations to give credit to the content's owner.

Copyright Basics

If you want to use content that is owned by someone else, you can verify its owner by locating the copyright symbol (figure 7).

Figure 7. *A work does not need to have a copyright symbol or be registered with the US Copyright Office to be protected under copyright. Work that you create, called an "original expression" in copyright law, is automatically protected.*

The name beside the copyright symbol will tell you who the owner is. For example, this textbook is owned by Chemeketa Community College, the parent organization of Chemeketa Press. The copyright symbol on the copyright page at the front of this book states, "© 2019 by Chemeketa Community College." To use content from this book in a professional setting, you would need to contact Chemeketa Community College and obtain legal permission. It's your responsibility to get permission for content before you use it.

Other common designations for ownership of content are public domain and Creative Commons. Content in the **public domain** can be used without permission, but like asking for permission, it's your responsibility to verify whether the content is free to use or not. The Copyright Office of the US government provides up-to-date information about locating public domain content and verifying its status at www.copyright.gov.

Creative Commons is a nonprofit organization aimed at providing legal and free alternatives to copyright to allow content creators to choose how their work is used or adapted. They have developed a set of licenses that designate what kinds of use are allowed for specific content so that the owner can choose a license that suits their needs. People who choose to use that content are responsible for following the rules of the license the owner chooses. There are four main Creative Commons licenses (figure 8).

These licenses can be found in any combination, and their names and symbols are simply listed after the letters "CC" to indicate what the license requires. It is your responsibility to identify which license the content is under and to follow the requirements of that license.

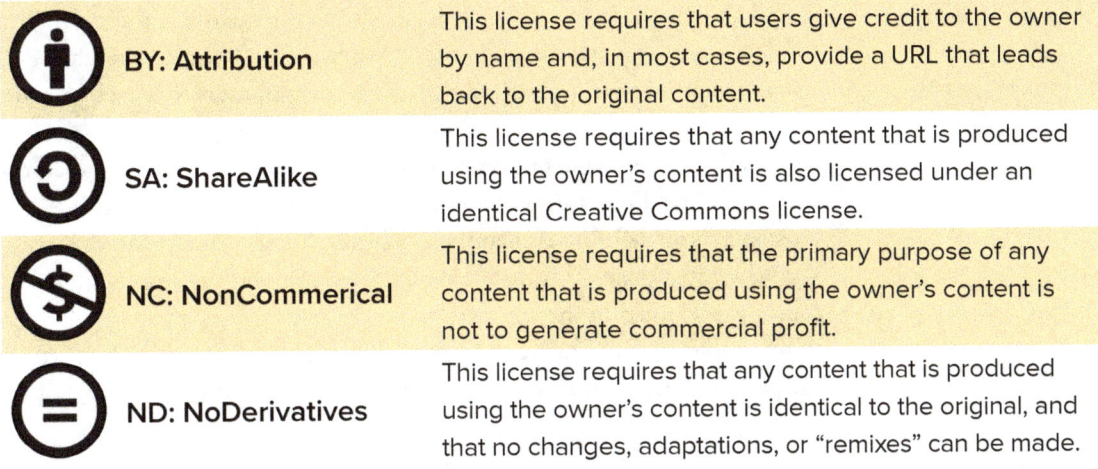

Figure 8. The four Creative Commons licenses were developed to provide additional means for content producers to grant permission and receive credit for their work.

Citations

Consult a handbook for college writing for additional guidance on citations.

In an academic setting, any content from outside source material must be acknowledged in the form of a source citation. If you've taken previous writing or communications courses in college, you should have experience with this. There are many citation styles for academic work, and each style has its own set of specific rules and requirements for what information is included in the citation and how it is formatted in your work.

What Should You Cite?

The short answer is you should cite everything you use in your research that you didn't personally generate. Some people say you only need to cite sources that you've quoted directly. That's not true. In technical communication, the chances that you need to quote any source directly are slim to none. You are much more likely to use data from studies, fieldwork, or meta-analyses and reserve direct quotes for instances in which you are using a source stating an idea in the best possible way. When you cite sources in your technical document, you are providing the user an opportunity to quickly find and review the original research.

How Should You Cite?

Academic citation standards are field-specific, which is why you will learn several citation styles in college. There are similarities between the styles, but the differences are what make the citation style useful for experts in that field. As a student, it's a good idea to check with your professors to see which style they expect you to use.

Modern Language Association (MLA) is the format used for literature, languages, and humanities and one of the two main formats you will use most in college. MLA uses an author/page number in-text citation style with a Works Cited page. This means the information you use from an outside source is identified in the text with the author's name and the page number of the original source enclosed in parenthesis. The information included in the parenthesis connects to a list of sources at the end of your essay.

Here are a few things to keep in mind about MLA style:

- You are unlikely to use MLA in the workplace because it is a scholarly format.
- You are most likely to use MLA in your English and composition courses because it works well for textual analysis.

American Psychological Association (APA) is used in behavioral and social sciences and is one of the other main academic styles you can expect to use in college. APA uses the author/date citation style with a reference page. This means that information you use from an outside source is followed by parentheses containing the author's name and the date of publication. The dates are an important part of the APA citation style because the fields that use this style want the reader to be aware of how recent the research is in the paper.

Here are a few things to keep in mind about APA style:

- You may use the APA format in sociology, anthropology, psychology, and some other science courses.
- You will see APA format in science writing and peer-reviewed scientific articles.
- You will encounter APA format in any number of fields, including nursing programs and exercise/fitness professions.

Chicago Manual of Style/Turabian (CMS) is used in the publishing industry for formatting books and citing references. Turabian Style refers to the student version of the CMS style that uses either the author/date/page number format or the (more common) footnote style and a bibliography. This style is used by a wide range of publishers and commonly used by business, history, and fine arts.

Here are a few things to keep in mind about Chicago/Turabian style:

- You will see CMS format used in fine arts, business, and history publications.
- You will likely use Turabian style in business and history courses.
- You will encounter CMS format in most textbooks, such as this one.

Institute for Electrical and Electronics Engineers (IEEE) sets research and citation standards for electrical, electronics, computer science, and computer programming fields. IEEE uses a bracketed number and corresponding reference list set in numerical order.

Here are a few things to keep in mind about IEEE style:

- You are most likely to use IEEE in computer science and programming fields or in electrical engineering.
- You are most likely to encounter this format in the aforementioned fields, but the place most people encounter IEEE is Wikipedia.

What does citing your sources have to do with ethics? It may seem like a flaming hoop you need to jump through in academic courses, but this habit of keeping track of your sources will benefit you in the professional world.

First and foremost, technical communication values accuracy and precision. Your sources of information must be carefully chosen to provide your audience with the best and most recent information. In-text references followed by a longer description of your source allow your audience to find and verify your sources. Second, documentation of sources shows your integrity—in other words, it shows that you are responsible with information and meticulous with your recordkeeping. Third, citations demonstrate confidence in your conclusions and reassure the audience that your recommendations are based on data. Finally, citing sources gives credit where credit is due and shows the reader your professional standards.

Conclusion

As you move forward in your study and practice of technical communication, remember the principles covered in this chapter. Like Kamaal, you will probably feel pressured to take an ethical shortcut, sooner or later. Recognize that the temporary advantages are not worth the long-term damage to your reputation. Follow the requirements of employers, as well as legal standards. Communicate clearly by avoiding approaches that confuse or exclude. Don't manipulate ideas to make your job easier. Get permission to use information that is not yours and give credit for that information.

Ethical considerations should not be an afterthought. Instead, make ethical communication the basis of all your work. Behaving ethically means technical communicators put the needs of clients and users above their own. Being an ethical communicator doesn't need to be complicated, but it does require a professional frame of mind. Your relationship with clients and users is based on trust. Honor that trust by looking to make your communication as clear, precise, accurate, and honest as you can.

Chapter 3
Design and Collaboration

Abstract: Technical communication requires harmony between distinct components of design. It also requires agreement among professionals with different skill sets. At its core, design is about organization. Collaboration is about synchronization. Words and images, much like the people creating the content, must work together to create meaning in a technical document. Whether you are a writer or a designer, your job is to make everything come together and create meaning for the user. This chapter explores design principles that produce accessible and engaging content that invites and guides a user through a document. Ultimately, technical communication involves collaboration, not just between people who create technical documents, but also between elements of design.

Looking Ahead

1. Why Design Matters

2. Principles of Document Design

3. Working with Others

Why Design Matters

More than ever before, design plays a major role in our lives. It impacts how you navigate a website, how you use the self-checkout stand at a store, and how you interpret the nutritional facts on the packaging of your favorite lunchtime burrito. Even if you don't think about the individual elements of product communication, you're still impacted by the design's effectiveness (or lack thereof). When the strategy is successful, you likely don't notice. But when it is poor—such as when a company doesn't properly define the functions of your new electronic device—it probably drives you crazy.

A poorly designed document becomes a source of frustration for users—now they must contend not just with the difficulty of their problem, but also with the difficulty of a challenging technical document. As a communicator, you need to consider how your organizational choices impact users. The extent to which you think directly about the impact of design on your content will directly influence the success of your communication. The extra effort you invest in designing accessible documents will significantly improve your users' experience.

Design Defined

Design is the structure or plan of anything that is used. In particular, design is what guides a person's interaction with an object and its features. Consider how you use applications on a phone or computer. Design makes the difference between an app that's easy to use and one that isn't. How easy is it to find what you're looking for? How do you know when the app is working properly? Design determines the quality of your experience.

Effective design in technical communication shares many qualities with a well-designed app: it should be easy to use, purposeful, and tailored to your needs. These qualities don't just happen. They result from the thoughtful application of design principles and elements that we'll explore in this chapter.

Design isn't just about how a document looks. Design refers to the underlying structure of your document and how you group and organize information to make it accessible to your user. While visuals are a part of that, other elements are equally important, such as balance, grouping, consistency, and contrast. This chapter takes a look at how these elements relate to readability, emphasis, and organization in technical communication.

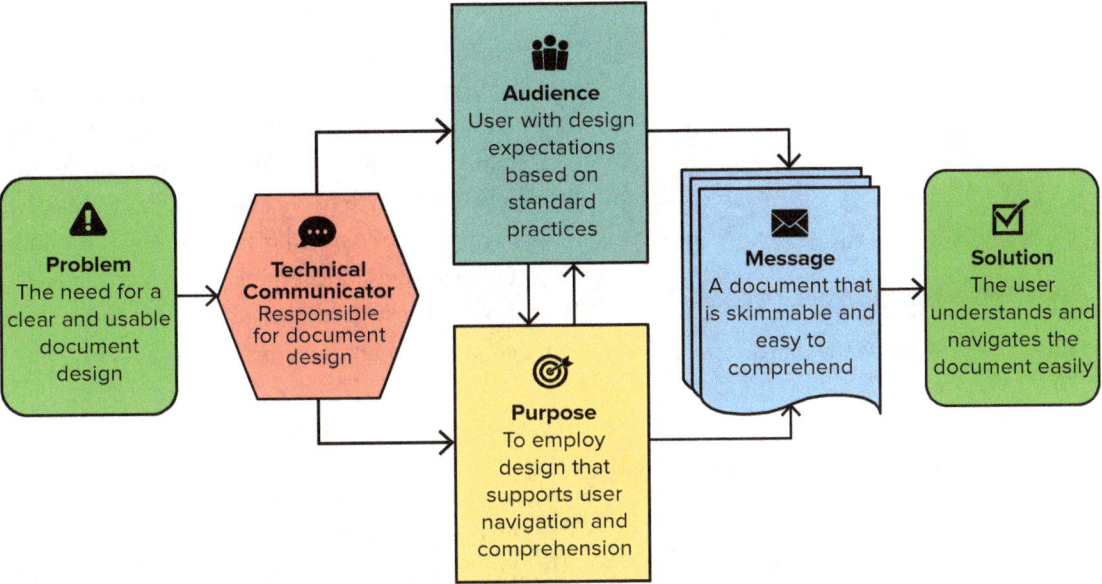

Figure 1. The Problem-Solution Framework can guide design decisions as well as decisions related to technical content.

Design and the Problem-Solution Framework

As discussed in previous chapters, the Problem-Solution Framework clarifies the construction process of technical documents (figure 1). With design, just as with other elements, your goal is to provide the user a solution to their problem. Your design choices should optimize the user's ability to quickly and easily navigate the document to find their solution. The Problem-Solution Framework demonstrates how audience and purpose lead to a message that solves the user's problem. Design factors into this solution.

Effective design is intentional. Haphazard or poor design obstructs user comprehension. Consider the designer who chooses a font with a fun or comic appearance, even though the subject matter is serious. In this case, the design can frustrate or mislead the user, rather than clarify the purpose. Poor design choices actually make it more difficult for the user to reach a solution. An effective message prioritizes user needs. Effective design makes it possible for a user to glance at a document and understand its intended purpose.

Purpose varies depending on the document type. In the case of instructions, for example, you should begin with the user's need to complete a

Figure 2. This sign clearly communicates what it wants.

Figure 3. This sign's design sends mixed messages.

specific task. Design choices should support that objective. Consider the order and arrangement to best aid user access. Also consider user expectations when making design choices. Be familiar with common design schemes, especially as they relate to the type of document you're creating. For example, the color red is associated with warnings or corrections in technical documents (figure 2). If you choose a red font just because you like the color, you might confuse users (figure 3).

Design at Work

The following scenario shows one way design is used in professional settings. Kenji works for Step-by-Step Advertising and PR. His client, Tavent Inc., wants to promote a new industry conference in India. Tavent has asked Kenji's team to design a printed brochure and a PDF version to promote the new conference. The brochures need to provide data that is compelling and easy to understand. They need to be organized and user-friendly.

Brochure design illustrates the ways images and text interact in a technical document. Even the simplest trifold brochure requires the technical communicator to juggle multiple design elements. Kenji needs to make the information accessible and appealing through a combination of words and images (figure 4).

He needs to choose a layout to organize relevant information. Relevant information, in this case, includes a description of the conference, the date, the schedule of events, registration details, and cost. People want to know when the new conference is happening, what it's all about, how much it will cost them, and if it's worth their time.

Thinking back to the relationship that design and the Problem-Solution Framework share, Kenji's team already has their purpose—to promote a new conference. The team understands the type of content needed—date, events, costs, etc. The team's next step includes choosing design elements that will help invite and guide the user through the document.

Chapter 3: Design and Collaboration

Figure 4. This brochure template shows Kenji's initial design plan with areas in gray reserved for images and areas in blue for text.

Principles of Document Design

Document design incorporates features of page layout that help users find their way through a document. Technical communication design differs from what you may have learned in academic writing. In other college courses, you can print a double-spaced page with one-inch margins in 12 pt. Times New Roman font with indented paragraphs and call it done. But with technical communication, you must craft the presentation of your document to your user's needs. Some documents' design will be more straightforward, as in a business letter. Others will be more complex. Don't get caught on that word *complex*, though. The key to effective design is simplicity and consistency. A document that is unnecessarily complex works against the goal of efficient access.

Page design is the deliberate organization of text and images on a page. A children's book is full of colorful images, short blocks of text, and larger font sizes. The book designer, in cooperation with the writer and publisher,

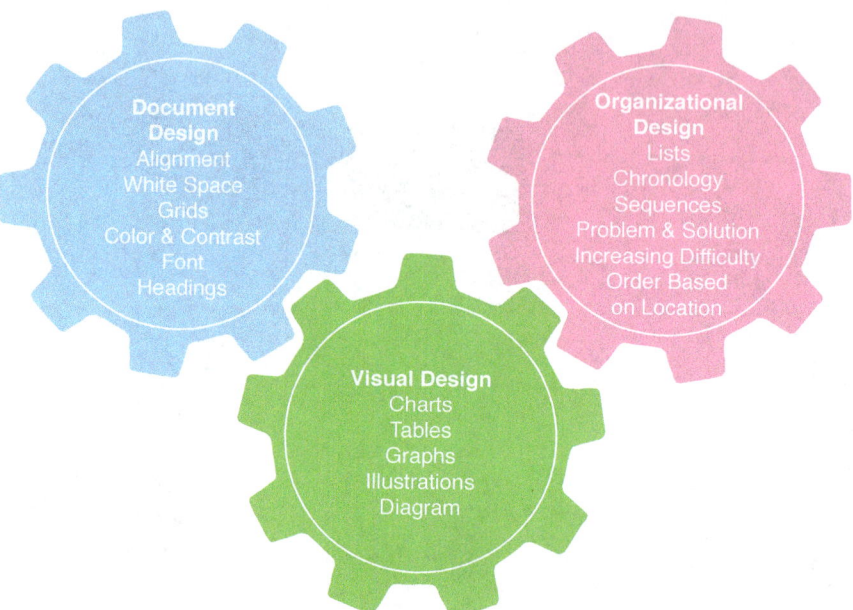

Figure 5. The elements of visual communication fit together much as these gears do. If the gears do not align, the entire document will not function properly.

makes deliberate design choices to ensure the audience, children in this case, can easily understand and use the material. As you can see in figure 5, the elements of document design, visual design, and organizational design must work together to create a functional document.

Design is equally important in the forms you fill out at the doctor's office. These black-and-white forms contain standard options, such as multiple choice, fill in the blank, or basic yes-or-no questions. For example, the forms might ask you to fill out your name, starting with your last name first. Why do this? Because official forms often use this layout, you've come to expect this element of design and invert your first and last name without much thought. This design choice also makes it easier for the doctor and office manager to keep track of and file multiple forms filled with valuable health information. The form leads with the critical information, your last name, to which all your medical records are attached.

Design choices are not limited to printed documents. Website designers also make choices that help users navigate their pages. If the purpose of a website is to sell you remote control cars, the designer might place an image of the car on the left-hand side of the page where our eyes naturally land. The designer might then orient the image of the car so that it points to the purchase button, which is set off by white space on the right-hand side of the page. Every design choice is designed to *drive* the user towards the site's main purpose: a sale.

Principles of design will help you make conscious decisions as you create documents. In the next sections, we look at how the general design principles of readability, emphasis, organization, and visual accessibility make for a more pleasant user experience.

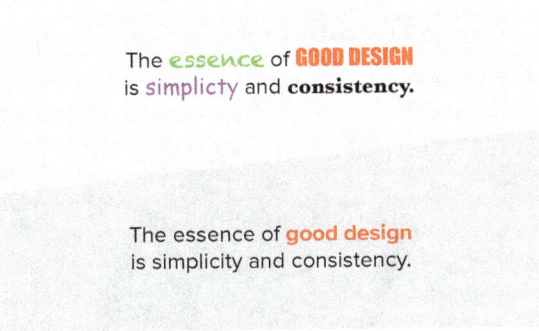

Figure 6. Fonts can add an element of playfulness to your document, but they may also be less readable and harder for the eye to track. Simple, universal fonts are preferable in technical communication.

Readability

Users want documents that are easy to read and help them understand the purpose and message. Using design elements can increase readability, especially font, color, contrast, alignment, and grids, but as you can see in figure 6, too much can distract from the message. For a better example, look at how Kenji uses design elements to increase readability in his brochure (figure 7).

Figure 7. Kenji's project is coming along. Notice how he uses a combination of visual elements to increase the readability of his conference brochure.

Font

All fonts fall into one of two categories: serif or sans serif fonts (figure 8).

Serif fonts are more decorative. You can identify a serif font by the additional stroke at the top or bottom of most letters. This textbook uses a serif font. Historically, serif fonts have been the font of choice in newspapers, books, and other printed material. Serif fonts are preferred for printed text because the small decorative flourishes guide the eye from letter to letter, allowing for faster reading. The most common serif font is Times New Roman, which you've probably used in your college writing classes.

Preferred Fonts in Technical Documents

Serif	Sans serif
• Garamond	• Arial
• Times New Roman	• Helvetica

Figure 8. Serif fonts are frequently used in newspapers and books. Sans serif fonts are often used for websites and headings.

Sans serif fonts, on the other hand, do not have these ornamental pieces (serifs). Sans serif fonts have a cleaner appearance. They are the no-nonsense fonts. Helvetica and Arial are the most common sans serif fonts. Electronic reading and increased screen time have popularized sans serif fonts because they are easier to read on different screen sizes and at different resolutions. Because of their simple appearance, they are also used for important words as in road signs, cautions and warnings, or instructions.

Font size and style draw attention to changes in a document. For example, Kenji knows that a heading's size helps readers rank the relative importance of the information. Kenji should be deliberate in his design choices involving fonts. Should the font be black or another color? How big or small should it be? A common rule says to use no more than three fonts per page.

Color and Contrast

Color and contrast guide readers through text and draw attention to particular areas. However, if used improperly, these same elements can distract readers (figure 9). As with fonts, you should avoid using more than three different colors in your design. Simplicity and consistency are key.

To make his brochure more inviting, Kenji uses Tavent's company colors. He asked for a style guide from the company so he can be sure to use

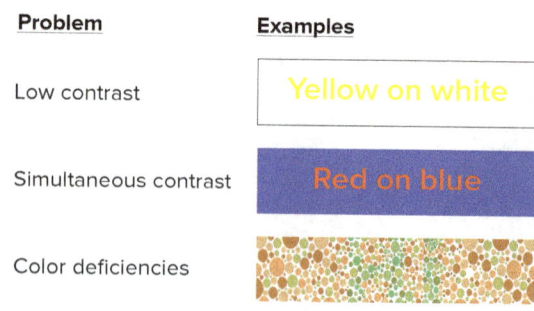

Figure 9. Avoid these problematic uses of color.

the company's signature color scheme. This will save the client time on their end because they won't need to edit as much before they incorporate the brochure into their larger proposal.

Color has different associations within different cultures. For instance, in Western cultures, such as North America and Europe, yellow represents warmth or caution depending on the context and is used in transportation systems for school buses and traffic signals. Yellow, however, represents death and mourning in some Latin American cultures. If Kenji were to create a brochure for a conference in Rio de Janeiro, for instance, he should probably avoid using yellow as a dominant color in his design.

Another design element that can create consistency within your document is alignment. Let's take a look at how it works.

Alignment

Alignment is one of the most basic and important features of document design. You might be so familiar with it that you take it for granted. **Alignment** means that every element should have some visual connection with every other element on the page. There are four basic types of alignment (figure 10).

In **left alignment**, the text lines up along the left margin. This alignment has a ragged edge on the right margin. You may recognize this alignment from other academic papers you have written. Kenji used this standard alignment on the market research report he submitted to Tavent because it allowed his client to easily read the multipage report.

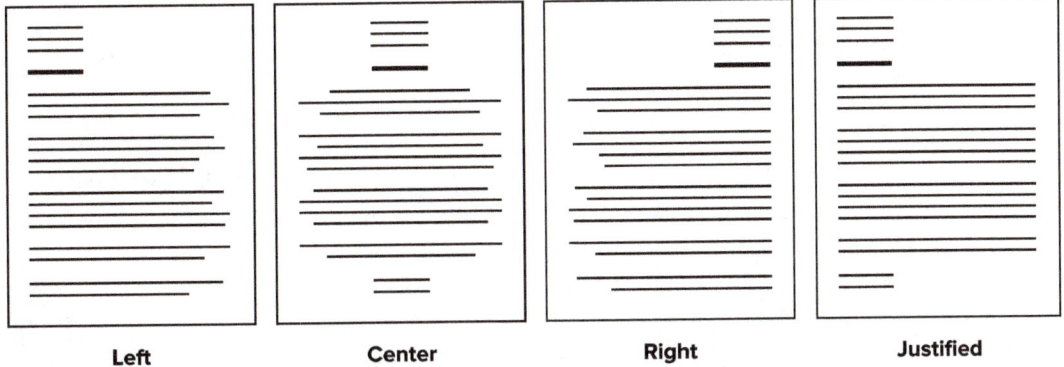

Figure 10. In the first three examples from the left, the content is either anchored to the left-hand margin, the center line, or the right-hand margin. With justified alignment, the content is distributed evenly between the left and right margins.

In **center alignment,** the text is anchored along the center line of your document. The result is text that creates a balanced mirror effect from one side to the other. This can be a great way to make sure your white space is balanced. Kenji will center the name of the conference on the front panel to make it stand out.

In **right alignment**, the text lines up along the right margin. This alignment is typically used to draw attention to a block of information. In the brochure's design, Kenji might align the date and time of the conference to the right-hand margin to draw attention to those details and to set them apart from the rest of the text.

In **full justification**, the text aligns along both left and right margins. It is most often used for book-length documents (like this textbook) and professional publications, such as journal articles and booklets. If Kenji includes descriptions for the break-out sessions in the brochure, this type of justification will create clean lines down both sides of the fold out.

In figure 11, you can see immediately how effective alignment helps the eye connect the different elements on the page. Ineffective alignment is the result of not considering how the placement of text and images affects the user's experience.

So, what is the best choice? Think about how the document will be used. Is it in print or online? Users read these types of documents in different ways. Does the document include long passages?

Effective Alignment

Notice how the grid lines reveal the structure of this document.

- Every element connects with every other element.

Alignment creates a sense of order and gives the reader a clear direction for what to read next.

- Most programs automatically align the text, so use this as a guide.

Ineffective Alignment

Here's a few things that happen when a document does not demonstrate effective alignment:

- Readability decreases
- The eye has to work harder

In this second document, the organization feels less intentional.

- It is more disorganized.

Figure 11. Compare these examples of effective and ineffective alignment.

Alignment helps users scan a document more effectively. Like most aspects of technical communication, keep your user's needs in mind. What you don't want to do is make your choice of alignment simply because you think it looks cool. Alignment won't benefit your technical documents if it's used without purpose or an understanding of your audience.

Grids

Grids are underlying structures used to help make sense of and create order within documents (figure 12). A grid also refers to how you set up the "rules" of your page, so that there is strength and consistency to your design. Most documents follow a standard horizontal grid as in a memo or email. A vertical grid is often used in brochures or manuals, like the one Kenji is designing.

When you don't use a grid, you can end up with a variety of alignment planes. Grids are like guardrails that help you stay on the right path. Take a look at these two résumé drafts (figure 13). In the model of effective alignment on the left, the text guides the reader's eyes down the page. In the right model, the text sends an unclear message to the reader about where to look. The path that you create through your document is an important part of readability. By choosing the lines for your design, you either give your reader a clear direction or create chaos.

Figure 12. Notice how the elements in Kenji's brochure line up with the grid, not just on a single page but throughout the entire document.

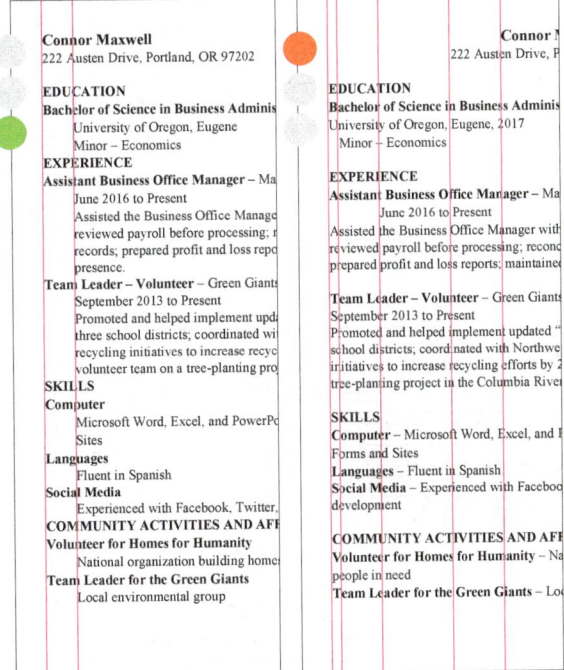

Figure 13. Scan these two versions of the same résumé. We're showing you just the left side of the page so you can see how the document is, or is not, aligning along the left margin.

Emphasis

Design in technical documentation is not decorative. Instead, design in technical communication focuses on guiding readers. One principle that helps communicators do this is through appropriate use of emphasis. Using specific design elements such as white space, contrast, headings, and proximity present users with a certain emphasis that helps them understand the message of a document.

Consistency, consistency, consistency. You need to have clear, repeated design choices to give stability and structure so that your design functions properly. The human brain works by pattern recognition. Your mind is so intent on this that it can even see patterns where there aren't any. This is why a bunch of random craters on the moon look like a face to us. It's also why it's so hard to proofread your own work— you see what you expect to be there rather than what is.

By using repetition to create emphasis, you give the user confidence in interpreting a document. Repetition works by using any single element multiple times. For example, can you see how this page, this chapter, this textbook use repetition? This use of repetition creates consistency and stability. Repetition can include color, shape, font, placement, line thickness, headers/footers, images, etc. Any element could be repeated to create this stabilizing effect. In Kenji's brochure, he uses the repetition of color, shape, and font to unify the document's design.

Figure 14. Use white space in technical documents to draw the user's eye to important information.

White Space

White space is any empty space surrounding figures, tables, visuals, or text. When used appropriately, it can direct a user's eye by isolating or emphasizing elements of document design (figure 14).

Don't neglect this "invisible" element. You have probably center justified the title of an academic paper, thus creating white space on each side. This draws attention to the title. On his brochure, Kenji uses white space around the date and location of the conference. The use of white space draws a reader's eye to the visual element more quickly. It is a great way to guide a user through a document without distracting them with unnecessary information. Don't tell a reader where to look, show them.

Contrast

Contrast can help with readability, as shown with the element of white space. Contrast can also help with emphasis by showing distinction between ideas. **Size** (a large font for headings uses contrast to set it apart from the body text), **dissimilarity** (a bold sans serif font as a heading will contrast with the serif font of the body text), and **color** (using a deep blue banner with white text will be visually striking) all provide an added level of contrast. As an element of emphasis, contrast centers around being aware of how your elements work together to make a visual impact.

In any document, there will be elements of marked space (text, images, shading, boxes, etc.) and unmarked space (white space). If you have too little contrast, your design will look muddy or indistinct. For instance, using multiple serif fonts in a single document looks wrong because the fonts are too similar. The lack of variety means that the document will lack contrast, and as a result, lack effectiveness. The same holds true for using a 13-pt. font for your headings and 12-pt. font for your body text. There is not enough difference between the two sizes to make the headings stand apart. On the other hand, be selective in your use of contrasting elements. You could also go too far and have too much contrast. You have likely been witness to a novice PowerPoint presentation where the designer uses too many colors, fonts, text boxes, words, and visuals. It's chaos at best and tends to be more distracting than useful.

Headings

Headings are used to group similar information within a document. The human brain likes to chunk information for understanding and retention. You can avoid the "wall of text" effect by using headings to break up the information into smaller sections. These headings are like roadmaps that guide your user and make the document more readable (figure 15). Kenji uses headings in his pamphlet to clearly divide the information into distinct sections. That way, users will be able to scan the different sections and see the structure and relationship between the big ideas.

Headings also help organize information into a hierarchy of ideas, with main concepts receiving a top-level heading and subtopics receiving a lower level heading, or **subheading.** When headings and subheadings are done well, you should be able to read just those elements and understand the scope and sequence of the document. In figure 15, the page on the right breaks up the "wall of text" using a first-level heading for "Recommendations." The three options being recommended are each labeled with a second-level heading.

Here are the recommendations. Given the relatively small size of the company, and its financial limitations in comparison to industry leaders, it would need to tread carefully into this area. The autonomous projects that require a driver's presence have been excluded from the discussion for safety and cost reasons. The following options are the most feasible at this time. The first option is partnership and pilot. "Corporation X" seems to be the U.S. automotive company most eager to release a fleet of AV's. They've developed partnerships with a few other companies in order to pilot their vehicles and are interested in using Tomorrow's Taxi Company as well. For the first year, they would provide the thirty-eight vehicles. Tomorrow's Taxi Company would be responsible for maintenance and energy costs, insurance, as well as monitoring staff. "Corporation X" would oversee any issues with the vehicles, make changes and upgrades, provide parts, and train staff. They would receive .5% of fare profits for this period for the use of the vehicles. At the end of the contract period, it could be renegotiated for another year if the technology is still needing improvement (which would likely be the case) or Tomorrow's Taxi Company would have the option to negotiate a purchase for the vehicles at a discounted rate. The second options is test vehicles. Under this scenario, Tomorrow's Taxi Company would lease-to-own two driverless vehicles from "Corporation A" at a rate of $20,000 per month for a period of six months. For the first six months, the corporation will handle the monitoring of the vehicles remotely. After the trial period, the company would have the option of extending for another six months or paying the balance on the vehicles and purchasing the monitoring equipment. If leased for an additional six months, an end-of-term buyout or return of the vehicles would be required. The third option is partial replacement. In this option, Tomorrow's Taxi Company would replace five of its vehicles that have the highest mileage with AV's and purchase the monitoring equipment at an estimated cost of $1,200,000. This would include replacing the two mini-vans currently used in the hilltop community, as these are experiencing significant

Recommendations

Here are the recommendations. Given the relatively small size of the company, and its financial limitations in comparison to industry leaders, it would need to tread carefully into this area. The autonomous projects that require a driver's presence have been excluded from the discussion for safety and cost reasons. The following options are the most feasible at this time:

Option One – Partnership and Pilot

"Corporation X" seems to be the U.S. automotive company most eager to release a fleet of AV's. They've developed partnerships with a few other companies in order to pilot their vehicles and are interested in using Tomorrow's Taxi Company as well. For the first year, they would provide the thirty-eight vehicles. Tomorrow's Taxi Company would be responsible for maintenance and energy costs, insurance, as well as monitoring staff. "Corporation X" would oversee any issues with the vehicles, make changes and upgrades, provide parts, and train staff. They would receive .5% of fare profits for this period for the use of the vehicles. At the end of the contract period, it could be renegotiated for another year if the technology is still needing improvement (which would likely be the case) or Tomorrow's Taxi Company would have the option to negotiate a purchase for the vehicles at a discounted rate.

Option Two – Test Vehicles

Under this scenario, Tomorrow's Taxi Company would lease-to-own two driverless vehicles from "Corporation A" at a rate of $20,000 per month for a period of six months. For the first six months, the corporation will handle the monitoring of the vehicles remotely. After the trial period, the company would have the option of extending for another six months or paying the balance on the vehicles and purchasing the monitoring equipment. If leased for an additional six months, an end-of-term buyout or return of the vehicles would be required.

Option Three – Partial Replacement

In this option, Tomorrow's Taxi Company would replace five of its vehicles that have the highest mileage with AV's and purchase the monitoring equipment at an estimated cost of $1,200,000. This would include replacing the two mini-vans currently used in the hilltop community, as these are experiencing significant

Figure 15. These documents contain the same information, but the first presents the reader with a "wall of text," while the second one uses headings and subheadings to break up the text and increase readability.

The contrasting size and font in the headings give users an immediate sense of the document's organization. Plus, if you want to create a table of contents for your document later, headings are your best friend.

Proximity

Proximity has to do with where things are placed in relation to one another. Similar ideas should be close to each other. Dissimilar ideas should be farther apart. White space and grids play a role in how this works because that is how you separate and group different elements. When proximity is logical in a document, the physical location of ideas relative to each other contributes to the user's understanding.

Kenji uses proximity in the brochure by keeping topics logically grouped. For example, the brochure will contain contact information such as a phone number and a web address for the conference. Kenji will keep this information together in close proximity. Users would expect all of the contact information to be collected in one place, not spread around the brochure. Kenji will also put similar content nearby, such as the address for the conference or directions. If Kenji hasn't created this kind of document before, he'll probably want to look at many examples to get a sense of what's typical. That way, he'll use proximity in a way that's similar to what users likely expect.

Organization

The organizational structure for a document is determined by the audience. Take the brochure Kenji is working on. The brochure covers the basic information the audience will want to know: when does the conference take place, where is it happening, and who should attend. The brochure should also include information about New Delhi to encourage international travelers to visit.

Once you know your audience, you can create an effective technical document that uses logical patterns of organization to enhance readability. Below are some preliminary questions that will help you choose the type of organization for your document.

Start by using the following questions as a guide:

- What is the purpose of this document?
- Who is my audience? What do they understand about the topic?
- What belongs where?
- How do I want the user to approach the material?
- What comes first? Next? Last?

This fact sheet from the Centers for Disease Control and Prevention (CDC) demonstrates audience awareness through its layout and organization (see figure 16).

The designers of the CDC fact sheet know their audience: athletic coaches who are concerned with preventing head injury. The document is sized to fit on a coach's clipboard and the symptoms and action plan are clearly bulleted to provide easy access to critical information.

An effective technical document uses logical patterns of organization to enhance readability. Think back to the medical forms discussed earlier. There is a consistent organization to most medical forms. You enter your name, address, and insurance information, and then you answer questions about your health. The predictability of these forms is based on logical patterns of information requested by health organizations.

Organization tends to follow a few familiar approaches. Three of the most common are chronology, sequence, and problem-solution.

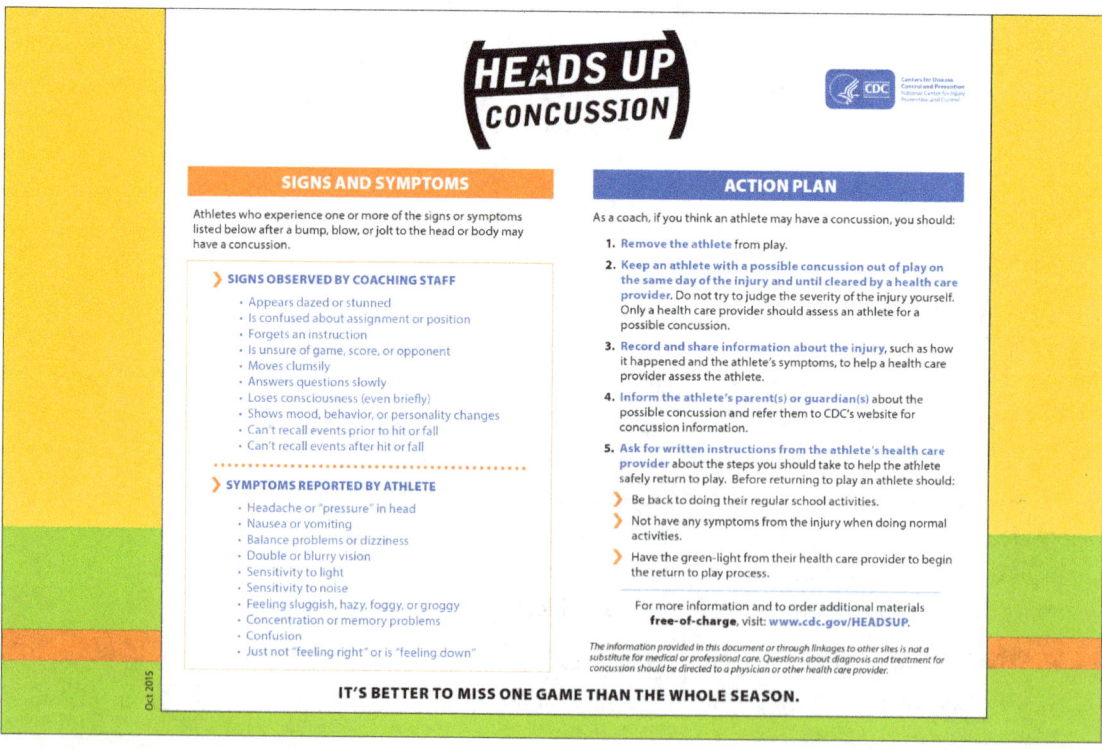

Figure 16. Look closely at this document to see if you can find "clues" that it has been written and designed for a specific audience.

Organization by Chronology

A **chronological pattern** of organization arranges information according to a progression of time, either forward or backward. Explanations of how something happened, how something currently happens, or how something may happen in the future follow a precise time sequence to guide users.

For example, Kenji's previous market research shows professional engineers are increasingly concerned over the safety of industrial control system cybersecurity. This type of cybersecurity is specialized to determine vulnerabilities not only for data, but also for the automated systems engineers design and oversee remotely and on location. Without cybersecurity to outpace hackers or vandals, systems could go down, placing whole communities in danger. Kenji knows that Tavent is creating a presentation on cybersecurity for the upcoming conference. In the conference description on the company's web site, Kenji suggests Tavent guide users through the past, present, and future of engineering conferences (figure 17).

Organization by Sequence

A **sequential pattern** of organization is similar to a chronological pattern but arranges information according to a logical step-by-step sequence that describes a particular process (see figure 18 on the next page). Using this pattern of organization requires each section of information to represent a main step in an actual process.

Often these steps are written from the user's perspective (in this case the implied second person "you"). This is done so that users can visualize themselves completing the process successfully. A user manual or set of instructions are the most common examples of this kind of organization.

Draft with Limited Guidance

Cybersecurity used to be part of conference seminars on other issues. Cybersecurity discussion at conferences increased after threats. Automated solutions began to be included, but engineers have to maintain those systems themselves. Engineers should be connected to cybersecurity consulting firms who provide maintenance services instead.

Draft Organized by Chronology

In past conferences, like those in the 90s, cybersecurity was an emerging topic mentioned as part of other relatable issues. Increased threats in the 2000s created an urgency for cybersecurity discussion. Present industry conferences offer seminars on automated solutions that engineers are responsible for maintaining. A future conference could connect engineers to cybersecurity consulting firms who could provide best practices for protection instead.

Figure 17. Using time-based and specific language makes it easier for your reader to understand the progression of events.

Step 1: Practice and prepare for the video interview
→ Practice your answers to the anticipated questions.
→ Prepare notes to prompt you at a glance during the video interview.

Step 2: Dress yourself and your setting for business
→ Dress nicely like you would for any interview and not just from the waist up.
→ Clear your background so viewers only see what you want them to see.

Step 3: Test equipment well in advance
→ Make sure your webcam, audio, and connection are all working beforehand.
→ Connect to your interview session ahead of time to avoid delays from logging in at the last minute.

Step 4: Captivate your viewer
→ Introduce yourself, continue to smile, and make eye contact with the webcam during the interview.
→ Answer questions to highlight your skills with a clear voice until ending with a fond farewell.

Step 5: Follow up in style
→ Send the interviewer a personal thank-you right away.
→ Check back with the interviewer in a few weeks.

Figure 18. Notice the use of parallelism in this example with the repetition of visual and verbal elements.

Organization by Problem-Solution

A **problem-solution organization** divides information into two main sections: one that describes a problem, and one that describes a solution (figure 19). There are standard sections for this kind of organization. For instance, in a problem-solution document, you will prepare a statement of issue, research, analysis, and recommendations for improvement.

This pattern of organization is typically used when the general purpose is to convince the reader to support a certain course of action. A **recommendation report** frequently uses this organization. In this kind of document, the technical communicator presents a suggested course of action in light of detailed research.

Visual Supplementation

Elements of visual design help users understand and remember pertinent information in a document. Visual design often follows social conventions that make material more user-friendly. Common visuals include images, photographs, tables, charts, and graphs. Visuals balance out text, provide another format for understanding, and connect the visual learning areas of the brain.

Tables, charts, and graphs are ways of displaying complex information in more accessible ways. You can think of each visual display as a tool with a specific use. It's important to recognize that each tool gives us a unique way of understanding the information. If you choose the wrong visual display, you risk confusing the user or even misrepresenting the facts.

As a professional, it is your job to make ethical choices in the visual presentation of data. Not doing so could have legal ramifications for you and your employer. Remember that visual data can be deliberately distorted, but it can also be misrepresented through lack of diligence. In either case, the technical communicator is at fault, so be vigilant about the accuracy and appropriateness of your visual communication.

Using Problem-Solution to Organize Information

Statement of Issue (Problem)
Traditional cars have shown a steady increase in driver accidents.

Research (Analysis)
Cars with autonomous features have shown a decrease in driver accidents

Solution (Recommendation)
Laws should be created to start phasing out cars manufactured before the year 2000 and require car manufacturers to produce vehicles with more autonomous features.

Figure 19. Using time-based and specific language makes it easier for your reader to understand the progression of events.

See **Chapter 2** *for more on ethical visual design.*

Tables

Tables organize data visually in columns and rows so that they can be easily compared. Tables can be used to organize numerical data or verbal communication (see figure 20). When is it best to use a table? If your purpose is to show facts and figures, a table might be your best bet. It's an efficient tool for organizing information so that the user can quickly scan and compare.

Numerical Table

Date of Conference	Attendance	Registration Fee
2014	5,216	$50
2015	6,844	$50
2016	4,988	$75
2017	7,176	$55
2018	8,000 (estimated)	$65

Prose Table

Problem	Contact	Solution
Conference room is locked	Conference center security	Post note on door until security arrives
Projector is not functioning/available	IT Support	Inform presenter and wait until IT support arrives
Not enough chairs	Maintenance	Obtain additional chairs from hallway and assist with setup when maintenance arrives

Figure 20. In the first table, Kenji uses a numerical table to show conference attendance in recent years and its relationship to the registration fee. The table allows for easy comparison of information and shows trends. In the second table, Kenji provides a prose table that allows conference volunteers to troubleshoot the most common problems they might encounter during the event.

Charts

Charts organize data to show relationships by using shapes, arrows, lines, and other design elements. There are many types of charts. Common examples are flowcharts, pie charts, and organizational charts (figure 21).

Kenji chooses a pie chart to show the types of activities that will be available at the conference. Pie charts are useful for displaying data for about six categories or fewer. Since Tavent is trying to increase its attendance numbers, Kenji breaks down the events as a way to persuade more people to attend.

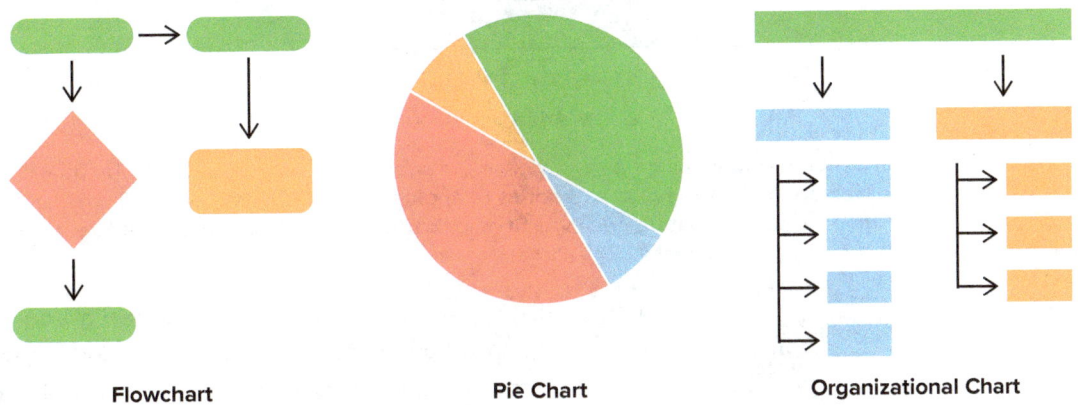

Flowchart   **Pie Chart**   **Organizational Chart**

Figure 21. Different charts serve different needs. Flowcharts show a process. Pie charts show how the parts relate to the whole. Organizational charts show relationships and hierarchy.

Graphs

This design element translates numbers into shapes, shades, and patterns. Graphs can display approximate values, a main point about those values, or the relationship between the two. There are generally two types of graphs: bar graphs and line graphs. In a simple **bar graph**, data is shown using either horizontal bars or vertical bars that correspond to how many items are in a particular category. This type of graph can help users see trends or changes over time. In Kenji's example of a bar graph, he defines the category he wants to measure: the types of engineers that attended last year's conference (see figure 22 on the next page).

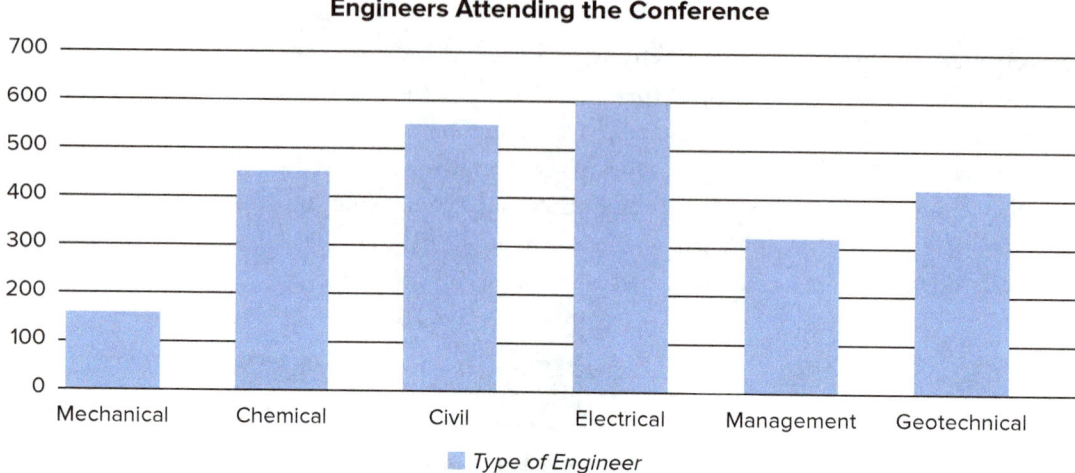

Figure 22. This example of a simple bar graph allows Kenji to see the categorical data of who attended the conference. If he wanted to show how the categories of engineers fluctuate over time, he could use a multiple bar graph. There would be a bar for each year in each category, and Kenji would need to create a key that explains what each bar represents.

A bar graph that displays its information horizontally is sometimes called a **line graph**. Line graphs display how one variable is affected as another rises or falls. In Kenji's market research, he examined how conference attendance has fluctuated over the past four years (see figure 23).

Illustrations and Diagrams

Illustrations rely on drawings and sketches rather than data or words. Technical illustrations often depict what words cannot. **Diagrams** show how parts of an object fit together. Common diagrams include cutaway, cluster, and cycle diagrams. Eventually, the conference organizers will need an illustration for their website and conference guide that shows the location of events in the multilevel convention center.

Kenji didn't make all of this happen on his own. First, he met with his client, Tavent, to figure out their needs. In that conversation Tavent most likely relayed the needs of their clients, the potential attendees. Once Kenji had information to work with, then he returned to his team to conduct market research. Next, he got his graphic designers on board to design the brochure and PDF. Lastly, he organized writers to create the content. It takes a team of people to create reliable and trustworthy content, which leads us to the topic of collaboration.

Chapter 3: Design and Collaboration

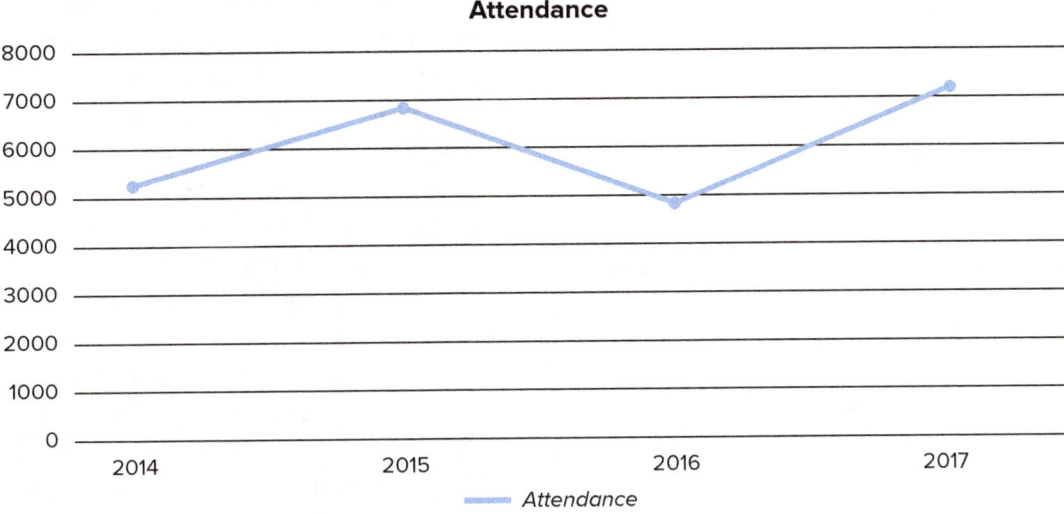

Figure 23. Kenji's line graph examines one data point: how many people attended the conference year by year. In a multiline graph, Kenji could examine the numbers of different types of engineers who attend year by year, assuming he has that data.

Working with Others

More often than not, technical documents are created by multiple communicators. This has become increasingly the case in the Information Age, as the pace of work and the complexity of communication has steadily increased. The involvement of multiple communicators typically gives a document greater quality and depth. Involving multiple people can allow a project to be completed faster, because the workload can be shared. But writing as a group comes with challenges, too. Success depends on **collaboration**, a specific style of project completion that involves multiple communicators. The success of a project also depends on the quality of communication among the various participants. In order for documents created by multiple people to succeed, both quality collaboration and communication must play a part.

Collaboration

While you may have written most of your academic papers on your own, much of what happens in the realm of technical communication happens collaboratively. Students sometimes think collaboration and group work are the same thing. They are not. In group work, a team of individuals is assigned a

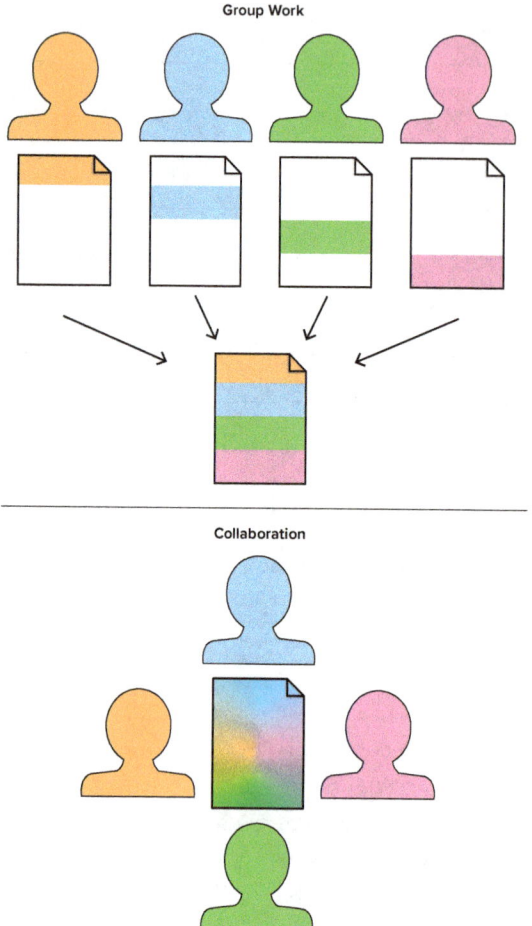

Figure 24. Though we frequently hear the terms "group work" (upper illustration) and "collaboration" (lower illustration) used interchangeably, they are not the same thing. As a professional, you will need seek out productive partnerships with your colleagues.

project, and each person works independently on their part of the project, as seen in the upper illustration of figure 24. Group members will check in with each other, but they do their work solo. Often most of the work falls to one or two people (usually the ones most invested in it). Miscommunication and missed deadlines are commonplace in group work scenarios.

Students who have tried group work often say they could do better work completing an entire project on their own. Research supports this. Studies have found that individual work creates higher quality documents than group work. This is because traditional group work is just multiple people doing independent work on the same project. When a group completes a document in this mode, the result is usually a document that is inconsistent. The differences in voice, style, and meaning can distract the user. Documents created by group work tend to lack unity. This is why individual work is often superior. Keeping a project on one person's plate means that the various sections are more likely to be consistent.

However, collaborative work generally creates higher quality products than individual work. This is because collaborative work blends the best characteristics of both group work and individual work. Collaborative work happens when each group member is assigned a different task, usually in their field of expertise. Collaboration means that every group member must participate in order to complete a project. Collaboration allows the participants to access higher levels of thought and creativity than they could on their own.

Figure 24 demonstrates the difference between a project completed via group work and a project completed via collaboration. Notice the visual distinction between the documents. Group work tends to produce a document that is characterized by distinct sections that do not form a cohesive unit. Collaboration, on the other hand, tends to produce a blended document that forms a unified whole.

To illustrate this idea, Kenji is an expert in market research, but he needs to consult with his graphic designer to complete an effective product for his client. Tavent probably consulted its sales team, event management team, conference team, and marketing team while completing their end of work. If Kenji had tried to complete the entire project by himself, it would likely have made some of the work easier or even more efficient, but it also would have impacted the overall quality. Because Kenji lacks the knowledge and experience possessed by his coworkers, the document would not have had the same depth. By leveraging the abilities of multiple people, a collaborative process results in a better final product.

Communication

Communication is the foundation of collaboration. When communication is going well, problems become opportunities for creative exploration. This means respecting the other participants' views and ideas. Ideally, you should view conflict as an opportunity for growth. Breakthroughs often happen in the spaces where collaborators see things differently. When a team allows its members to engage in constructive and respectful disagreements, the result is a collective ownership of what is created.

Varying commitment levels can tip the dynamics of the process in ways that might send you hurtling back towards group work. To keep your collaboration on track, talk about what success looks like for your project. Being direct from the start about commitment levels can spare you the frustration of bringing someone onto your team who is intending to do group work rather than collaboration. Timeframes and deadlines form an important part of collaboration. Participants need to communicate regularly about if and how they will meet their deadlines.

Differences of opinion can be difficult to navigate in a collaboration, but they are also important. One of the reasons group work often fails is because it typically avoids controversy, resulting in a document that is inconsistent in its message. Working through differences in a collaboration takes hard work and effective communication, but the result is typically a stronger document that better reflects the nuances and complexity of the topic.

The flip side of the difficulties involved in communicating with others is that the end result is a better document. Effective communication requires time and energy, but it is still a vital part of a successful collaboration. You will grow more valuable as a technical communicator as you develop your ability to respectfully and consistently interact with coworkers.

Conclusion

To be successful in both design and collaboration, you must skillfully blend multiple components. In design, you must balance multiple principles of layout and emphasis. In collaboration, you balance a multiplicity of voices. In both areas, the key is to focus on the common goal of creating a document that meets the needs of users. How users benefit from the document is what ultimately matters.

Remember that all design—whether it's technical communication or something as ordinary as a paper clip—seeks to simplify user experience. The principles of readability, emphasis, organization, and visual supplementation make it easy to design documents for users to understand.

When collaborating, remember that the blend of differing opinions and differing abilities will typically lead to a stronger document. The added perspective can help a broader range of users. Even when collaboration seems like extra work, the added effort will contribute to a better user experience.

In a technical communication course, you will likely be graded on your individual understanding of the concepts in this textbook as well as the ideas presented by your professor. Beyond the classroom, however, technical communication is a complex field that requires collaboration as well as thoughtful, purposeful design. Just as words and images must work together in a technical document to create meaning, you need to sharpen your ability to work with tools and in teams to create the best possible product.

Chapter 4
Multimodal and Multimedia Communication

Abstract: Multimodal documents use a combination of written, auditory, spatial, gestural, and visual choices to help convey and deepen a document's message. Technical communication requires that you understand the choices a writer/designer makes and be able to explain the chosen output. In professional workplaces, your boss will expect you to be able to explain why and how you chose a certain mode of expression for the information and how it benefits the end user. To be successful, you will need to understand and apply a range of communication modes and media.

Looking Ahead

1. Why Multimodal and Multimedia Communication Matter

2. Multimodal Communication at Work

3. Rhetorical Awareness and Digital Literacy

4. Output Options

Why Multimodal and Multimedia Communication Matter

Think about the many ways you absorb information daily. Maybe you read your news online, stay updated on family and friends via social media, or get tips on how to perfect your standup routine through podcasts. You interact with different modes—simply put, a variety of communication methods—when you take in ideas through multiple channels, such as text, images, videos, or podcasts

Multimodal communication is a system of relaying information that includes gestural (movements), linguistic (words), aural (sounds), visual (images), and spatial (physical arrangement) modes (figure 1). Because the use of multiple modes of communication is so common, you may not recognize it at first. Ever play charades? Or create a home budget on a spreadsheet to track your monthly expenses? Congrats. You're already living a multimodal life.

The digital age has produced an increased interest in multimodal communication. Your phone, computer, and Instagram account provide different avenues for you to make meaning. Even if you don't own a cell phone or personal computer, you still participate in a multimodal life because it's all around you.

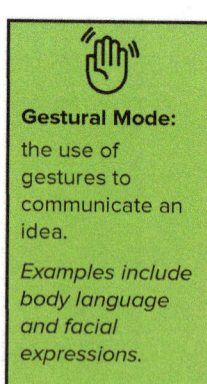
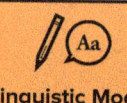

Gestural Mode: the use of gestures to communicate an idea.

Examples include body language and facial expressions.

Linguistic Mode: the use of words, whether written or spoken, to communicate an idea.

Examples include a business letter, an email, or a podcast.

Aural Mode: the use of sound and music to communicate an idea.

Examples include sound effects, pauses, and songs.

Visual Mode: the use of visual elements (color, layout, design, etc.) to communicate an idea.

Examples include charts, infographics, and diagrams.

Spatial Mode: the use of organization, design, and physical arrangement to communicate an idea.

Examples include using proximity or contrast of elements to express an idea.

Figure 1. Multimodal communication mixes together different ways of conveying meaning, mainly gestural, linguistic, aural, visual, and spatial modes.

Think about your last trip to the mall. You were surrounded by multimodal communication whether you knew it or not. When you visit a mall, or any modern retail space, you are presented with multiple modes. When you pass a store playing loud, danceable music, that store is using the aural mode to indicate the store is full of fresh styles you'd feel good wearing to a club. If you walk in, employees use the gestural mode of smiling at you to indicate you are welcome and belong in the store. The spatial mode is used to arrange the store so you will pass points of interest in a specific order—the clearance rack is never by the door and accessories are on the way to the register. Meanwhile, you experience the visual mode through images of people looking good in the latest fashions. Even the flattering mirror shape and lighting in the fitting rooms are designed for a purpose. You encounter the textual mode via exciting buzzwords, information, and price tags. A lot of careful consideration and expertise is behind how the store brand is communicated. Take a moment to consider what multimodal elements might make you choose one store over another.

The pervasiveness of multimodal communication means that modern audiences expect it. As a technical communicator, you should be ready to satisfy this expectation. As a student and developing professional, you should understand *why* the choices you make about the process (your mode) and *how* the finished product is distributed (your medium) both create meaning for the user. This sequence requires you to focus specifically on how to transfer meaning to a user. You must think about what your audience understands and how they need to receive new information to make it useful.

Multimodal and Multimedia Communication Defined

Multimodal and multimedia sound similar, but don't let that fool you. **Modes** are broad categories for how meaning is created and experienced. **Media** (the plural form of medium) is the final product that serves as a container for the information. The difference between mode and medium can be confusing because both terms can be applied to a single form of communication. The next two sections will help break down the difference even more.

Every piece of communication has a mode and a medium. For example, the TED Talk by Suchitra Krishnan-Sarin called "What You Should Know about Vaping and E-cigarettes" combines linguistic, aural, visual and gestural modes, but it also has a medium (online digital video). You might find it helpful to think of mode as the larger, general category and medium as the narrower, specific category (figure 2).

In this TED Talk, Krishnan-Sarin talks about the feeling of raising children, her expertise studying the biology of addiction, and the popularity of vaping while debunking myths about the safety of e-cigarettes. Her speech combines linguistic and aural modes, just as her slides showing different types of vapes, diagrams of e-cigarettes, and the definition of "chasing smoke" use the visual mode. Her body language, facial expressions, and hand movements aren't emphasized in the talk, but these do represent the gestural mode—especially when Krishnan-Sarin makes an "opening the door" gesture with her hand while presenting a new slide. The video offers an excellent example of a multimodal approach to presenting a technical topic to a broad audience.

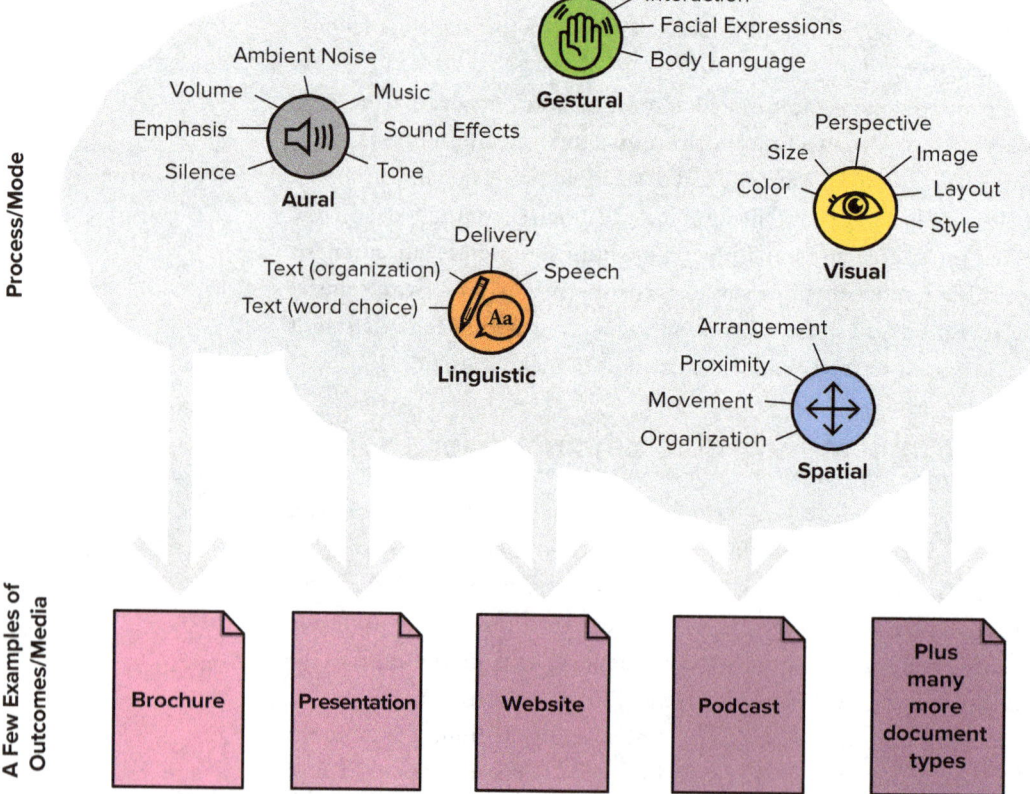

Figure 2. One way to help distinguish between modes and media is to think about where the action takes place. The choices you make while composing a business letter or assembling a presentation are part of a sophisticated internal process. The medium is the outward-facing product that carries your idea to the user.

Modes

Mode is the style or way content is presented. Mode can be text, images, sound, movement, or anything that creates and conveys meaning. An interpretive dance is an example of a movement-based mode that is useful for describing complex emotional landscapes difficult to put into words. However, this mode would be useless when trying to efficiently describe the safety precautions necessary to operate a forklift.

Multimodal describes using more than one mode at the same time. For example, if you give a presentation to your class, you'll likely write an outline beforehand (text). You'll vocally deliver your ideas in front of the class (speech). To make your presentation interesting, you add in a visual aid or animated slides with sound effects (color, image, movement, sound). You use the room as your stage and invite audience participation (gesture, movement). You might not have thought about it directly in these terms, but by incorporating all these elements, you've given a multimodal presentation.

Medium/Media

A **medium** is a means of transmitting information or data. A résumé is an example of a medium. So is a website. Both examples deliver information. They are the result of a process. **Media** is the plural of medium. Multimedia refers to more than one medium being used in the same application. For example, a multimedia presentation might feature printed handouts, video clips from a documentary, or audio recordings from an album.

For the sake of simplicity, the remainder of this chapter will use the term multimodal in a collective sense. Understand that when you read multimodal from now on, the idea of multimedia is implied. When you apply multimodal communication, it will inevitably take the form of a medium.

Multimodal Communication at Work

Prathita is a graduate student about to complete her education in forensic psychology. In Prathita's last quarter of graduate school, she is assigned a presentation about what forensic psychologists do. The instructor created this task to ensure students have the software skills to create effective visual presentations and can articulate their thoughts to a public audience.

Prathita will be graded on the layout, design, and visuals she chooses for her presentation. She needs to show that she can choose visuals that complement her text on each slide. Her instructor requested students to use text, visuals, and short video clips. Prathita and her classmates still have autonomy in how they choose to display those modes, but the instructor has limited students to a specific medium, PowerPoint or Google Slides.

During this same quarter, Prathita was selected for a position at a local community health organization that provides mental health access and services to the county's citizens. As you follow Prathita's transition in this chapter from student to working professional, consider how the focus of her projects expand from development choices to include distribution choices.

Multimodal Communication and the Problem-Solution Framework

Think about how multimodal composition fits in the Problem-Solution Framework (figure 3). As always, the relationship between audience, purpose, and message should move the communicator from problem to solution. Consider Prathita's ongoing situation.

After Prathita meets the requirements of her final project and graduates, she lands her first job. Prathita soon discovers that her manager doesn't provide guidelines like her professors did. Where her professor would have offered Prathita detailed instructions and considerable help, Prathita's boss leaves her to figure things out by herself. Prathita needs to be resourceful and collaborate with her colleagues.

Prathita's job is funded by a grant and that means her department needs to show a return on investment (ROI) to remain funded in the future. She must report on the number of calls her department receives per month and the type of services provided. The problem that Prathita faces is how to best communicate all of the information she is reporting. Based on her research, Prathita knows that reports like hers are typically presented in a multimodal format. She needs to determine how to combine modes in a way that will best communicate her findings. She needs to consider multiple factors to complete her task.

Prathita must consider the fact that her audience is composed of a diverse set of individuals. Not all of her audience will be physically present when she delivers her report, so she needs to consider how audience members will

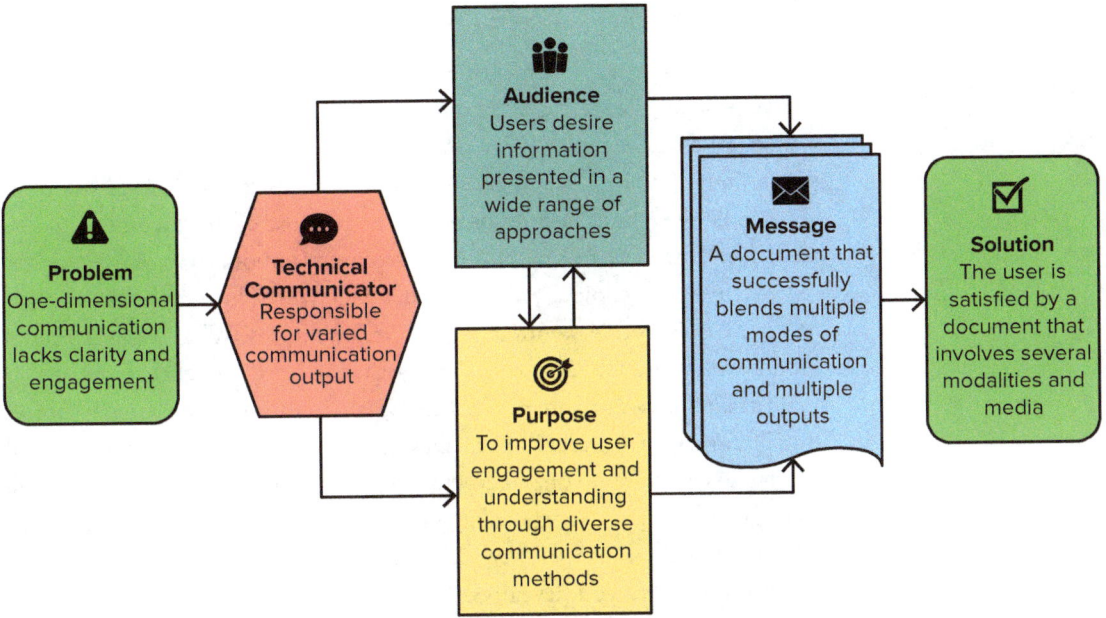

Figure 3. The Problem-Solution Framework is useful in thinking through the steps of creating multimodal communication.

interact with the report from a distance. Prathita also learns that some of her audience speak English as a second language, so she needs to communicate using clear and assessible language. Unlike an academic audience, who might not expect a multimodal presentation, Prathita's audience will likely expect multimodal documents as a standard.

The purpose of the report is to convince her manager, funders, and other stakeholders that Prathita's work remains valuable. As a result, her report must be persuasive. The message Prathita creates must combine the needs of her audience and her persuasive objective. Because this particular report must also take a multimodal format, Prathita needs to find a variety of methods to engage her audience.

If Prathita can do all of this successfully, she will reach a solution to her problem. To accomplish this, she will need to deepen her understanding and mastery of multimodal communication.

Rhetorical Awareness and Digital Literacy

Technical communicators make decisions about how they will communicate. You've probably heard the word rhetoric in other communication or writing classes. Rhetoric is the study of how to best communicate, especially when persuasion is involved. **Rhetorical awareness** means that an individual thinks about how they make choices based on the purpose of the document and its audience. When it comes to multimodal communication, you need to consider the value of your choices. Are the modes effective? Why are you choosing as you do? Could you make alternative, superior choices? What combination of modes will create the most meaning for the intended audience?

In school, you are often asked to explain why you made certain choices in a document. Consideration of these choices is important to your overall success. As a student, your instructor might ask why you chose to use a full color graphic spread in a report for your civil engineering class. Or, they might ask why you chose to use a vertical grid on your digital education blog that tracks lesson plans you developed.

However, as a professional, your responsibilities will go beyond the process to include production and distribution choices. In the workplace, you most likely won't be asked to explain rhetorical principles. Instead, you may be asked to explain the medium (or communication platform) you chose. Your employer isn't as interested in why you chose certain colors for your civil engineering graphic, but they are interested in the usefulness of an interactive blog your created for a neighborhood roadway restructuring project. Rhetorical awareness in this circumstance is understanding the situation and the needs that arise. It's not that understanding the process or product is more important than the other, it's that you need to understand the connection, extension, and impact of the choices you make about both mode and medium.

Digital Literacy

Digital literacy is your ability to locate, interpret, or generate information using a range of digital and online tools. Communication in the twenty-first century is about more than writing. Cell phones, tablets, computers, games, and virtual reality have changed the way people communicate and make meaning. If you want to remain relevant, you need to understand how to use and create multimodal content.

Digital literacy includes six essential skills:
- Knowing how to operate a computer or other digital device
- Knowing how to use a range of hardware and software
- Knowing how to keep your information secure online
- Knowing how to conduct an online search
- Knowing how to evaluate online information
- Knowing how to communicate and collaborate online

Hiller Spires, a professor of literacy and technology at North Carolina State University, provides another way to look at digital literacy. Spires says you can think of digital literacy as having three buckets: 1) finding and consuming digital content; 2) creating digital content; and 3) communicating or sharing that content. Each step of digital literacy flows into the next (figure 4).

Prathita thinks about the essential skills of digital literacy and concludes that she lacks expertise keeping information secure online. As a result, she does some research to learn more about how to improve the security of her information, as well as the sensitive information belonging to her department. She finds ways to improve her passwords, to add login securities, and to save sensitive data more securely.

Because technology moves so quickly, it's inevitable that you will discover gaps in digital literacy even if you grew up knowing how to code computers or hack into your sister's Twitter account. Digital literacy is not just about knowing how to use these tools. It's also knowing when and how to use them, how to evaluate the information you receive, and how to translate this information into forms that are useful for others. These skills can be developed and will be important for the rest of your life. Ensure that you have a strong foundation by keeping up with changes in technology, and your capacity for multimodal communication will be much stronger.

Subscribing to publications that discuss new technologies is also a good way to keep yourself from falling behind in your field. If there are

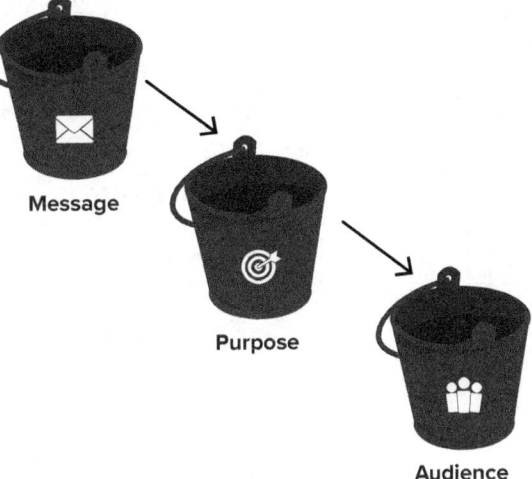

Figure 4. Digital literacy requires three different sets of skills, represented by the buckets here. First, you must know how to access information digitally (the message). Once you've found it, you must learn how to use or adapt the information for your needs (the purpose). Finally, you need to engage in the creative process of translating that information into something that can be shared with others (the audience).

significant changes to technology or something completely new is introduced into your profession, it's not a bad idea to take classes that give you a safe way to experiment with new technology while guided by experts. As misinformation becomes more prevalent and convincing, remembering to triple verify facts via the most credible, relevant sources should always be your top priority as a technical communicator.

Output Options

Many types of output (media) exist, and the options continue to grow and change at a rapid rate. This section discusses why and how you might choose one or more to create meaning for the user. This is in no way a complete list of options. This section offers a sampling of what might be at your disposal.

Choose your media thoughtfully. As a technical communicator, you need to make users confident in their interpretation. You can build this confidence by using media in ways that are consistent with a user's experience. The more you look at good examples of media application and familiarize yourself with what makes them effective, the greater the likelihood that users will understand your documents. The output options covered in this section are storyboards, photography, podcasts, social media, presentations, virtual reality, and websites.

Storyboards

Storyboarding is one of the more collaborative efforts in this list. It involves illustrations that help visualize a line of thought or a sequence of events (figure 5). Storyboards are used by writers, designers, and others who have an interest in the project. Marketing executives use storyboards to create advertisement or public relations campaigns. The basic framework of the storyboard facilitates communication by bringing together the separate elements of the story into a single document.

Photography

Photography provides us an example of how media is interpreted by different people. You may look at a photograph of a sunset and think it's romantic. Your neighbor may look at the same photograph and see darkness encroaching.

Chapter 4: Multimodal and Multimedia Communication

Storyboard Template

Shot # _____	Shot # _____	Shot # _____
Image	Image	Image
Action	Action	Action
Narration	Narration	Narration
Music/Sound	Music/Sound	Music/Sound
Transition	Transition	Transition

Figure 5. A storyboard template allows a group of people working on the same project to identify the elements that are needed to create a cohesive product.

While photographs can add interest and emphasis to a document, they can also provide specific technical information (figure 6). In a recipe, a photograph can tell the user how the lasagna should look when it's finished. In a user's manual, a photograph of the toaster oven can be labeled to show its parts and functions. In assembly instructions, photographs can provide step-by-step guidance for the assembly of your new bookcase. In technical definitions or indexes, a photograph can aid in visual identification of a specific item.

Podcasts

Podcasts are collections of digital audio files that can be accessed online or downloaded to a smartphone, tablet, or computer. Podcasts come in many different genres (categories), including fiction, nonfiction, news, humor, how-to,

Figure 6. A picture is worth one thousand words, the saying goes. Here, a photograph provides an overview of the ingredients the user will need to begin making a tasty meal. In this situation, the photography is not merely decorative. It communicates technical information that the user needs in order to complete a specific action.

and more. Podcasts are generally recorded and edited, but they can also be performed and recorded live for an audience. There are even podcasts about technical communication, such as "I'd Rather Be Writing," a podcast by Tom Johnson that explores trends and innovations in technical communication (figure 7).

Though mainly an auditory experience for the listener, the creation of a podcast is multimodal. Most podcasts have formats and recurring segments that listeners come to expect. These components are frequently outlined and planned in advance. Online show notes are paired with the podcast to document the show's content and to allow for additional information, links, images, and interactivity.

Figure 7. This screenshot shows an example of show notes from "I'd Rather Be Writing." As you can see, the show notes summarize the show, highlight key content within the show, and provide a link to the audio file.

Social Media

Social media includes websites and applications that allow users to generate and share content in highly interactive online environments. The most common social media site is Facebook with 1.52 billion daily active users (DAU), according to their publicly available 2018 fourth quarter earnings statement.

Certain social media sites are better suited for certain kinds of content. When you use social media professionally, review your company's social media policy and guidelines. As always, select the platform that best suits your purpose, audience, and message (figure 8).

Prathita, like most people, is familiar with casually posting content to Facebook and Instagram about her personal and professional experiences. She received an amusing call from a client while at work, which she's pretty sure her friends and followers would like and pulls out her phone to record the story. *Wait a minute*, she thinks, *this is a new job, I should check the policy first*. After looking at the social media policy, she realizes that talking about clients online violates her confidentiality agreement and she might get in trouble for being on social media while on the clock (her boss, Annabelle, is already one of her Facebook friends and a stickler about not posting anything before 5 pm).

Presentations

A presentation is a verbal performance that is delivered to an audience, either in person or virtually. A presentation might happen as part of a weekly production meeting. Or it may be an external meeting to keep stakeholders informed. You may give a presentation using a web conferencing tool to an audience

Platform	Audience	Purpose	Message
Instagram	Potential customer	Image sharing	New product announcement
YouTube	New customer	Video sharing	Step-by-step assembly demonstration
Twitter	Existing customer	Content sharing	Software update with link

Figure 8. Social media platforms may change, but the big three (audience, purpose, and message) remain essential for anyone who wants to communicate effectively.

you will never meet. Many presentation styles exist, but most incorporate a combination of modes, including spoken and written language, visuals, sounds, gestures, and movement.

One familiar and accessible form of presentation is the TED Talk. TED (short for technology, education, and design) is a nonprofit organization known for its idea-based talks and conferences. One reason these talks are so popular is that they distill complex and timely topics into segments of less than twenty minutes. This brief format makes them easy to share. According to Chris Anderson, owner of TED, the common element that all successful talks share is a singular new idea, which he describes as "a pattern of information that helps you understand and navigate the world."

Here are four tips from Anderson for giving a successful presentation:

- Limit your talk to one major idea.
- Give your listeners a reason to care.
- Use familiar concepts.
- Make your idea worth sharing.

You might never give a TED talk, but the same principles apply to a presentation you might give to a room of four people. Limiting the presentation to one major idea is important because it won't make much sense otherwise — it's too easy to start rambling and talking about irrelevant issues. All technical communication puts the user first, so it's your job to make sure the audience has reasons to care. Otherwise, they'll think you're wasting their time. If the idea is complex and the presentation is for people who aren't familiar with the topic, you need to find concepts or analogies that can help them make the connection to your topic. Finally, you should be confident the idea is important enough, developed enough, and worthy enough to share.

Virtual Reality

Virtual reality is a computer-generated environment that creates the illusion that the user is somewhere else. Visual and auditory stimuli produced by the program via a headset combines with the user's physical and sensory experience to create an immersive and believable setting (figure 9).

Just as the invention of the telephone allowed for communication to take place between individuals in separate locations, virtual reality communicates the details of a distant (or even fictional) location to recreate it in the user's

Figure 9. Could this headset be used for more than fun and games? Imagine being able to see complex procedures conducted in three dimensions. Virtual reality has potential within technical communication for training, usability testing, demonstrations, simulations and walk-throughs, or whatever else you can dream up.

perceptions. In practice, virtual reality could be used to simulate just about any activity or model any scenario. If once you had to read the instructions to figure out how to use your new blender, now you can don a headset and see a master chef assemble it and use it in your own kitchen. Virtual reality is multimodal communication to the extreme, and its use for the purpose of technical communication is still being explored.

Figure 10. The homepage for Chemeketa Community College's website gives visitors everything they need to know at a glance.

The images used on the website's homepage communicate volumes about the college's values and mission without saying a word.

Chemeketa's logo occurs in the top left quadrant of the webpage and is used as a watermark in the center of the page to give added emphasis to the text.

The top three navigation links correspond to different users of the site. The orange tabs are designed for students and donors. The second level of navigation links are for specific audiences. The bottom navigation links appeal to general audiences or prospective students.

Websites

The first webpage went live in 1991, and since then websites have evolved in design, functionality, and mobile responsiveness. You can chat with someone on the other side of the world. You can order products and have them delivered in a matter of days. You can watch a video on your phone. The amount of data created and uploaded each day is staggering. Every second, 40,000 Google searches are conducted. About half the world's population (3.7 billion people) have internet access as of 2018.

When you create content for an online medium, you must keep in mind how people interact with information. Because most people scan websites rather than read them, websites are often organized visually and spatially (figure 10). Web-based text needs to be short, clear, and well-balanced with images.

Conclusion

The ever-expanding digital landscape is rooted in the concept of multimodality. If you didn't grow up with this constant flow of information and changing technology, the pace of it all can feel daunting. Even digital natives—individuals who have used technology from an early age—sometimes have a hard time keeping up. Whenever you feel awash in the sea of information overload, remember that the foundations of communication are timeless. Just apply these classic ideas to new contexts and situations and you're ready for a multimodal world.

Chapter 5
Research Methods for Technical Communication

Abstract: Although the fundamentals of doing research for technical documents are the same as for other types of documents, technical communication tends to focus less on research for rhetorical goals and more on research for analytical purposes. The primary purpose of research in technical communication is to test a hypothesis. Because research quite often will turn up information that disproves your hypothesis, you need to allow ample time to revise and narrow your research question. But even a "failed" hypothesis can produce useful results. Effective research for most technical documents includes analyzing data and studies. Researchers always keep detailed notes so they can cite their sources and avoid claims of plagiarism or theft of intellectual property. Ultimately, this chapter guides you in taking responsibility for finding answers, evaluating the answers proposed by others, and delivering the best answer to those who need them to make informed decisions.

Looking Ahead

1. Why Research Matters
2. Steps for Research
3. Primary and Secondary Research
4. Using Sources Effectively
5. Citing Sources
6. Intellectual Property
7. Advanced Research

Why Research Matters

As a college student, you've likely had considerable experience with conducting research. This forms a good basis for your research skills as a technical communicator. This chapter reinforces what you already know about effective research, but it takes research a step farther by showing you what's important and unique in technical communication.

Here's another scenario to demonstrate how one might conduct the research process. Jessamyn works for Tomorrow's Taxi Company. It's Jessamyn's job to research issues for the company and put her findings into technical documents that will help her boss make decisions. Jessamyn's boss has asked her to research the feasibility of adding electric cars to the company's fleet of vehicles. Jessamyn will need to do considerable research about the cost associated with adding these vehicles before she can create a deliverable.

Research Defined

Researching for technical documents differs from research for academic papers. Fundamentally, research functions the same way regardless of your field or industry: you look for the most credible evidence that supports a conclusion and present it in a format that meets the audience's needs and expectations. The techniques you may employ while researching an argumentative academic paper and those you would use for technical communication are similar enough that you shouldn't feel lost while reading this chapter. There are, however, some differences to take into consideration.

The big difference is that there is less room for ideological concerns or biases in technical communication. When writing in an academic setting, your opinion often contributes to your conclusions. Frequently, in academic writing, your goals are rhetorical—that means your purpose is to convince an audience to see the topic your way. Technical communicators, on the other hand, must let the research lead them to the best conclusion instead of finding the research that best fits their preexisting assumptions. For technical communicators, sometimes a failed thesis is as useful as a successful one. Ultimately, the technical document you create may recommend further study or taking a different course of action than originally planned.

Research at Work

Back at Tomorrow's Taxi Company, Jessamyn begins her research on electric vehicles. Her company has identified an issue with its fleet of cars. Its traditional gasoline cars continue to break down and contribute to air pollution, costing the company money on repairs and missed revenue opportunities. Jessamyn's boss asks her to investigate whether it is economically justifiable to add electric cars to the company's fleet.

Taking a professional approach to this assignment means that Jessamyn does not simply make up her mind about the recommendation she'd like to give and then try to find evidence to back up that opinion. Jessamyn will need to do a considerable amount of research to establish whether adding the electric vehicles makes sense. Rather than making up her mind ahead of time, she needs to start with the question of whether the decision is wise and allow the data to inform her conclusions.

Like most people, Jessamyn has a personal preference when it comes to gas-powered versus electric-powered vehicles. These preferences came into play when she decided to purchase her own car. When it comes to the recommendation she offers Tomorrow's Taxi, however, she needs to be guided by data. Which choice is better for the company?

Jessamyn's job in this situation is to help her company make the best decision. Ultimately, she is solving a problem. The next section will unpack how this relates to the Problem-Solution Framework that you've seen in other chapters. After that, you'll encounter a series of steps to follow when conducting research.

Research and the Problem-Solution Framework

Jessamyn thinks through the Problem-Solution Framework as it relates to her research project (see figure 1 on the next page). In the case of Tomorrow's Taxi Company, the problem is the cost of vehicle maintenance and fuel. This problem is observed via quarterly expense reports by the owners, who would like to see a solution. Jessamyn's boss has narrowed the possible solutions that she could consider by directing her to investigate electric vehicles. So, her problem has been made more particular—she must find a solution in the form of an answer. Her answer must explain whether or not electric vehicles will save money.

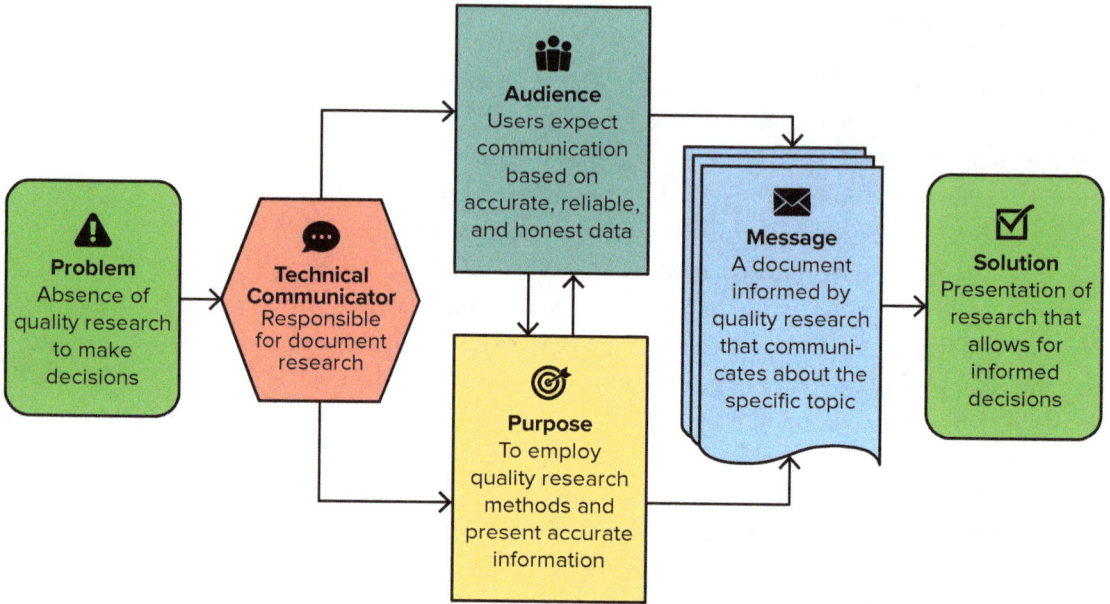

Figure 1. Use the Problem-Solution Framework to organize your research process for technical documents.

Jessamyn needs to consider the interplay between audience, purpose, and message as she researches a solution. The members of her audience are decision makers in her business, people such as her boss, other administrators, and investors in the company. These people aren't interested in Jessamyn's feelings on the subject. Instead, they want to be convinced by the evidence that Jessamyn finds.

The purpose of Jessamyn's project is to provide the administrators with a recommendation regarding the suitability of adding electric vehicles to the taxi fleet. This purpose will help focus her research. Even if she finds other information that could be useful to the company, she needs to guard against distractions and getting off topic in her research. She'll also need to avoid sources of information that are biased or inaccurate, even if they confirm her suspicions about whether or not electric vehicles are a good idea.

Jessamyn's message needs to be a clear recommendation in favor of or against adding electric vehicles. She needs to present this message in a way that is rooted in the research she's done. Her recommendation will only be respected by her audience if she can demonstrate that it is warranted by data and clear reasoning.

Having established how to solve the problem, Jessamyn can proceed to doing her research. She'll follow a set of steps in her research. The next section explains how you can follow a similar methodology.

Steps for Research

Just like in Jessamyn's scenario, you need to determine what problem needs solving. Sometimes this is easy: you receive an assignment from your boss or instructor. The assignment has a clear outcome, such as "determine the feasibility of switching to electric vehicles."

In your case, you may get an open-ended research project from your instructor. Your instructor may assign you a topic or give you the option to decide what you want to research and why. In your professional life, you can expect to encounter any combination of reasons to do research that range from putting a bid on a work contract to submitting a business plan to qualify for a small business loan. Doing effective, honest, ethical research is a part of everyday life in the professional world.

Step One: Observe the Problem

To begin the research process, you need to spend some time observing the problem.

For the purposes of illustration, let's say your problem is that you're waking up exhausted. During this stage of research, you begin by making observations and collecting data about your energy levels. Are there certain days you're more tired than others? Does it correspond to the number of hours you slept or to the amount of caffeine you did or did not consume? Do you notice that you're more tired on the mornings you don't have breakfast? Does the temperature of the room affect your sleep quality? Are you more or less tired when you exercise the day before? What about screen time? Do you get better sleep when you turn off the tablet an hour before your bedtime? Do you even have a bedtime? As you collect your data points, look for patterns, trends, correlations, or changes that can lead you toward the formulation of a more precise research question.

Step Two: Form a Question

To refine your research, you need to come up with a question to answer.

You could ask yourself, "Why am I so exhausted?" but you're unlikely to find research that will be able to provide a suitable answer. Instead, you need to narrow your question to one of the data points you observed earlier. Let's say that you noticed you woke up multiple times during the night because you were too hot. A researchable question might be, "What is the ideal temperature for better quality sleep?" This process will keep you from getting distracted by too many possibilities. Effective research requires an appropriate level of focus. Don't overlook the usefulness of the five Ws: who, what, where, when, and why.

Step Three: Propose an Answer

Those of you familiar with the scientific method probably see where we're going with this. You need to form a hypothesis.

A **hypothesis** is an educated guess. At this stage, you come up with an answer to the question based on what you may already know (or think you know) about the issue you're researching. Your experience of tossing and turning at night suggests that room temperature plays a part in sleep quality. Your hypothesis, then, is this: "Cooler room temperatures contribute to better sleep quality." The value of a hypothesis is that it tells you what you are and, more importantly, are *not* researching.

Step Four: Test the Hypothesis

This step is the biggest difference between some of the academic research you do and research in technical communication. In technical fields, you should view the research more like a test of the hypothesis. Your goal isn't to prove you are right. Instead, the goal is to determine whether the solution will work. To test your hypothesis about cooler room temperatures, you could turn down your thermostat and keep a record of your sleep quality over the course of several weeks. Better yet, you can find a researcher who has already tested this hypothesis on a larger group of test subjects and published the results.

In your search for a better night's sleep, your preliminary research may lead you to change your hypothesis. Maybe sleep quality is equally impacted by the temperature of the room and the amount of artificial light in the room. You will get better results if your research explores these two factors rather than a single one.

Step Five: Draw Conclusions

The next two steps require a bit of discipline. Many of us don't like being wrong, which can lead to questionable choices during the research process. As in all areas of communication, honesty is the best policy. If you manipulate or exaggerate your results, you may have to deal with serious negative consequences.

If your hypothesis doesn't work out, simply say so and suggest an alternative solution or new research angle. The user will then take the appropriate action based on your well-informed advice.

See **Chapter 2** for more on ethics in technical communication.

Preliminary Research

Dividing research into two stages can help you save time. The first stage is preliminary research, which you use to accomplish the following:

- **Find useful search terms.** Take time to figure out how professionals in the field refer to what you're looking for. This is one of the better uses for sites like Wikipedia—you can scroll through and look for terms that might get better search results. For instance, the more common term for myocardial infarction is heart attack. If you're looking for recent medical research on heart attacks using the search term "heart attack," you will get limited results. You have to figure out how experts in the field talk about the topic.
- **Take your research to the next level.** It's pretty rare to come up with a research project that hasn't already been explored on some level. If you find yourself at a loss for sources, it probably has more to do with what's going into the search bar than a lack of existing research covering the topic. If this is the case, consider reaching out to your reference librarian. Most reference librarians staff 24-7 chat sessions, have direct lines, or respond to emails.
- **Collect possible sources.** Since most topics you might research have already been researched by someone else, you can use this preliminary stage to collect the material you want to examine more closely.

Chances are you will read more than what you directly reference in your report. Jessamyn will collect information about the problem of gasoline vehicles and potential solutions of electric vehicles so she can provide a level of expertise about the topic. That means she will read all types of articles, trade journals, and scholarly sources to inform her recommendation.

You will do a lot of skimming at the preliminary stage, concentrating on secondary sources and determining whether you will need to do any field work (see primary and secondary research later in the chapter).

Final Research

The final research stage is where you do a deep dive. Effective research tends to be a little like increasing the power on a microscope to see the details of your project better. You'll need to have a solid grasp of the big picture alongside the granular details because you'll probably be tasked with explaining your findings when necessary. If your document is longer, like a technical research report, part of the document will show the granular details you discovered through your research.

As you develop your research, you will most likely encounter new questions, new answers, and further research. This is where having a focused question and clear hypothesis comes in handy: it helps to organize your research according to relevance.

Step Six: Narrow the Research Topic

Let's revisit the scenario above and imagine that you are waking up tired every day. This may or may not be a *technical* issue, but it provides some background for a possible technical research topic.

First, you need to observe the pattern and eliminate multiple possibilities. Your bedroom temperature runs hot in the summer, cold in the winter. This variation doesn't affect your sleep quality. Beyond your firsthand experience, your preliminary research on room temperature and artificial light didn't produce useful results.

Your next step is to narrow your topic. The common factor in all your sleepless nights has been your old mattress—the one you've been sleeping on for most of your adult life. Now you have a somewhat technical research question: What mattress will give you the best rest for your money? The scope and focus of your research may change as you start making progress. Simple problems get simple solutions—now you're on to a much more complicated topic: choosing a good mattress.

This topic triangle can help you visualize how to narrow your topic as you conduct research (figure 2).

Step Seven: Locate Credible Sources

If you're reading this textbook because you're in college, you are in luck: a chunk of your tuition pays for access to many highly credible resources you can use to conduct research on any topic. In short, you probably have access to independent sleep and mattress studies via the college library that no one without that access could read. It would make Jessamyn's life a lot easier, too, if she could still access her college's database to find recent research on electric vehicles. After you've narrowed your topic, you can take advantage of these resources to find the studies you need to make your final assessment.

Figure 2. Inexperienced researchers often begin with an overly broad topic. Effective research requires narrowing down to a specific topic to produce a focused search.

Another resource you can use to help you find relevant material are reference librarians. Sometimes jokingly referred to as "the original search engine," reference librarians offer so much more than a mere Google search. They can advise you on anything from search techniques to citation methods, and they can help you ensure your report on mattresses is the best, most comprehensive mattress report ever.

If you, like Jessamyn, are using a regular internet search, you should limit your search to weed out all the false results you're likely to get. A basic Google search algorithm privileges paid advertising (usually marked) and so-called relevant search results, which are governed by how frequently the sites are linked or clicked. To get on the top results lists, some businesses buy clicks.

Save time with these three ways to restrict your search:

- Do most of your searches using Google Scholar (see figure 3 on the next page).
- Use quotations around your search phrases to restrict the search to that exact word combination (see figure 4 on the next page).
- Restrict your search to .gov or .edu sites to find independently conducted research by using the "site:" function (figure 5).

Figure 3. Google Scholar compiles resources from academic literature, such as journals, university publishers, and other sites it identifies as scholarly.

Figure 4. The quotation marks tell Google to search for these words as a distinct unit.

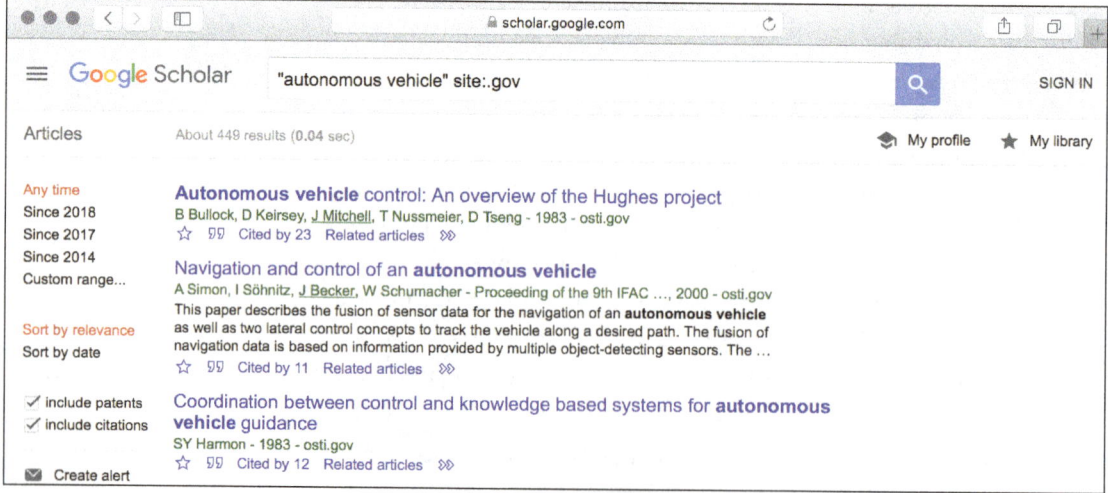

Figure 5. Websites with a domain of .edu are linked to educational institutions. Websites with a domain of .gov are linked to government institutions. This search limits the sites to those produced by the government.

You will have to determine the relevance, accuracy, and credibility of your search results. Don't simply use whatever you find on your first try—dig a little deeper. If you use all these tools to locate sources and come up short, you may have to conduct primary research.

Step Eight: Skim for Relevant Information

When you find a source, evaluate it quickly to determine whether it's relevant or useful to your research. Take notes as you do so to make sure you don't lose the source or your impressions of it as you make your evaluation. If you aren't taking notes, you aren't retaining information. Studies show that handwritten notes help you retain information better than taking notes on your phone or a laptop.

Tips for Skimming

When you skim your document, evaluate the source first. We cover this process later in this chapter. Where possible, take the following steps:
- Check for and read the abstract.
- Look for the scope of the research, methods, and check for sources, usually listed at the end of the document.
- Read enough of the intro and the conclusion to determine the reasons and outcomes for the document.
- Determine whether the source uses language you can't understand, such as a lot of jargon or formulas you haven't learned to interpret. Do you really want to spend time reading someone's dissertation on mattresses? An industry report in a peer-reviewed journal may be much easier to digest.

Tips for Taking Notes

It's said that the weakest ink is better than the strongest memory. This is why you take notes whenever you do research. It can save you a lot of time and effort to jot down even a few key terms while working through your sources.

Whatever note-taking style you use is up to you, but follow these fundamentals while doing research:

- Make sure you can find the source again. Make a bibliography as you find sources instead of waiting until the very end of your project. Keep track of important information (author, title, publication) that may get lost otherwise. At minimum, write this information down in your research notes.
- Write down keywords you may need to look up. You'll need to hit the dictionary a lot more when you use peer-reviewed or scholarly articles. Write down any thoughts you have about the research materials, such as how the source is relevant to your research. This can be part of your screening technique for sorting material quickly.
- Record useful statistics and data you'll use. Jot down a quick note reminding yourself why you chose the information.
- Make sure you have the page numbers for information if you're using a citation style that requires them.

Notes like these require diligence, but ultimately they save you a lot more time and effort when you compile research for your technical document.

Primary and Secondary Research

Research in technical communication follows two methods, primary and secondary research. For your project to succeed, you need to quickly determine what kind of research is required based on time constraints and availability of resources. Contrary to the implied order of their names, you will most likely start by skimming secondary research before engaging in primary research.

Primary Research

Primary research is new data that has not been collected before. This is often called fieldwork because it requires running experiments, doing interviews, collecting surveys, and getting out into the world. If you want to do a research project that develops primary research, you'll need to consider the following:

- **Fieldwork takes time.** You need to account for how much time you have to complete a project before deciding fieldwork is your best option. Often effective fieldwork requires exposure to statistics and advanced research methods. If you're unfamiliar with these, leave it to the experts.

- **Effective surveys and interview questions are difficult to write.** Leading survey questions can produce false results, throwing all your work into question. Think about online surveys you encounter periodically. Can you detect that there is a question the author wants you to answer? If so, that's an invalid survey.
- **Self-reported data is less reliable than other more objective means of data collection.** This is another potential problem you may encounter. If you were doing research on sexual activity among teens as part of a health study, you would have to account for the possibility that some of the survey responses are probably untrue. This is why you see margins of error listed in polls or surveys conducted by experienced, credible sources such as Pew Research.
- **Don't redo it.** Chances are high that the fieldwork you'd like to do has been performed already. Check before you decide to venture out on your own.

An example of fieldwork when choosing a mattress might include conducting stress tests to determine durability, sleeping on the mattress for a hundred days or more to see if you feel more rested, setting the mattress on fire to check flammability, etc. This takes time and might be expensive.

Secondary Research

Secondary research involves data that already exists. Trade journals, industry publications, and government reports are types of secondary research. This is the kind of research you do most of the time. Before deciding to tackle primary research, look at the literature in the field to see if people have already done some (or all) of the research for you. An appropriate time to move from secondary research to primary research is when you discover there is a serious gap in information that you think will prevent you from making a clear, ethical conclusion.

Secondary research exists in several strata, or levels, of credibility and depth (figure 6).

Figure 6. In the pyramid of sources for secondary research, notice how the bulk of sources are at the bottom. As a researcher, your job is to sort out what's reliable from what's not. And there's a lot that's not.

Level One: Blogs, Personal Websites, Propaganda

The sources on this level have little-to-no editorial oversight. Frequently this means that the person writing is responsible for producing, fact-checking, editing, and publishing the content. The source might be a message board or other user-generated site that has few restrictions on content. You'll need to do some serious background checks if you plan to use these sources. Does the source have an "about" page that defines its stance, publishing standards, or code of ethics? Watch out for sources that have weird URLs, come from personal blogs, are articles from hyper-partisan fringe platforms like US Uncut (on the left) or Breitbart (on the right). The chances that you can use any source from this research strata are slim to none, since this level is dominated by opinion, misrepresented data, and amateur reportage.

Level Two: General News Publications

News media is where we usually make first contact with a research topic we'd like to pursue. If we're assigned a project though work or school, this is a good place to get an overview and to find the language to use as we dive deeper. These are sources with a history of following standards of ethics, like triple verifying sources before publishing them. Wikipedia articles can fall into this category, since it gives you basic information and useful search terms. These sources are probably not viable for deeper technical reports, but they can put you on a trail, especially if you focus on publications that do objective analysis and heavily cover science and industry.

Level Three: Trade or Specialized Publications

Now you're getting into more credible sources. This is where you start to find trade-oriented publications that are still accessible to a general audience and a good place to go when you need help understanding the experts. *Wired*, *Popular Science*, and *Scientific American* are examples of publications that focus on general STEM topics and print articles that the layperson can understand. These publications do long-form journalism or researched articles that take months (or years) of research and usually employ writers with expertise in their subjects.

Level Four: Scholarly Publications

This level features the highest form of credible research. Peer-reviewed sources are written by experts in their field, and the articles are reviewed by other experts for potential flaws prior to publication. This process is standard practice in most scholarly works that reach publication. Peer-reviewed journals are tightly focused on specific fields of inquiry and you can usually find a publication for the field you need to research. For instance, there are at least six US-based peer-reviewed journals that cover fisheries alone and at least one peer-reviewed journal covering baseball. This is the best resource for deep dives into your favorite topics.

This level is also where you may find meta-analyses, which are the collected findings of multiple independent research projects into the same or similar subjects to determine statistical significance. Score!

Checklist for Research

Read the following statements and check off the box as you complete each step of the research process:

- [ ] I know what the problem is and can explain it in a single sentence.
- [ ] I have made observations about this problem to help me formulate a research question.
- [ ] I have made an educated guess (hypothesis) about how to solve this problem.
- [ ] I have tested my hypothesis by comparing it with research I find.
- [ ] I have found credible sources of secondary research.
- [ ] I have conducted primary research if needed.
- [ ] I have evaluated the credibility of my sources.
- [ ] I have documented my research and tested my hypothesis against it.
- [ ] I have taken useful notes that remind me what the research is about and where I can find it later.
- [ ] I have collected the information I needed to cite my sources.
- [ ] I have used only the material that is relevant to my research topic.
- [ ] I did not ignore material that challenged my hypothesis.

Using Sources Effectively

But how do you use sources effectively? This is the big question many students have while working with sources. It takes a little getting used to, but anyone can use sources effectively with a little practice.

In technical communication, unlike academic essay writing, you are less likely to use direct quotation. Rather, you will summarize, paraphrase, or pull

---

Introduction

Currently, electricity accounts for just 0.1% of all transportation-related energy consumption in the U.S., while 92% of transportation-related energy consumption is still derived from petroleum (0.03 and 25.7, respectively, out of a total 27.9 quads[1] consumed for transportation) (LLNL/DOE, 2017). However, in recent years, sales of plug-in electric vehicles (PEVs)—both battery electric vehicles (BEVs) and plug-in hybrid electric vehicles (PHEVs)—have begun to accelerate, with sales of each vehicle type increasing by more than 700% since 2011 (AFDC, 2017g). This rapid increase in sales for these relatively new (and still evolving) vehicle technologies was due in part to the need for automobile manufacturers to begin to meet the increasingly stringent requirements to lower CO_2 and other greenhouse gas (GHG) emissions (and the corresponding performance gains in fuel economy) to help comply with current and future CAFE standards.[2] Zero-emission vehicles (ZEVs) such as BEVs have played an important role in recent years to help manufacturers achieve their CAFE targets; California and several other states have recently required the sale of such vehicles (Carley, Duncan, Esposito, Graham, Siddiki, and Zirogiannis, 2016).

Battery electric vehicles (BEVs) operate entirely on electricity stored in on-board battery systems that are charged from the main electrical grid, usually via a special high-voltage charging station and using special electrical connectors. Plug-in hybrid electric vehicles (PHEVs) can also operate on electricity stored in on-board battery systems that are charged from the main electrical grid or by an internal combustion engine (ICE), but with the option of switching to the internal combustion engine for power when the battery runs low. Example illustrations of the key differentiating components for each vehicle type are shown in Figure 1 (AFDC, 2017e, 2017f). The advantage offered by PEVs over conventional ICE vehicles is their ability to operate on little to no petroleum (depending on the vehicle design and operating mode). Correspondingly, little to no CO_2 emissions are associated with such vehicles when calculating CAFE compliance.

---

[1] One quad (one quadrillion Btu) is equal to approximately 8 billion U.S. gallons of gasoline or 293 billion kWh of electricity.
[2] In March of 2017, the EPA and NHTSA officially announced that the midterm review of CAFE targets for model years 2022-2025 would be re-reviewed (EPA/NHTSA, 2017), reversing the decision to confirm the targets set by the previous administration (EPA, 2017c). Therefore, it is possible that the CAFE targets for 2022-2025 could be altered or eliminated during the upcoming midterm re-review.

1

Figure 7. Compare this document with the summary Jessamyn creates from it in figure 8. Notice how a summary is significantly shorter than the original.

data from your sources. None of these three techniques uses quotation marks, but all require some form of citation.

In the following section, we'll take a look at how Jessamyn summarizes and paraphrases information she found from the University of Michigan's Transportation Research Institute. Figure 7 is an excerpt of the source she found.

Summarizing Sources

A **summary** is approximately one paragraph (seldom more) that describes the source. Think of writing the summary a little like explaining to a friend what a movie is about. It works the same way. You've read an article on your topic and now you must describe the article to someone who hasn't read it in fewer than 150 words. When you write a summary, you typically include the following information:

- Name of the author and title of the work.
- The main point (conclusion or thesis) of the article.
- Key useful details (such as methodology or study size).

Take a look at how Jessamyn summarizes the research she found (figure 8). Like her, you should avoid writing long summaries. In early drafts, you

> The University of Michigan Transportation Research Institute examines common misnomers of electric vehicles in the U.S, including battery-electric vehicles (BEV), plug-in electric vehicles (PEV), and plug-in hybrid electric vehicles (PHEV). The extensive report cites current drawbacks including vehicle costs and accessibility. The research also identifies several benefits of owning electric vehicles (EV). The personal paybacks include less maintenance and fewer overall costs. Because electric energy converts more efficiently than a conventional vehicle, demand is expected to increase. This increase should help lower the purchase price. Once more electric cars are on the road, the U. S. should reap more environmental benefits, such as a reduction in overall emissions compared to gas-powered vehicles and a stronger nationwide security around energy.

- The research institute that released the report is considered the author.
- This section indicates which vehicles are included in the study.
- The summary identifies the conclusion of the original report.

Figure 8. An effective summary will contain the original document's most essential information, including the author, main conclusion, and other details that describe the purpose or scope of the research.

might be tempted to fill pages with a "play-by-play" summary of your sources. The research isn't there to provide filler for a report—it's there to help you (and your audience) better understand your subject so you can provide a well-reasoned solution to the problem. Think of the summary as answering the question "what is this source about?" and nothing else.

Effective Summary

To write an effective summary, you must read the source well enough to be able to relay the information confidently to the audience. A telltale sign that the source was not read or understood is that the writer uses vague, imprecise language that doesn't adequately describe the source. The audience should have a good idea what the article is about after reading the summary.

One way to summarize a source is to answer the following questions:
- What is the topic of this research?
- Who conducted the research?
- Why was this research conducted?
- What were the major findings?
- What were the requirements or limits of the research?

Paraphrasing Sources

See **Chapter 8** for more on writing definitions.

It can be easy to confuse a paraphrase and a summary until you learn how they are different. A summary describes a source, focusing on providing an overview of the material. A **paraphrase** recasts a specific author's ideas into your language. There are a lot of good reasons to paraphrase a source. Chief among them is that you may need to translate technical concepts into language that a general audience can understand. You can use some of the techniques we cover in writing definitions to help you paraphrase.

When you paraphrase a source, it's a little like when you tell a story to someone but you don't remember exactly what someone said, so you relate the general idea to your listener. In Jessamyn's paraphrase, she translates the report's information into her own words (figure 9).

Effective Paraphrase

Like summary, an effective paraphrase requires you to really know your source material. Read the passage you want to paraphrase several times and then write

> In addition to research funding, various government agencies at both the national and state level have enacted legislation specific to PEVs, often with the goal of encouraging or incentivizing vehicle owners (including government, commercial, and individuals) to consider purchasing PEVs.

This is an excerpt from the original report.

> Ongoing government support and legislation from both the state and national levels continue to encourage adoption of electric vehicles for individuals, government agencies, and commercial drivers.

This is Jessamyn's paraphrase of the original source.

Figure 9. In addition to paraphrasing the original research, Jessamyn also simplifies the language by avoiding the use of technical jargon ("PEV") to make the paraphrase more understandable for her general audience.

the passage in your own words. Be sure to set aside the original and don't look at it until you have your own version.

If you translate the original word by word or phrase by phrase into your own version, you may end up with a version that is too close to the original. You might be tempted to copy the passage from the original and swap out similar words. But don't. This is not just an example of sloppy research—it's plagiarism.

When you are happy that the paraphrase is in your own words, reread the original to make sure you haven't altered the original idea. Finally, cite the paraphrase according to the citation method required by your professor or employer. This allows the user to find the sources that you used to arrive at your hypothesis.

Citing Sources

Throughout college you'll encounter a variety of citation styles. Eventually you will settle on the one that is most heavily used in your field. The two you are probably most familiar with are MLA and APA, but you will likely encounter Chicago and IEEE, if you haven't already. Citation standards are the agreed-upon system for creating a paper trail for your research. They help

Find a handbook of college writing for more examples of how to cite sources.

other researchers see where your information comes from so they can more fully understand your conclusions. Citation also acts as a kind of insurance against claims of plagiarism or copyright violation.

In most instances, general audiences will be satisfied that you use one clear system to identify your sources. Choose the citation system that works best for your audience and use that system exclusively. You don't want your audience distracted by inconsistencies in your formatting.

In the workplace, no one's going to fault you for citing your sources. Your colleagues and even your future self may thank you for pointing them in the direction of sources they can use for similar projects. When in doubt, use the citation method most common to your industry.

MLA Style

MLA stands for "Modern Language Association," which is the organization founded in 1883 to promote the study of language and literature in the US. The MLA citation standards are used by English and World Language classes in US colleges and universities.

Works Cited

To create a works cited entry in MLA, you only need to remember four main categories:

- Author name (Last, First)
- Title (in quotation marks if it's an article)
- Container (publication, usually in italics)
- Additional information (volume and issue number, publisher, date, and page numbers for shorter works)

The works cited page is formatted with a hanging indentation and organized alphabetically.

Format

Author. "Title." *Title of Container* (self-contained if book), Other contributors (translators or editors), Version (edition), Number (vol. and/or no.), Date, Location (pp.).

Example

Doe, Jane. "Flight of the Killer Alpacas: An Examination of Early Alpaca Literature in Post-Colonial Andean Cultures." *Journal of Historical Alpaca Studies*, vol. 25, no. 3, 2017, pp. 325–415.

In-Text Citation

The in-text (or parenthetical) citation is where you tag the source you've used in the body of your document. The basic expectation for in-text citation is that the name and page number of the author appear after using the source, like this: (Doe 34). If there is no page number, you can use the author name alone (Doe) or the paragraph number (Doe Par. 5). If you have already mentioned the author name in a signal phrase, you can just use the page number (34). Notice that the period always goes after the parenthetical citation.

APA Style

APA stands for "American Psychological Association" and is used primarily by social sciences, such as psychology and sociology.

References

The list of sources for your APA formatted research document is called "references." Like MLA, the references are listed in alphabetical order by last name and are formatted with a hanging indent. The difference is that you follow this organization:

Format
Author, A. A., Author, B. B., & Author, C. C. (Year). Title of article. *Title of Periodical,* volume number (issue number), pages (print sources) or https://doi.org/xx.xxx/yyyy (online sources)

Example
Doe, J. (2017). Flight of the killer alpacas: An examination of early alpaca literature in post-colonial Andean cultures. *Journal of Historical Alpaca Studies,* 25(3), 325–415.

In-Text Citation

APA style also uses a parenthetical citation, but there is a comma in the citation and APA uses the publication year instead of the page number, like this: (Doe, 2018). Also, like MLA, APA leaves the name out of the citation if the author is already mentioned, as shown here (2018).

Chicago Style

The Chicago Manual of Style is a large text that defines what is called Chicago style. It is used most often in the humanities and within the publishing industry. The Notes-Bibliography system (NB) is used in humanities, especially history.

Bibliography

The list of sources in NB is called the bibliography and organized alphabetically by author. Chicago does not use the hanging indent for the bibliography.
Format
Author. "Title." *Title of Container* Edition Number, Volume, Issue Number (Date of publication) Location.
Example
Doe, Jane. "Flight of the Killer Alpacas: An Examination of Early Alpaca Literature in Post-Colonial Andean Cultures." *Journal of Historical Alpaca Studies* 25, no. 3 (2017) 325–415.

Notes

Chicago style uses footnotes instead of parenthetical citation. The number appears as a superscript number within the body of the text, as in this sample sentence: "The history of alpacas in post-colonial Andean cultures[1] shows that these hairy creatures are part of a long-standing literary tradition."

At the bottom of the page, you will see the source information next to the corresponding number.
Format
1. Author's name (first then last). "Title." *Title of Container* Edition, Volume, Issue (Date of publication): Location.
Example
1. Jane Doe. "Flight of the Killer Alpacas: An Examination of Early Alpaca Literature in Post-Colonial Andean Cultures." *Journal of Historical Alpaca Studies* 25, no. 3 (2017): 325–415.

IEEE System

The Institute for Electrical and Electronics Engineers (IEEE) is a professional organization that has created industry standards for the fields of computer science, engineering, and information technology. IEEE citation style is most often used for publications in these areas as well as technical articles and periodicals.

References

The reference page is ordered numerically by the order in which the sources have been cited in the paper. The author name appears with the first initial, followed by the last name.

Format
[1] A. Author. "Title." *Title of Container* Edition, Volume, Issue (Date of publication) Location.

Example:
[1] J. Doe. "Flight of the Killer Alpacas: An Examination of Early Alpaca Literature in Post-Colonial Andean Cultures." *Journal of Historical Alpaca Studies*, vol. 25, issue 3 (2017) 325–415.

In-Text Citation

IEEE uses a square bracket citation that corresponds to a numbered list of sources on the reference page, like this: [1]. You might be familiar with the variant of this system from visiting Wikipedia. Number your sources as you cite them in the paper.

Intellectual Property

By the time you take a technical communication course, you probably know what plagiarism is and know that your instructors will probably give you an F for the course if you do it. Using someone else's ideas as if they are your own is bad form, but you aren't breaking any laws.

If Jessamyn finds a study on electric vehicles and presents it as her own original research, her boss might not appreciate her lack of resourcefulness. But do you know who really won't like it? The researcher who invested her time and research budget to create the original report. During a late-night research session, she googles herself and finds that Jessamyn has posted the research on Tomorrow's Taxi Company's blog. Tomorrow's Taxi Company might be on the receiving end of a cease and desist letter, a demand for them

*See **Chapter 2** for more information about technical communication ethics.*

to take down the stolen research or be sued.

As an expert in your field, you need to understand the nuances of intellectual property. Intellectual property is defined by the Legal Information Institute at Cornell Law School as "any product of the human intellect that the law protects from unauthorized use by others." For our purposes, we'll touch on copyright, work for hire, fair use and public domain, and Creative Commons.

Copyright

Copyright law governs who owns intellectual property, which can include images and text. The law is simple: if you made it, you own it for the duration of your life, plus seventy years. You don't have to do anything special to show you own your copyrighted material, such as stamp a © symbol on every page of your diary, because the law covers your work as soon as you commit it to paper or recording, even if you don't publish it publicly. Copyright law allows designers to seek compensation for their intellectual property. Without copyright laws, anyone could steal your ideas and make money off them.

When someone uploads an image, text, recording, or other content to the internet, that person retains copyright unless they make it clear that they are giving away those rights. What this means is that you cannot use this content in its entirety without written permission from the creator. The same is true for any content you create.

Keep in mind that someone else could easily have the same idea at roughly the same time as you and publish their material first. If you claim they've violated your copyright, but all you have is a private journal as proof, you may not win this suit.

Work for Hire

If you've entered a **work for hire** contract, which is common in the technical communication field, you don't own what you create for that job. Examples that automatically fall under this contract are workplace communication such as memos, emails, and presentations created as part of your regular job duties. For example, as an employee of Tomorrow's Taxi Company, Jessamyn does not own the rights to her report on electric vehicles. The report belongs to her employer because they paid her to produce it.

If you are involved in a specialized project or working as an independent contractor, you would agree to a price for the project and how much copyright the client owns. If you get into a career like graphic or web design, understanding these agreements is vital to your livelihood.

Fair Use and Public Domain

Just because you found it online, doesn't mean it's free. A common mistake people make is assuming they can use whatever they find on the internet for free. This isn't true. Designers cannot use copyrighted materials without seeking permission or paying under the fair use clause. **Fair use** is narrowly defined as using parts of copyrighted material for specific purposes, such as critique or a short quotation from the original. To use the whole document or major parts of a copyrighted document requires permission from the owner, which often involves payment.

When copyright on material ends, it enters the **public domain**. You can use any source in the public domain, which is why so many movie plots are minor variations on Shakespeare plays or fairy tales. It's useful to know that all research published through government channels, such as CDC or USDA, are in the public domain.

Creative Commons

Some people are interested in freely sharing information and apply "Creative Commons" copyright licenses to their work (figure 10). This type of copyright is free to use but may come with conditions. A common condition is that you can only use the Creative Commons material for noncommercial purposes.

Whether you use copyrighted material via the fair use clause, a source in the public domain, or material with a Creative Commons license, you should clearly identify your sources and provide adequate citation.

Figure 10. A Creative Commons license is one of several methods that allows people to use copyrighted material without requiring additional permission.

Advanced Research

Some of the skills required for technical communication research go beyond traditional approaches. You will likely need to develop a skillful approach to learning about broad topics. You will also need to learn how to deal with subject matter experts as sources of information. And you'll need to conduct usability testing for certain documents as a gauge of their effectiveness.

Learn How to Learn

Your primary skill as a technical communicator is the ability to use language in a way that makes your topic easy to understand. Another valuable skill possessed by capable communicators is the ability to learn new topics and relate them to existing knowledge. This is why technical communicators are always in demand. Not everyone has the ability to do this well.

Technical communicators are often required to learn quickly about new subject areas. The eight research skills discussed in this chapter provide a good starting place for any topic. Your primary skill is in the ability to communicate, not the ability to possess exhaustive knowledge. It's the communication expertise that your employer values the most in your skillset.

Develop an understanding of the difference between key ideas and details or examples. Look for connections between new areas of knowledge and existing knowledge. Often you'll find that topics about which you know little have a similarity to topics about which you know a lot. Use this to your advantage. The similarities between the known and the unknown can facilitate understanding.

Sometimes, you'll need outside help to learn about a new topic or to check your understanding of a new topic. In these cases, you'll need to look for a subject matter expert.

Consult a Subject Matter Expert

While learning as much as possible about the topics that you communicate about is always important, don't assume that you need to be the ultimate authority to effectively create documents for an audience. If you lack mastery of a subject and need to check your accuracy, you will likely need to work with a **subject matter expert** (SME). Collaborating with a SME is common for technical communicators. You should learn to rely on them, particularly during the research process.

If you embark on a new project in an unfamiliar topic area, find a SME to interview early. Often your employer will arrange this for you. The SME might be a coworker in a different department of your company. If you are working for a company via a temporary contract, the SME might be a full-time employee for that company or another freelancer on a contract. Once the relationship has been established, ask the SME questions to help you in your research. It is likely the SME will save you considerable time and effort by pointing you in the right direction. You also need to consult with the SME at the end of your project—their perspective will be invaluable in fact-checking your work.

Don't be intimidated to work with SMEs or to complete technical writing in new topics. While most technical communicators have specialized skills and knowledge beyond technical communication, most will be asked to create materials outside of that specialized skill or knowledge. This is because the ability to communicate clearly about complex ideas is such a challenging task and because technical communicators do it so well.

Conduct Usability Testing

Sometimes part of your research will involve getting feedback from future users of the document. This is called "usability testing." The goal in this task is to determine whether the communication is understood by users. If it isn't, further research and revision will likely need to happen. Allowing the additional time needed for usability testing is an important part of planning the research phase of a project, as well as finding willing and unbiased volunteers.

See **Chapter 9** for more information on usability testing.

Conclusion

Just because you know how to use Google doesn't mean you know how to research. There's a lot of information out there, and there's a lot at stake. As a student, you can use your course assignments and research papers to help you get a handle on how to conduct research effectively and efficiently. If you're good at your job, chances are high that this won't be the last time you need to do research.

And if you really love hunting down information, keep developing that skill. How we find and access information is constantly changing. Employers need people like you who are both creative and systematic in the search for answers or new conclusions.

Chapter 6
Job Materials

Abstract: Job materials are technical documents that serve as the first point of contact with a potential employer. This chapter introduces the idea of adapting one's job materials (message) to the particular needs of the job (audience) in order to move to the next stage of the hiring process (purpose). Applying the fundamentals of technical communication can help you design documents that are persuasive and professional. As you'll see, creating effective job materials is not a one-and-done activity. These are living documents that you will build on throughout your career. Like all technical documents, they should be precise, clear, concise, accurate, and scannable.

Looking Ahead

1. Why Job Materials Matter

2. Organize Your Materials

3. Steps for Creating Job Materials

4. Cover Letters

5. Characteristics of Effective Job Materials

6. Job Materials Best Practices

7. Ethical Considerations

8. Putting It All Together

Why Job Materials Matter

Recent reports from the US Bureau of Labor Statistics show that the average worker holds ten different jobs before the age of forty. Younger workers are three times more likely than previous generations to move from job to job, according to a recent Gallup poll. That means creating job materials — résumés, cover letters, and the like — is not just a task for recent graduates. Your job materials will likely be a type of technical communication you'll do several times throughout your working life.

Almost everyone has spent time looking for a job, so you'd think the average person should be confident in this activity. Not so. Most people feel uneasy when preparing job materials. A survey conducted by Hired, an online employment site, found that eight in ten working adults find the job search stressful. In fact, the same survey found that most people feel looking for a job is more nerve wracking than a root canal.

The job hunt is stressful, true, but it doesn't need to be painful. This chapter deals with the technical skills you need to be successful and addresses some of the myths and misconceptions about the job search. When you create engaging and effective job materials, not only do you increase your chances of getting the job you want, but you gain confidence in yourself as well.

The Applicant Situation

Your college writing courses likely taught you how to make a claim and support it with evidence. The documents you provide when applying for a job should do the same. Your claim should be a professionally stated version of "I'm the right person for the job." You must support this claim by illustrating your qualifications with your job materials.

Your degree, experience, goals, and skills should work together to provide solid evidence that you are a good candidate for the position. Fortunately, your coursework in technical communication teaches you to design documents that grab attention and direct a reader's eye for maximum impact.

Let's take a look at someone looking for a job right now. Connor will graduate with a bachelor's degree in Business Administration. He has many high school accolades and spent summers working as a lifeguard. He works part-time in the business office at his uncle's hardware store, but he does not want to work for the family business forever. Recently, he saw a job at Eco-Thrive,

> **Business Development Manager**
>
> **Summary**
> Eco-Thrive, a leading-edge builder of tiny homes, seeks a Business Development Manager to join its team of dedicated, environmentally-conscious employees. The position will oversee daily business operations, maintain accounts, and focus on development and strategic analysis. The ideal candidate will have a degree in business or related field and know the difference between a flat head and Phillips screwdriver.
>
> **Qualifications and Skills**
> - BA or BS degree
> - Three years in business sales or related market
> - Excellent organizational skills
> - Proficiency in Microsoft Word, Excel, PowerPoint
> - Superior communication skills, both written and verbal
> - Ability to communicate technical information in a clear and concise manner
>
> **To Apply:** Send cover letter, résumé, and three professional references.
> **Questions?** Contact Human Resources at 503-555-5555.

Annotations:
- Whether or not Connor feels ready for a managerial position, he does fit the description.
- The ability to communicate well is vital to all types of companies.

Figure 1. The first step in Connor's job search begins with the job posting. Compare the description of this job with Connor's experience.

a company that builds sustainable tiny homes (figure 1). This could be his dream job, but Connor has some work to do first.

Even with his degree and work experience, Connor is nervous about preparing personal marketing materials. Yes, you read that correctly. These documents should attempt to "sell" your skills to potential employers. Connor needs to figure out how to translate his limited work experience and love of the environment into a compelling argument to get him an interview.

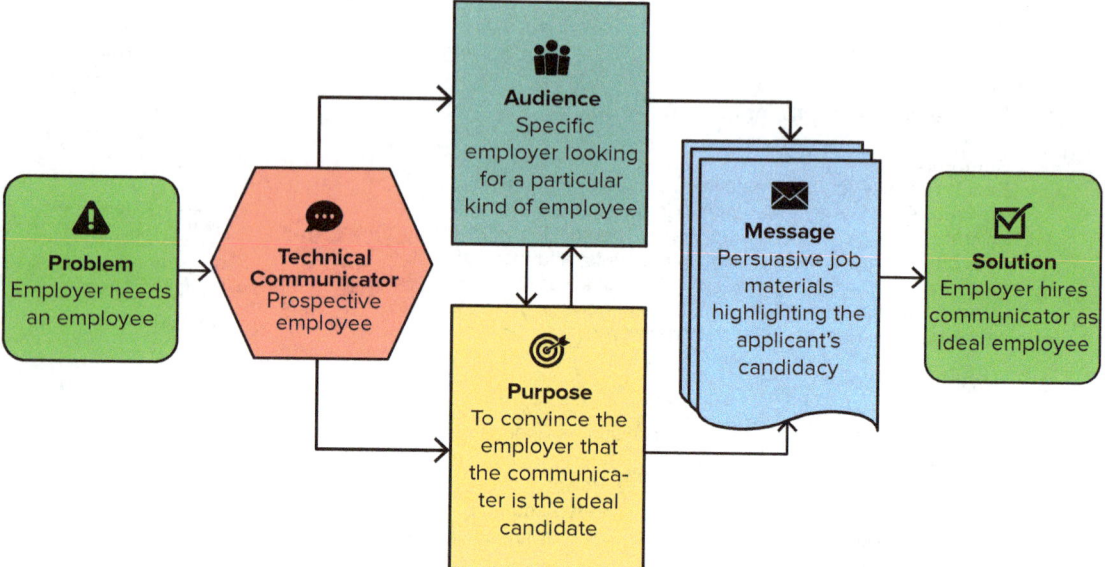

Figure 2. The Problem-Solution Framework can help you break down the steps of creating job materials. They have the same structure as all other forms of technical communication.

Job Materials and the Problem-Solution Framework

The Problem-Solution Framework can provide you with some perspective when creating job materials. Just as with the other kinds of deliverables, job materials will be better if you keep your focus on your audience, purpose, and message (figure 2).

The fact that your job materials always have the same subject (namely, you) doesn't change the need to tailor the documents to the specific job. Great job materials are written for a specific audience. No matter how much time you might save by creating a generic set of job materials that are targeted at an average employer, don't do it. Human resource managers and the other administrators who review applications are highly experienced. They typically deal with hundreds of applications for every job opening. If you write generic content for your documents, you will not stand out from the competition. Instead, you need to revise the documents for each application and customize them for the particular employer.

This impacts your purpose, as well. Although your objective may simply be to find a job, your specific purpose will change given the employer and position. This does not mean that you swap out a few keywords on your résumé and call it good. Businesses want employees who are committed to their jobs.

The way you think about and communicate purpose should reflect that you are sincerely interested in that position. If you rely on the generic purpose of "I need a job," it's unlikely that you'll make a compelling argument for your hire.

Considering your audience and your purpose together will help you to arrive at a precise message: your job materials. The nature of the message should be targeted to the particular audience and purpose as much as possible. This doesn't mean that you need to completely rewrite every job document from scratch, but it does mean that you need to avoid sending the same generic documents to every potential employer.

Organize Your Materials

Job materials can take on various forms, so you should be familiar with multiple methods of organizing your experience so you can create a useful document for your potential new boss.

For example, a person applying for a job as a nurse or nursing assistant may complete an online or paper application. An applicant for a position as the Director of Nursing at a hospital may have to prepare a résumé. Why the difference? The first two jobs rely heavily on licensure and experience, while the third also requires the ability to lead, supervise, and communicate well in writing. A résumé will help employers determine a candidate's abilities in these areas. Here are a few industry-specific job materials that you may encounter (figure 3).

Job Materials	Industry	Purpose
Application	General	Minimum requirements and specific job-related qualifications
Curriculum vita	Academic	Comprehensive presentation of qualifications
Résumé	Professional	Concise overview of employment history and qualifications
Portfolio	Creative or Professional	Work samples

Figure 3. Different job materials serve different purposes. Make sure you understand what kind of document the position requires. Some jobs may require combinations of these materials.

Organize by Purpose

One way to begin organizing your experience is to consider your goals. Many career experts recommend starting with goal setting before you create a résumé or cover letter. Why would anyone recommend this? Isn't it just an extra, unnecessary step?

Actually, this process is similar to other kinds of research and writing. Think back to what you've learned about thesis statements in your past classes in writing or communication. Just as a strong thesis provides a foundation for your essay or your speech, your goal statement can form the basis of your job materials. Just like a thesis statement, this is a short phrase or sentence that relates to your career objective.

If you know what you're aiming for it will help you with decisions and choices along the way. Think of it like a mantra, a repeated phrase that some people use to remind them of what's most important to them. Your goal statement serves a similar purpose in your job search.

To craft goals for yourself, you need to think about what you want. It might help to break your goals into current, short-term, and long-term goals. Consider making your goals S.M.A.R.T., an acronym that stands for specific, measurable, attractive, realistic, and time-based. The farther you've gone in your thinking for this, the easier it will be to articulate your goals in writing and in an interview.

Consider how S.M.A.R.T. goals can help you identify what you want in each of the following categories (figure 4).

Goals to Set	Areas to Consider	Questions to Ask
S – Specific	Job Type/ Industry	What is my preferred job title or industry?
M – Measurable	Income	How much do I want or need to make?
A – Attractive	Workplace Values/ Relationships	What is my ideal working situation?
R – Realistic	Location	Where are the jobs? Am I willing to travel?
T – Time-Based	Advancement	What do I hope to accomplish in the next five or ten years?

Figure 4. Reflecting on what you want will allow you to craft a goal statement that can guide your job search.

It's important to make a distinction between the goals you set for yourself and the goal statement you might include at the top of a résumé. Your personal goal may be to earn as much money doing as little as possible so you can retire early and live in a windmill. But your goal statement should express not what *you want*, but instead why that specific company would *want you* to be their next hire.

The practice of including a goal statement on a résumé is far from universal, however. In fact, some job experts discourage applicants from including the goal statement because it is seen as a statement of the obvious that takes up valuable space on the résumé. When in doubt, look for quality résumé examples in your target job market. Do they use a goal statement? If possible, ask the HR manager at your target place of employment. Do they prefer résumés with a goal statement?

Whether or not you include a goal statement in your application packet, the process of articulating who you are and what you want will help you identify the positions where you would be a good fit.

Select Relevant Details

Be intentional when you choose what details to share in your job materials. Whether you've been working for twenty years or haven't yet held a full-time job, your résumé should stick to a single page. If your experience is deep, you should limit your résumé to the most recent and relevant parts of your work history. If you're new to the job market, organize your experience in other ways by including volunteer work, coursework, skill sets, or activities that relate to the job.

Resist the urge to list everything you can think of on your résumé and instead be selective. Your goal should be to show that you're an ideal candidate for that specific job, not to overwhelm the person looking at the document with your list of unrelated accomplishments.

Create a Distinct Header

Your résumé may be in a folder of many. The header of your résumé will be the first data point the hiring manager sees. You need to make it stand out.

Take a look at Connor's first attempts at his résumé header (figure 5). Connor wants to highlight his proficiency with social media, and he has multiple social media accounts that he posts on regularly. Which ones should he include?

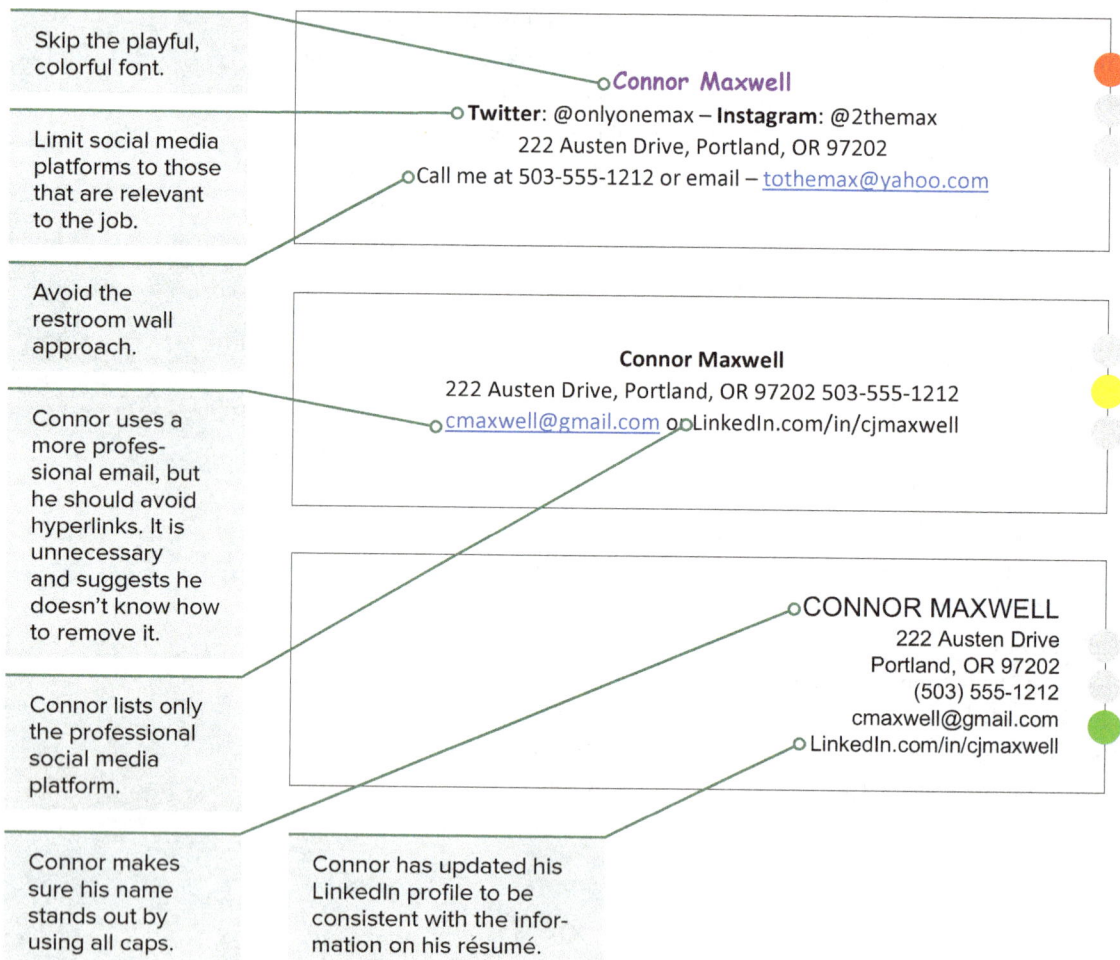

Figure 5. You want your résumé to stand out, but in a good way. Consider the effectiveness of these three variations for Connor's header.

Connor should only include the social media account that is geared toward the workplace and will help market his skills. It's best if he leaves off those that show where he ate last night or his hobby of knitting sweaters for his pet Yorkie.

Let's take another look at two versions of the header for Connor's résumé (figure 6). Notice how the first example gives prime real estate to his career objective. Not only is this objective loaded with general terms that the HR manager sees several hundred times a day, but it makes a statement of the obvious. In the second example, Connor ditches the obvious objective, which allows his education and current position to take its place.

Connor Maxwell
222 Austen Drive, Portland, OR 97202
(503) 555-1212 – cmaxwell@gmail.com – LinkedIn.com/in/cjmaxwell

Candidate with two years of industry experience, an education in business administration, and a working knowledge and interest in sustainable programs seeks an economic or financial business development position within a company focused on environmental concerns and sustainability.

EDUCATION
Bachelor of Science in Business Administration

This layout doesn't allow much room for the eye. Compare this version with the second format Connor uses.

Connor uses key words from the job description to highlight his experience with this summary.

CONNOR MAXWELL
222 Austen Drive
Portland, OR 97202
(503) 555-1212
cmaxwell@gmail.com
LinkedIn.com/in/cjmaxwell

EDUCATION

BS in Business Administration, Minor in Economics   2017–2019
University of Oregon, Eugene, OR

Relevant Course Work:
- Project Planning and Communities
- Special Topics in Sustainable Development
- Environmental Economics and Policy

The use of white space draws attention to Connor's contact information and the headings of his resume.

Figure 6. These headers use different approaches to direct the reader's eye. The first is a bit crowded, while the second makes use of white space.

Organize by Function

A functional résumé design groups similar items together. Your education, work experience, military experience, skills, and so on are all grouped in their own sections, usually beginning with the most relevant or the most recent. Someone with extensive work experience might begin there. A person right out of college, like Connor, would likely start with his education as the most valuable and then his work experience. Military experience could be placed in its own section or divided between education and experience depending on the nature of the knowledge or experience gained during enlistment.

This list provides some categories to help you think about how to organize your experience by function (figure 7).

Maybe inexperience is not your problem. You volunteer every weekend at the Humane Society, have always had a job if not two, and you got a 4.0 in school, a full-ride scholarship, multiple accolades, and employee of the month for four months running. Well, good for you. Your challenge, then, is to decide what to leave off your résumé. Do not reduce the font size so you can cram it all in. Choose the most relevant and recent. You can sum up the depth of your experience in your cover letter and, with luck, the interview itself.

Education	Related coursework
	Certifications
	Professional licenses
Experience	Military service
	Internships
	Related course projects
Activities	Community involvement
	Volunteer work
	Leadership experience
Special Skills	Social media experience
	Computer skills
	Fluency in another language

Figure 7. These standard categories will help you think about how to organize your experience by function.

Organize by Theme

A thematic résumé design groups items together by categories like publications, sales, or management—whatever relates to the field. This enables experienced individuals to highlight specific aspects of their career and areas of knowledge. It usually connects directly to key requirements listed on the job posting.

Look for the common threads between your education, work experiences, seminars, and other skills that connect you with the skills the company wants to see. For example, if the posting mentions market analysis, you might list the jobs where you performed that skill, the seminar you completed, and the courses you took on marketing and statistics. On a résumé, these might be listed under the thematic heading "Market Analysis."

For both approaches, it comes down to preparing the document that best suits the needs of the audience. It also matters what information you have to present. The functional approach is the most common and works well for many jobs and many people. The thematic approach can help set you apart or organize your document when you have significant experience to relay.

Steps for Creating Job Materials

A plan with a side of research will save you time in the long run and likely result in a more successful job hunt. Start by thinking about your background, and then research the potential employer. After taking these steps, you can begin creating your job materials.

Step One: Assess Your Background

Brainstorm all the relevant skills and traits you possess that make you qualified for the job:

- **Experience:** What jobs have you held that show your knowledge in the field and demonstrate a solid work ethic? Did you complete any internships or practicums?
- **Education:** What degrees, professional licenses, or certifications do you hold? Do you have additional college credits or partial degrees? Does any of your coursework show a specific focus in the field?
- **Skills and abilities:** Do you understand how to use computers and various software programs? Are you fluent in a language or languages other than English? Are there field or trade-specific skills you possess?
- **Activities:** Are you part of any professional organizations or clubs? Have you volunteered anywhere that would show knowledge in the field, work ethic, or character?
- **Personal attributes:** What traits would make you suited for the position? Are you levelheaded? Organized? Good at time management? Do you work well with a team?

Your audience wants to know what makes you qualified, not what makes you interesting. For example, Connor is fluent in Spanish. He highlights his bilingual skills and notes his international travel experience. Connor also likes to hike and considers himself a tea connoisseur. Should he include that information? Probably not. Is his experience as a lifeguard relevant? If Connor highlights the skills he acquired during his time at the community pool, it could be. His lifeguard position required an eye for detail, constant vigilance, and calm reactions to potentially life-threatening situations. Those qualities could definitely set him apart.

Step Two: Consider the Employer

Job materials, like the other technical documents, require research, audience awareness, and thoughtful design. If possible, call the HR department to find out more about the position. In just few minutes, you could learn valuable information about the hiring process for the job.

The first stage of the application might be reviewed by a recruitment manager in the company's HR department. You might gain other valuable information, such as the correct spelling of a manager's name or the closing date for the position. A few minutes of primary research will save you time down the road. Here are some questions to consider:

- **Research the position:** What are the minimum and preferred qualifications? What are the job duties?

- **Research the company:** How does the company describe itself? Are they local, national, or global?

- **Research the field/industry:** What are the trends in the field? What are the latest developments?

Connor looks at Eco-Thrive's job posting and finds that he barely meets the minimum qualifications. He checks out Eco-Thrive's website, reads their mission statement, learns about their recent expansion into California, and finds out that they are a nonprofit supported by government grants. He finds some comparable jobs online to determine what the salary might be. With a little digging, Connor gains valuable knowledge to help him tailor his job materials and prepare for a possible interview.

Step Three: Prepare Your Materials

From the point you see a job posting that fits your qualifications, you may not have much time to prepare and submit your materials. It pays to think ahead.

Connor has taken stock of his relevant qualifications and done his homework. He now has a good feel for the company, the position, and the type of person Eco-Thrive may be looking to hire. The job posting asks applicants to submit a résumé, cover letter, references, and a college transcript online. Connor puts in a few calls to his current and former employers and people under whom he volunteered, along with a few of his college professors, to ask if they would serve as a reference. He requests an official transcript from his university. He then begins the process of drafting his materials, keeping audience, purpose, and message in mind.

As you prepare your own job materials, refer to the three steps in this chapter. Remember the important attributes for all job documents are clarity, simplicity, organization, and concision.

Cover Letters

The cover letter is a strategic document in which you personalize your qualifications. If you don't make it too long and boring, someone will actually read it. One page is usually preferred. The cover letter should be memorable and not just a restatement of your résumé. For example, Amira is applying for a position at a nursing home. She grew up helping take care of her brother who has Down Syndrome. The personal experience fuels her professional commitment to providing quality care to others. Amira can't put that on a résumé, but she can describe the experience in her cover letter.

When you're picking the item from your résumé or your life to highlight, you need to select the characteristics that recommend you most. If employers can see you in action in the cover letter, they are one step closer to seeing you do the job.

To begin, think of one defining moment you've had in the workplace. How did it test you? What did you learn? Connor could describe his split-second reaction when he noticed a five-year-old girl struggling to keep her head above water in the community pool's deep end. He could describe how his lifeguard training, his decisiveness, and his attention to the situation allowed him to prevent a potential tragedy. Don't mistake this for bragging. Connor's not telling everyone he's an awesome person who saved a little girl's life. He's showing himself in action, and the user is left to conclude that he's attentive and calm under pressure.

As with the résumé, cover letters must be tailored for the specific job application. Does this mean that you must write a completely different cover letter every time you apply for a different job? Not exactly. Certainly, your cover letter will have similar information in almost every version you write, but the specific combination of details will vary depending on the job. You need to mix and match the information you share.

Think of all of the potential details that you could include like toppings in a taco bar. You don't use all of the ingredients every time you make a taco, right? You choose different toppings. In the same way, don't throw all of your potential information into every cover letter. Sprinkle different information like seasoning into that cover letter, and tailor it to the job that you're applying to. Take a look at the three cover letters that Connor has created for this job (figures 8–10).

Connor Maxwell
222 Austen Drive
Portland, Oregon 97202

December 1, 2019

Taylor Lombard
Director of Human Resources
Eco-Thrive Industries
5555 Greentree Drive, Suite 100
Salem, OR 97301

Dear Mr. Lombardo:

I recently came across Eco-Thrive's posting for an Assistant Business Development Analyst and would like to be considered for the position. My résumé is enclosed for your review. If you need any additional information, please don't hesitate to ask. I can be reached at (503) 555-1212 or tothemax@yahoo.com.
Thank you in advance for your time and consideration.

Sincerely,

Connor Maxwell

> Connor correctly includes the name and title of the contact person and the complete address for the company.

> The title Connor uses does not match the job posting.

> Connor has misspelled the director's last name and has also assumed that Taylor is a man.

> Connor's email address is unprofessional.

Figure 8. This first letter is polite but offers very little information and assumes the résumé speaks for itself. The letter also contains several avoidable mistakes.

> Connor's formatting is inconsistent. His name and return address should be aligned to the left-hand margin.

> Connor has verified the spelling of the HR director's name and has chosen to use the full name instead of making an assumption about the director's gender.

> Connor has identified the correct title that Eco-Thrive used.

> Connor's letter focuses on what the company can do for him rather than what he can do for Eco-Thrive.

Connor Maxwell
222 Austen Drive
Portland, Oregon 97202

December 1, 2019

Dear Taylor Lombard:

I recently came across Eco-Thrive's posting for a Business Development Manager on the company's website and would like to be considered for the position. I graduated from the University of Oregon in 2015 with a Bachelor of Science in Business Administration and a 3.6 GPA. I have two years of experience as an Assistant Office Manager for Buck's Hardware and completed an internship for Kelly Motors. In both of these positions, I worked to develop the company's social media presence. At Buck's, I focused on bookkeeping, accounts receivable, accounts payable, and some payroll entry, as well as the preparation of P & L reports. During my internship with Kelly Motors, I had the opportunity to conduct market research and help develop the companies economic strategies and goals for their new line of hybrid vehicles. I would like to venture more into economics with a growing organization and believe your company could help me to expand my knowledge and skills in an environmental area.

Ever since I was a little boy, I have had a strong passion for the environment. I volunteer with the Green Giants, a program focused on promoting reduce, reuse, and recycle programs across Oregon. I have also done work with Homes for Humanity, an organization that builds homes for families in need. Your company sounds like the perfect fit for someone with my interests and I would love to join your team. I look forward to speaking with you at your earliest convenience. If you need any additional information, please do not hesitate to contact me. I can be reached by phone at (555) 555-1212 or by email at cmaxwell@gmail.com. Thank you in advance for your time and consideration.

Sincerely,

Connor Maxwell

Figure 9. The second letter provides more detail but uses large, blocky paragraphs that are hard to read. The letter also contains jargon, typos, and inconsistent formatting.

December 1, 2019

Taylor Lombard, Director of HR
Eco-Thrive Industries
5555 Greentree Drive, Suite 100
Salem, OR 97301

Dear Taylor Lombard:

I am writing to apply for Eco-Thrive's Business Development Manager position in your community outreach department. I have two years of industry experience, an education in business administration, and a working knowledge and interest in sustainable programs. I believe I can bring a current approach and consistent dedication to the growth of your organization.

My résumé shows that I have put my education to good use even before graduation. An internship with Kelly Motors taught me about economic strategy through performing market analysis studies. At Buck's Hardware, I have gained more technical experience by monitoring the inflow and outflow of cash, taking inventory, and preparing monthly profit and loss reports.

My volunteer work has driven me to focus on environmental sustainability. I served as a Team Leader with the Green Giants, a local environmental group, for two years. Together, we planted 200 new trees in the Columbia River Valley and helped to clear trails in the gorge after devastating wildfires. This experience, combined with my formal work and education, have cultivated a strong work ethic and commitment that I would like to bring to your organization.

I would enjoy the opportunity to hear more about your company in person. If you need any additional information, please do not hesitate to contact me. I can be reached by phone at (555) 555-1212 or by email at cmaxwell@gmail.com. Thank you in advance for your time and consideration.

Sincerely,

Connor Maxwell

- Be specific about what you can bring to the position and company. Don't use clichés or be vague.
- Your opening paragraph should focus on what you can offer the company.
- Connor refers to his résumé but offers additional specific information about these experiences.
- Connor tells the audience what he can do for the organization.
- Make sure your email matches the one you used on the résumé.

Figure 10. The final letter demonstrates professionalism through a formal but clear tone that shows effective communication.

Characteristics of Effective Job Materials

The principles of designing a user-centered document apply equally here as they do to all forms of technical communication. Presenting your information efficiently makes a positive impression on potential employers. Keep the following principles in mind to ensure your job materials get you the best chance at scoring an interview. Designing job materials offer a practical way to put the following principles into practice.

Clarity

In the formatting of all job materials, clarity is king. You need to clearly display your credentials. Consistent formatting helps the reader find information efficiently (figure 11).

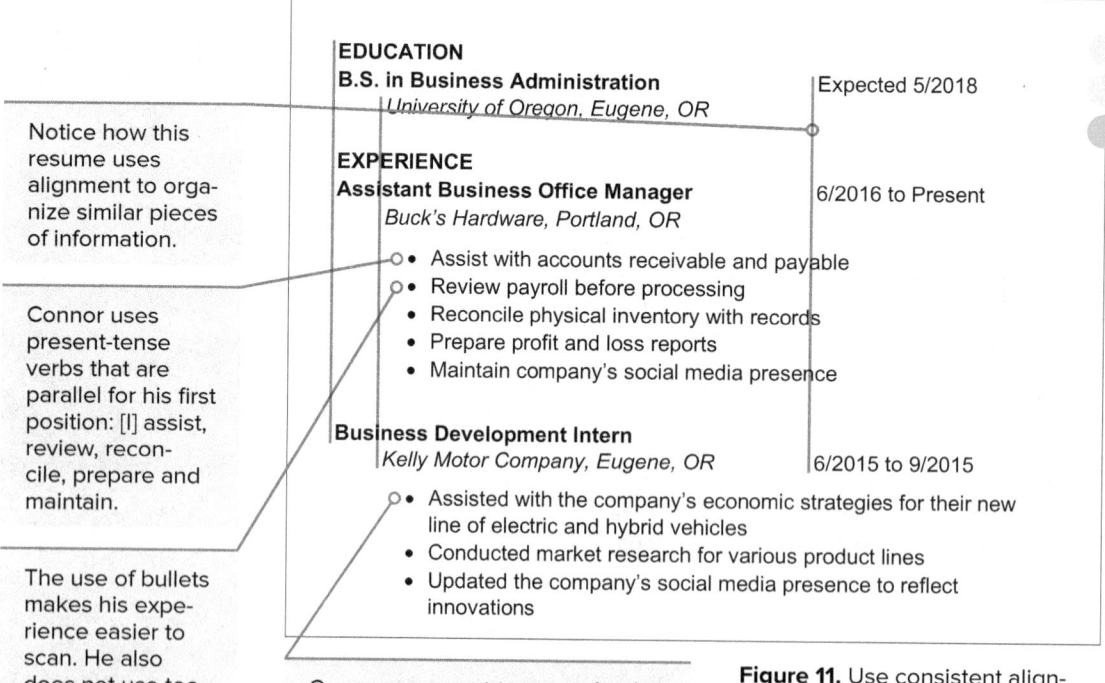

Notice how this resume uses alignment to organize similar pieces of information.

Connor uses present-tense verbs that are parallel for his first position: [I] assist, review, reconcile, prepare and maintain.

The use of bullets makes his experience easier to scan. He also does not use too many. Seven is the max.

Connor uses past-tense verbs that are parallel for his past position: [I] assisted, conducted, updated.

Figure 11. Use consistent alignment in résumés to create a clean, clear design.

Professional language does not need to show off. Keep it formal but accessible. Only use trade lingo or field-specific jargon if they are useful on job materials. The person doing the recruiting may not understand these terms. For instance, Connor spends time completing P & L reports for his current job. Most people in business understand this means "profit and loss." The person doing the initial scan of the materials may not be familiar with this term. The recruitment manager may be confused or annoyed rather than impressed.

Simplicity

Clean-looking, standard fonts in one or two colors read easier for most materials (figure 12). Avoid pictures or images for most job materials, and keep them to a minimum on web-based portfolios. Occasionally, creators of job materials assume that elaborate page design will attract the attention of potential employers. This isn't a good strategy. Employers want to be impressed by the content of your materials, not by the appearance.

Your choice of font is important when considering simplicity in your job materials. Do not use fancy, uncommon fonts to draw attention to your documents. Employers typically see this as desperate, rather than creative. Stick to using simple, familiar fonts that have a professional appearance. Traditional

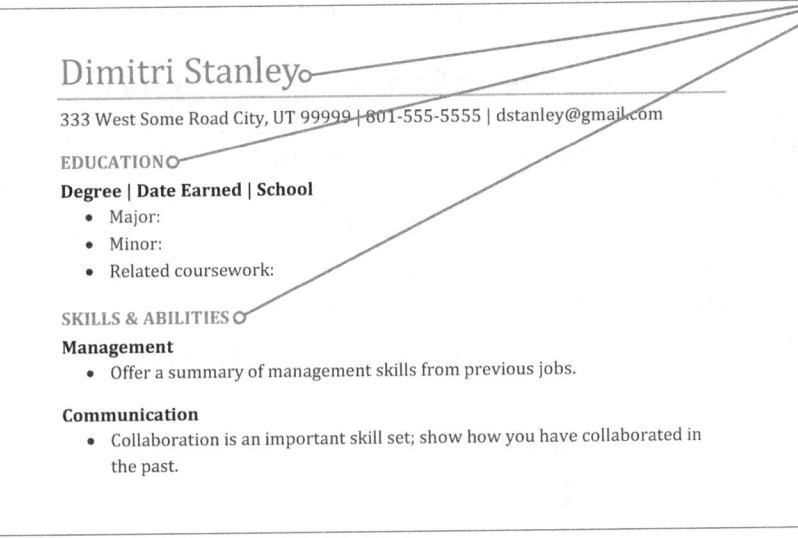

Figure 12. Avoid using too many colors or fonts in your résumé. Keep the design simple.

> See **Chapter 3** for more on serif and sans serif fonts.

job materials favor a serif font, such as Times New Roman. The use of sans serif fonts has become more acceptable in job documents, however. If you're in doubt, research examples of job documents in your specific field. Not every job industry has the same standards or expectations when it comes to font choice, so do your homework.

Organization

Intentional organization helps your reader navigate your job materials quickly to find the information that they need.

You can begin doing this by thinking carefully about headings. Consistent and deliberate patterns with no more than three heading levels will help the reader scan the document easily. The content of your headings is important, so don't just use what immediately comes to mind. Instead, craft your headings to draw attention to themes that are most relevant for the job to which you're applying.

Headings can vary depending on the field, so don't assume that the best headings are always the same. For example, if you're preparing a résumé for a job at a nonprofit organization, it would be appropriate to list your previous volunteer work beneath a heading entitled, "Volunteer Work." In the case of many other jobs, listing your volunteer work would be less relevant, so you might want to skip that heading and dedicate the space to a more appropriate category of experience.

Bullets and lists are valuable for sharing multiple related ideas that don't require elaboration. Bullet lists are useful for keeping the reader's eye moving down the page because they are highly scannable. As with all lists, be sure to use similar wording for the items being shared.

White space can help chunk related information together without having to use fancy separators or text boxes. Be intentional with your use of white space. Good usage of white space has a few specific benefits:

- It keeps the reader's eye moving through the document in a logical pattern.
- It emphasizes the separation and organization of topics.
- It makes the document more attractive by improving visual balance.

Alignment ensures that each element on the page lines up with other similar items on the page, such as dates and work locations. Don't get too creative and make the reader work to find the information. Give them a traditional layout that their eyes expect. The key is to use a consistent pattern of alignment so the reader can easily recognize the different sections and locate information throughout the document. Notice how these organizational elements come to together in this model (figure 13).

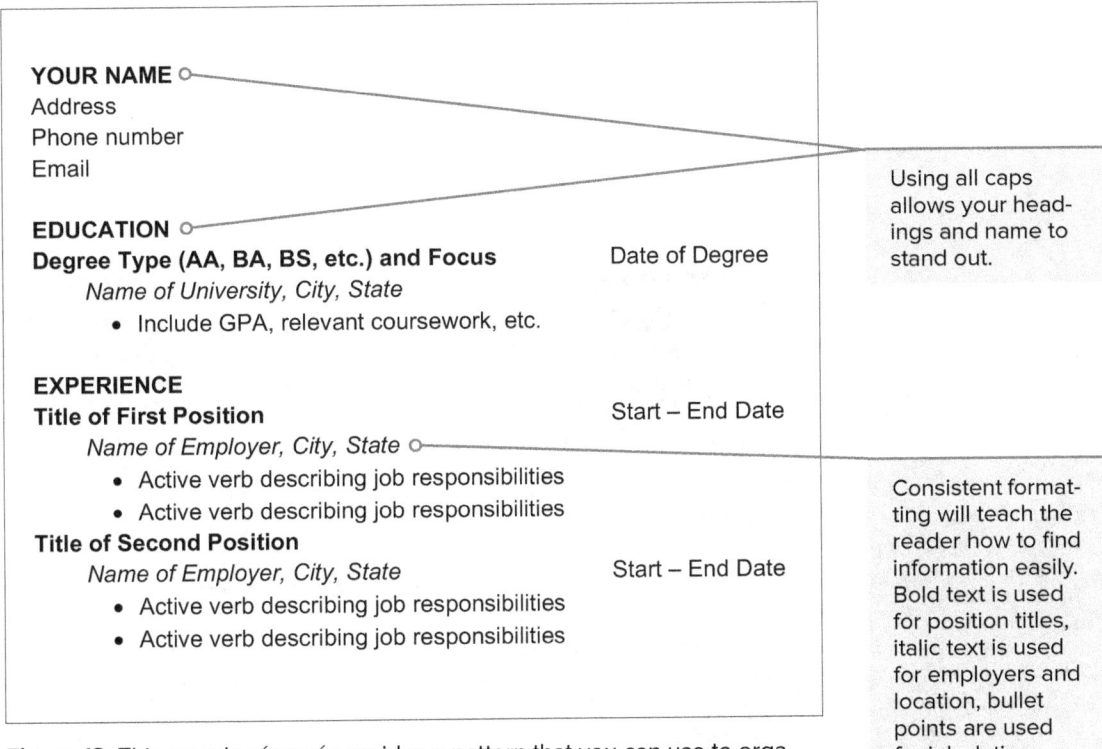

Figure 13. This sample résumé provides a pattern that you can use to organize your work experience.

Concision

There's a reason most résumés are a single page. Employers don't have time to read your life story. Make sure your job materials include only what your audience needs to make an informed decision. Do not give them excess or irrelevant information. Most importantly, avoid including personal data like your gender, race, age, or how many children you have. Employers should not ask for this information, and you should not volunteer it.

You would not want the conscious or unconscious biases of the reader to affect your chances of getting an interview. Also, leave off hobbies or clubs that don't increase your qualifications for the job. Employers won't be impressed by your knitting skills or Connor's participation in a Dungeons and Dragons group. Anything irrelevant could be off-putting.

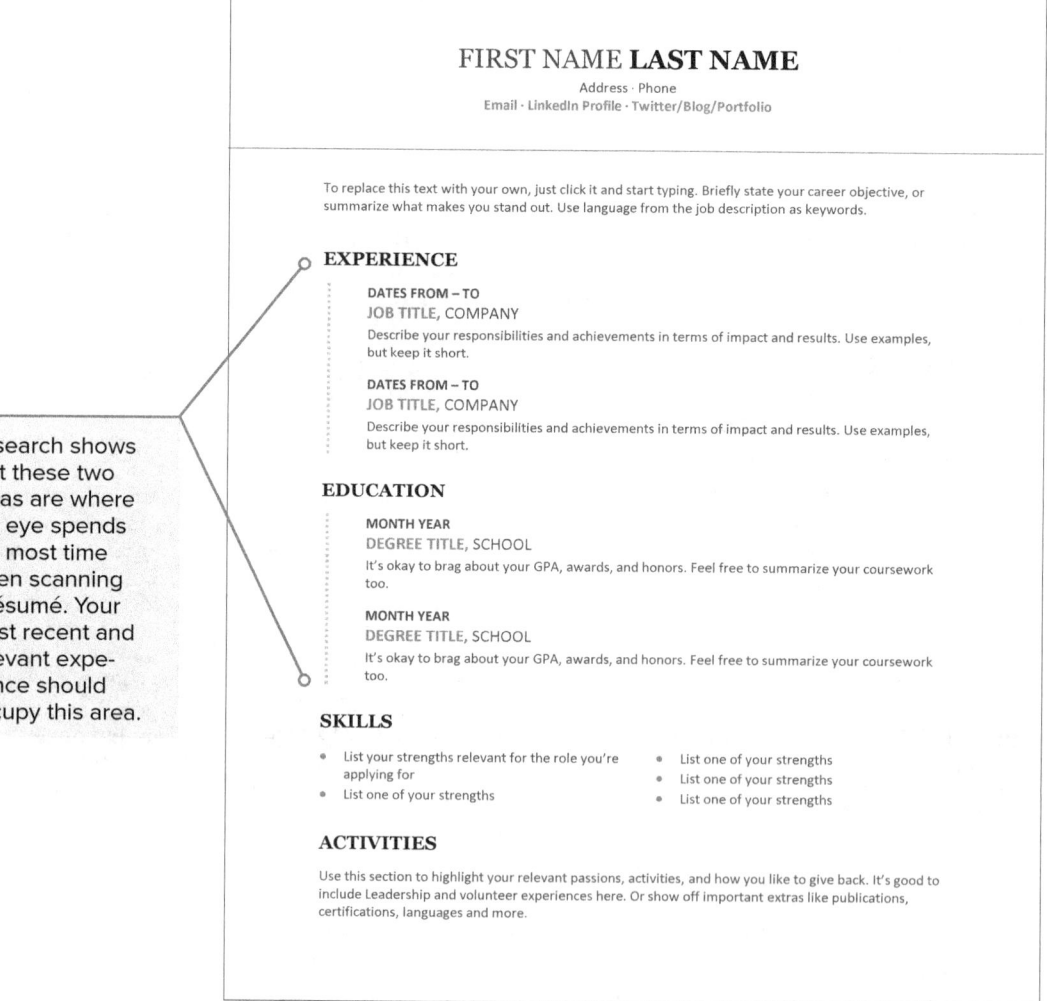

Research shows that these two areas are where the eye spends the most time when scanning a résumé. Your most recent and relevant experience should occupy this area.

Figure 14. Make good use of the area where the eye tends to concentrate. Place your most recent and relevant experience here.

Job Materials Best Practices

Following a few best practices can help your job materials stand out. Be mindful of how the following elements might impact your audience's response to your materials. Make documents that are easy to scan, include active verbs, avoid clichés, and point to references who can vouch for your work.

Design for Scanning

Research shows that employers spend as little as six seconds scanning job materials to determine if you might be the right person for the job. Their eye tracks quickly through a résumé, looking at the pattern of information and for data points that show whether the applicant meets the job qualifications (figure 14). Once you have grabbed the employer's interest, they are likely to spend five minutes or fewer looking over a résumé. Notice we use the word "looking" and not "reading."

Research tells us that the recruiters spend 80 percent of their time scanning for these data points:

- Candidate name
- Current position/company/employment dates
- Previous position/company/employment dates
- Education

Recognizing how your audience will scan your document will prepare you to design documents that are more effective and efficient. Your job is to keep the eye moving down the entire page and avoid any design elements or white spaces that stall or stop the reader's gaze (figure 15). You need to communicate a lot of information in a small amount of space, but extending the margins of your document and creating a wall of text will ensure that your résumé, at best, goes to the bottom of the pile. Too spare of a design can likewise shuffle your résumé to the bottom.

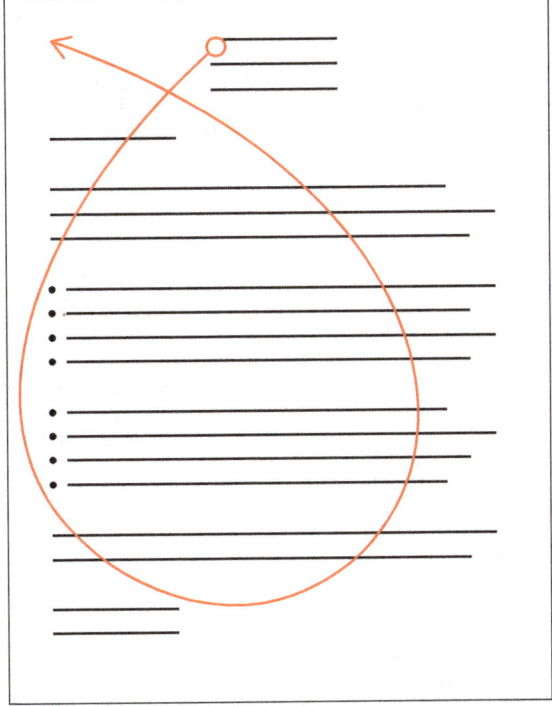

Figure 15. This graphic illustrates the way a recruiter's eye flows over the text. Bullet points and white space can help direct the eye and keep the reader moving down the page.

Once a recruiter has determined a candidate possesses the required experience and education, they scan for keywords related to the position. A **keyword** is a specific word or phrase that relates directly to the open position. Some companies use software, such as applicant tracking systems (ATS) to filter résumés based on keywords. Build your vocabulary list of keywords by completing the following:

- Search the job posting for important words that describe the kind of work required for the position.
- Search professional profiles of people who hold similar positions for how they describe their position.
- Search the company's website and "about us" page for how they describe their work and company culture.

Notice how Connor uses the job posting and the company's website to define his keywords (figures 16 and 17). In the first example, the highlighted words provide him with a vocabulary list with which to describe his skills and experience on his résumé. In the second example, the highlighted words help Connor tailor his cover letter so that he can show how his interests align with the company's mission.

The highlighted words in this job posting are potential keywords an applicant could use. These specific skills and experiences could to make a résumé more scannable.

Business Development Manager

Summary
Eco-Thrive, a leading-edge builder of tiny homes, seeks a Business Development Manager to join its team of dedicated, environmentally-conscious employees. The position will oversee daily business operations, maintain accounts, and focus on development and strategic analysis. The ideal candidate will have a degree in business or related field and know the difference between a flat head and Phillips screwdriver.

Qualifications and Skills
- BA or BS degree
- Three years in business sales or related market
- Excellent organizational skills
- Proficiency in Microsoft Word, Excel, PowerPoint
- Superior communication skills, both written and verbal
- Ability to communicate technical information in a clear and concise manner

To Apply: Send cover letter, résumé, and three professional references.
Questions? Contact Human Resources at 503-555-5555.

Figure 16. The highlighted words indicate potential keywords in the job posting.

> **About Us**
>
> Eco-Thrive is a ==grassroots== organization that got its start ten years ago when co-founders Ron and Brian ran into each other at a ==local== hardware store and bemoaned the lack of ==affordable== housing in their ==community==. Combining their love of nature and proficiency with power tools, Eco-Thrive was born. The company has a small but ==dedicated== staff of ==environmentally-conscious== employees who are ==committed== to making their community better. Eco-Thrive's mission is to think big but make small by building homes that are affordable and ==sustainable== for all.

Look at the company's website for clues about their culture. The highlighted words will help you understand what the company values in their work and employees.

Figure 17. The highlighted words indicate ways to tailor job materials to the specific employer.

Use Active and Specific Verbs

You can enliven your technical documents by using active and specific verbs. Doing this helps to convey the importance of what you've done in previous roles, rather than simply mentioning that you were employed somewhere. For example, if you say that you "worked in sales" at a particular job, it doesn't sound particularly impressive. On the other hand, if you say that you "managed the sales accounts for forty commercial customers," the reader has a much better impression of your role and responsibilities.

On your résumé, use a variety of specific action verbs to convey your past experiences as accurately as possible. Use the past tense, such as "managed," for past jobs. Use the present tense, such as "manage," for jobs you still hold. Here are some verbs to give oomph to your résumé:

- Adapted
- Advised
- Analyzed
- Chaired
- Communicated
- Composed
- Conducted
- Consulted
- Coordinated
- Developed
- Evaluated
- Formulated
- Generated
- Improved
- Increased
- Initiated
- Led
- Maintained
- Negotiated
- Organized
- Oversaw
- Promoted
- Resolved
- Specialized

In your cover letter, go one step farther. Provide evidence of your qualifications that is specific and measurable. For example, Connor volunteered with the Green Giants and helped grow its recycling programs by 20 percent. Generalities, such as "I'm a hard worker" or "I have good leadership skills," tend to fall flat. But statements like "I served as a team leader with the Green Giants for two years" and "We planted 200 new trees in the Columbia River Valley" offer evidence to support his claim.

Avoid Clichés

A **cliché** is a sentence or phrase that is overused and shows a lack of originality. How many times can you hear someone tell you to "make lemonade out of lemons" or that they "love you to the moon and back?" It might be cute, but cute is not the trait you're marketing. It may seem like employers want to know that you're a leader, excellent at interpersonal communication, and detail oriented, but everyone says this. Do your research and find the overused phrases for the specific job document you're completing. Find a different way to convey that information without employing the clichés.

What you need, instead, are keywords. As mentioned earlier, these are words that are functional rather than descriptive. An example of functional keywords would be to say you are a "social media expert" instead of saying you have "excellent communication skills." Employers use keywords to find matches, particularly when your materials are part of a database. Saying you

Clichés to Avoid	Attention-Grabbing Alternatives
Strong leadership skills	Led department to a 30 percent increase in client satisfaction
Good communicator	Excellent at generating approved grant proposals
Excellent team player	Worked with a team to increase company revenues by 10 percent
Self-motivated	Independently implemented a new customer satisfaction program
Track record of success	Consistently surpassed department goals by 5–10 percent

Figure 18. If you want to stand out, don't use the tired phrases and buzz words everyone else will be using.

are a "strong leader" will lump you in with a ton of other people. This table outlines phrases overused by job seekers (figure 18).

Include specifics when possible as further evidence of your claim. Don't underestimate this. Anyone can describe themselves using adjectives, but competitive applicants can point to what they've *done* as a way of demonstrating their character and abilities. Even without data to measure your success, specific language builds more credibility with your audience. It also proves that you're a "good communicator" without you having to say it.

Maintain Strong Connections

Most job postings will ask for around three references or recommendations, either as part of the application process or part of the interview. It's important that you don't wait until you're looking for a job to build your bench of supporters who are familiar with your work ethic and abilities. Keep in touch and stay on good terms with previous supervisors and teachers. These are the people most likely to be able to provide a recommendation.

Connor has already asked two of his current instructors to serve as a reference. He's considering using his uncle as a reference, since Uncle Buck is his current employer and direct supervisor. However, a family member isn't usually the best, unbiased choice, and his uncle does not know he is job hunting. So, what does he do?

Most potential employers do not expect you to use your current employer as a reference. Many people look for a new job while they still have one, often without telling their boss. You do not need to jeopardize your current position by sharing this information. Connor can leave his uncle off his reference list without alarming anyone. Instead, he contacts the coach of his swim team who can speak to his commitment to continuous improvement and his ability to work well with others.

Ethical Considerations

Tailoring your job materials does not mean exaggerating your abilities or past jobs. It means sending the right materials for the right position, not altering history. Even simple adjustments, like referring to your hostess position at a restaurant as a "Client Services Manager" distorts the truth and implies an unproven level of skill. Your dishonesty will eventually be exposed when it is time to do the work.

Connor does not supervise anyone in his current job but knows leadership skills will look good on his résumé. Rather than counting the times he has kept his uncle's children from destroying the office as supervisory, he highlights his ability to work as part of a team and his leadership in his volunteer groups.

Business Etiquette

Every field has a certain level of etiquette. You may not know what is conventional in your field yet, but there are general guidelines to follow.

- **Use standard written English:** Your letters and emails should always consider your audience and be well-edited. Even when the potential employer is a bit more relaxed, you should maintain a professional tone. Avoid slang, abbreviations, shortcuts (LOL), politically incorrect terms, and emojis. You never know when you are being tested.
- **Be polite:** You may not like that the Human Resources manager does not respond promptly to your calls or emails or is a bit of a know-it-all. Right now, your focus should be on getting the job, not giving criticism—always use please and thank you.
- **Don't go overboard:** Too many colors or fancy fonts, scented or colored paper, and unnecessary images or graphics can be tacky and make your documents hard to read. You want your materials to stand out for the right reasons.
- **Follow up:** If you receive an interview, send a thank you letter or email to the person you met with immediately after the interview.

Putting It All Together

Let's take a look at how Connor pulls together his final résumé. It takes him a couple tries to strike the right note, but after some research and revision, Connor is now prepared to make a good case for himself. Look closely at how these documents change and how you can apply these principles to job materials and other technical documents you may create (figures 19 and 20).

Draft Résumé

Connor Maxwell

222 Austen Drive, Portland, OR 97202
(503) 555-1212 – cmaxwell@gmail.com – LinkedIn.com/in/cjmaxwell

> Candidate with good customer service, interpersonal, and communication skills seeks employment in a growing company where I can make use of my education and work experience and grow my skills.

EDUCATION
Bachelor of Science in Business Administration – University of Oregon, Eugene
Minor – Economics
Grade Point Average – 3.6 out of possible 4.0

EXPERIENCE
Assistant Business Office Manager – Buck's Hardware, Portland, OR June 2016 to Present
Business Development Intern – Kelly Motor Company, Eugene, OR June 2015 to September 2015
Team Leader – Volunteer – Green Giants, Eugene, OR
September 2013 to Present
COMMUNITY ACTIVITIES & AFFILIATIONS
Volunteer for Homes for Humanity – National organization building homes for people in need   2016 to Present
Team Leader for the Green Giants – Local environmental group
          2013 to Present
Member of the Future Leaders of America – Oregon Chapter focused on developing youth leadership   2014 to 2017

Annotations:
- Connor's name definitely stands out, but at the expense of detail later on.
- This career objective does not provide specific key terms from the job description and takes up valuable space on the résumé.
- Irregular formatting looks messy and unprofessional.

Figure 19. What changes would you recommend Connor make to this résumé?

Final Résumé

Without increasing the font size to grab attention, Connor can make his name and the categories of his resume stand out by placing them in all caps.

Aligning your contact information to the right-hand margin draws attention to your heading.

By indenting this information your document becomes more scannable for the user.

Bullet points use parallel verbs to describe Connor's work duties.

CONNOR MAXWELL
222 Austen Drive
Portland, OR 97202
(503) 555-1212
cmaxwell@gmail.com
LinkedIn.com/in/cjmaxwell

EDUCATION

BS in Business Administration, Minor in Economics 2017–2019
University of Oregon, Eugene, OR

Relevant Course Work:

- Project Planning and Communities
- Special Topics in Sustainable Development
- Environmental Economics and Policy

EXPERIENCE

Assistant Business Office Manager June 2016–Present
Buck's Hardware, Portland, OR

- Assist with accounts receivable and payable
- Review payroll before processing
- Reconcile physical inventory with records
- Prepare profit and loss reports
- Maintain company's social media presence

Business Development Intern June 2015–Sept. 2015
Kelly Motor Company, Eugene, OR

- Assisted with economic strategies for the company's new line of electric and hybrid vehicles

Figure 20. It may take a few attempts, but a solid résumé is worth the effort.

Final Résumé continued

- Updated the company's social media presence to reflect innovations
- Conducted market research for various product lines

Team Leader, Volunteer   Sept. 2013–Present
Green Giants, Eugene, OR

- Promoted and helped update recycling programs in three school districts
- Led a volunteer team on a tree-planting project in the Columbia River Valley in 2016

[Just because he didn't get paid to do this work doesn't mean it's not important to a future employer. It belongs under "Experience."]

COMMUNITY ACTIVITIES & AFFILIATIONS

Volunteer for Homes for Humanity   2016–Present
National organization building homes for people in need

Team Leader for the Green Giants   2013– Present
Local environmental group

Member of the Future Leaders of America   2014–2017
Oregon Chapter focused on developing youth leadership

SKILLS

Computer: Proficient with Microsoft Word, Excel, and PowerPoint
Social Media: Experienced with Facebook, Twitter, Instagram
Languages: Fluent in Spanish

[Note that each section handles lists differently. But each section is consistent. For example, this section bolds first words but doesn't use bullet points. The section before uses spaces in between, but no bullet points.]

Conclusion

The fact that so many people find applying for a job stressful can work to your advantage. This chapter demonstrates the techniques you can use to be confident and competitive in the creation of your job materials. If you are mindful of the recommendations in this chapter and thoughtfully create your job documents, you can set yourself apart from the competition. Producing clear and engaging job materials is not as difficult as many people think. Doing so just requires clarity and an awareness of your audience, as with all technical communication.

Your job materials are strategic marketing tools. You may feel uncomfortable with that idea, but if you consider how many other people may be applying for the same position, it should be clear that you must strategically promote yourself and your skills. Most colleges offer additional job material workshops. Take advantage of your resources. Your qualifications will not speak for themselves. Your document must do the talking and build the claim that you are the right person for the job.

And what if you're not yet the right person for the job? This is your clue to start looking for opportunities, courses, mentors, and internships that will allow you to build the skills that employers are seeking.

Chapter 7
Workplace Communication

Abstract: This chapter explores the purpose, types, etiquette, and ethics of workplace communication. The conventions, format, and style of documents used in daily workplace communications, including text messages, emails, memos, and business letters, are an essential part of technical communication. While technology continues to change how we communicate in the workplace, the fundamentals of communication etiquette and format remain the same.

Looking Ahead

1. Why Workplace Communication Matters

2. Types of Workplace Communication

3. Communicating Professionally

4. Checklist for Business Etiquette

Why Workplace Communication Matters

Many people may not think of workplace communication as a form of technical communication. But remember: technical communication is about delivering specialized information to a particular audience. In the workplace, both the message and the audience are specialized. As a result, communication in the workplace demands a technical approach.

Take the humble email, for example. You use these all the time, right? Frank, an executive assistant, uses them all the time, too. When he's asked in a planning session that he email everyone vital information about the project, he does so by finding a group email sent from the supervisor that's been sitting in his inbox for a few weeks and hits "reply all" to send the message. He cuts and pastes information from some data tables without explaining what the tables represent, forgetting that two of the teams working on the project aren't in the field that uses data in the style presented in the table. What do you think happens?

Frank sends the email and leaves for the day. Most of the team either doesn't read the email because the subject line is out of date and appears unimportant. The people who need the information and realize this "out of date" email is the one they're waiting for can't understand the content.

A strong technical communicator (not Frank, apparently) knows the data needs interpretation to be useful and will start a new email thread with a relevant subject line. The body text will lead with the most important information first and provide clear language explaining the information to whomever needs it.

To communicate effectively in the workplace, you must be aware of the audience's expectations. Beyond this broad consideration, however, communicators in the workplace also have expectations regarding typical communication formats, such as emails, letters, or minutes from meetings. As a professional, you're likely to spend most of your career communicating with others in a work environment. You can master the expectations and conventions of communication in the workplace to distinguish yourself and help create an efficient work environment.

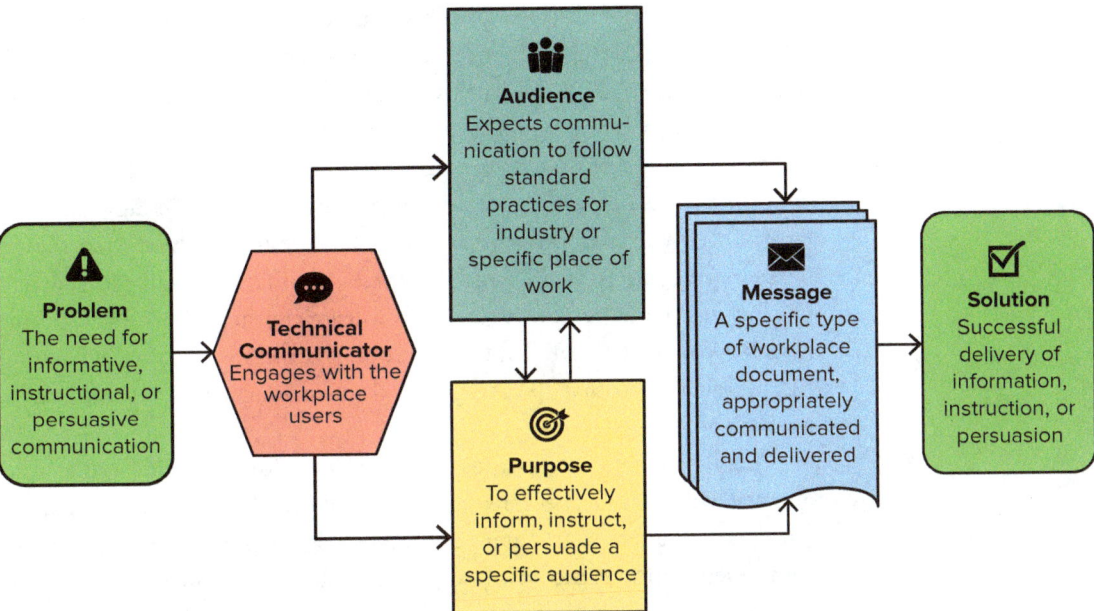

Figure 1. Within the context of workplace communication, the Problem-Solution Framework aims to fulfill a need by informing, instructing, or persuading.

Workplace Communication Defined

Workplace communication involves the transfer of information from one person to another. This is accomplished through a variety of modes and technical documents, such as staff meetings, emails, memos, business letters, and more. You've certainly written emails to your family, led a scout meeting, or typed up a letter to your landlord to complain about the leaky roof. But the workplace equivalent of these communication tools requires a technical approach.

The Problem-Solution Framework applies to workplace communication just as it does to other forms of technical communication (figure 1). As with other situations, workplace communication seeks to solve a problem, which takes the form of a need. These workplace needs can be sorted into the following categories:

- A need for information
- A need for instruction
- A need for persuasion

For example, your coworker missed a meeting due to illness. They need information (having missed the meeting), so you compose a memo and give it to them. Alternatively, consider this scenario: your research at work convinces you that a policy in the employee handbook needs to be updated, so you send an email to persuade the HR manager regarding the issue.

The success of a workplace document hinges on considering your audience. When you're working with others, be sure to remember that they're people. They have strengths and weaknesses and families and problems — just like you. Consider how your words will affect others. Realize that people have limited time — and limited attention spans. Keeping your document tightly focused on that specific goal will make your communication more likely to be successful.

Taking audience and purpose into consideration will guide you to your message, which will be delivered in the form of the most appropriate medium (an email, a letter, etc.). Later sections in this chapter discuss the normal components and characteristics of these documents. Don't forget to apply the lessons you've learned so far. Who is your audience? Is it the executive board or your department's bowling team? What voice is appropriate for your message? Formal? Technical? Chummy? What is the purpose of your communication? Knowing your audience, message, and purpose will get you moving in the right direction.

Types of Workplace Communication

Preferred modes of workplace communication keep changing and expanding. According to a 2014 Gallup poll, texts, phone calls, and emails are the most common types of communication. In fact, between 37 and 39 percent of Americans report they've sent texts, calls, and emails "a lot" in the previous day.

To function in the professional world effectively, you need to be familiar with a broad range of communication tools. You need to have a basic knowledge of the different advantages of these tools, as well as a sense of how to use them appropriately.

Text Messages

Using a cell phone to send text messages is a common type of personal communication, and it is becoming more common within workplaces as well. Structurally, a text has more in common with speech than written language, according to Dr. Caroline Tagg, a British linguist who began studying text messages in 2009. We use informal words such as "dunno," quick phonetic spellings, and the now-ubiquitous emoji to create the tonal context we'd normally provide when speaking in person.

Texting is great for quick, back-and-forth messages. It combines the benefits of spoken and written language into a compact message that can be sent and responded to almost instantaneously. Unlike a face-to-face conversation or phone call, texting creates a record of the dialogue and you can put the dialogue on pause while completing a task.

Professional Use

We all know how to text, some of us better than others. It's easy to forget, however, that you can't text professionally the way you do with your pals. The act of adjusting how you communicate based on your audience is called **code-switching.** This is simply a matter of changing the way you speak to fit the situation. If you fail to recognize the need to adjust your communication style, even if the change is slight, the result could be confusion, as seen in these text messages. Notice what happens when the message is too casual or too formal for the situation (figure 2).

What's happening here? This is a realtor (Linda) asking her clients to sign a counteroffer on the home they're selling. Neither of these texts represent a career-ending mistake, but they

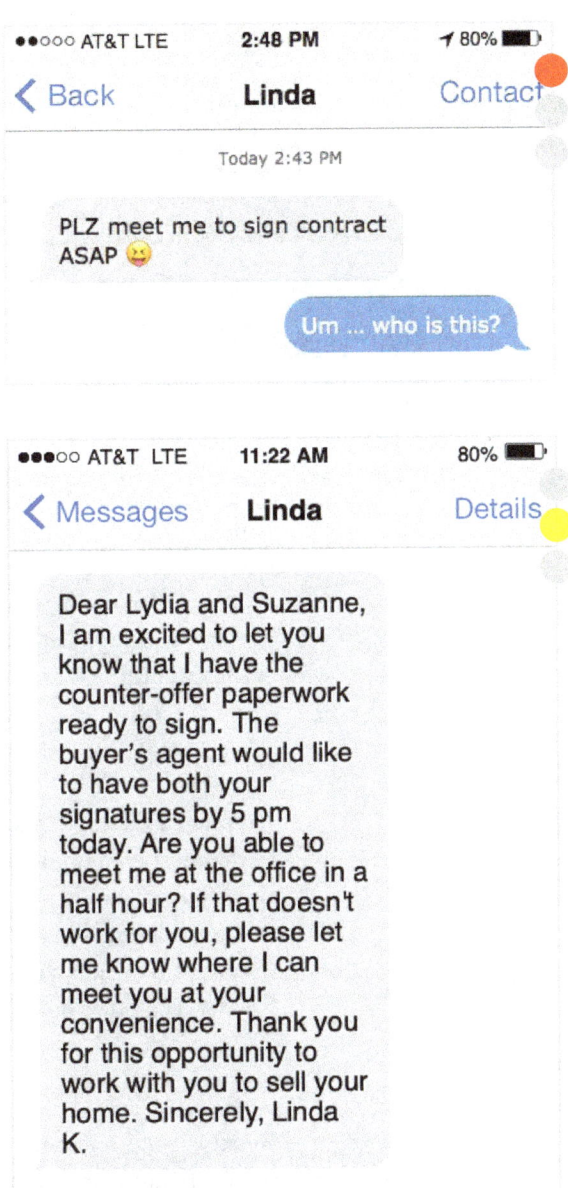

Figure 2. The first text message makes assumptions that the recipient will immediately recognize who is sending it. The second text message sounds unnatural because it's using the conventions of email, which is not a good fit for this medium.

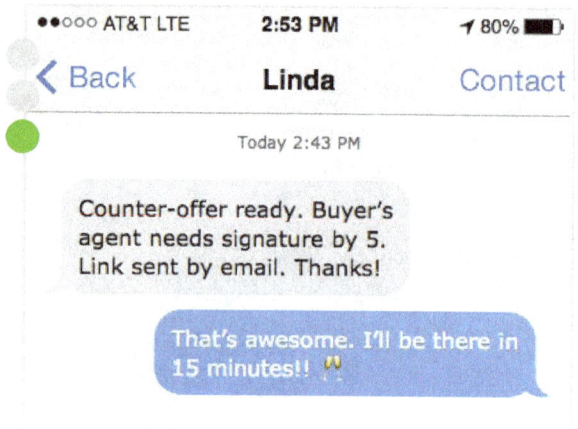

Figure 3. This text message is casual yet provides information so the recipient knows how to respond.

do chip away at her credibility. Linda's clients trust her to handle complex transactions that involve their finances and determine how soon they can make the move into their new home. When a message strikes the wrong tone or creates confusion, it can slowly erode that trust.

So, let's give Linda another shot. Here's a professional text that strikes the right tone (figure 3). The message isn't exactly using the kind of language you'd want to use in a business letter, but it's perfect for a text message, assuming she's not sending it at 11:30 p.m.

Formatting

Text messages are designed to be brief. The technology that allows messages to be sent by cell phone is called SMS (short message service), which can contain up to 160 characters. You can of course text more, but the message will be broken up into multiple smaller messages. When texting professionally, limit yourself to short messages.

Email

Despite all the spam and surveys overloading our inboxes, email is still one of the most commonly used forms of workplace communication. Just like a text, an email easily becomes unprofessional if you're not careful. Have you ever sent an email to an instructor or potential employer and never received a reply? After reading this section, take another look at your sent folder to see what you could've done differently.

Professional Use

Email is good for short messages of about one to three paragraphs and for delivering attachments. A solid practice, if you want the recipient to read your email, is to use the content window in which you enter your message as a guide. The goal is to write messages that do not require scrolling. If you must scroll up and down too much to proofread your email, your reader is unlikely to read the whole message. As with most technical communication, you want to lead with the most important information first.

Email dialogues are called **threads.** One person starts the thread and, as long as the topic is relevant, recipients will respond back and forth within it. Responding to a relevant thread, instead of starting a new email on the same topic, makes finding important information easier for everyone involved. If you want to email someone with a new topic, you should always start a new thread. Otherwise, expect the email to go unanswered when you hit "reply" to an email that person sent three weeks ago on a totally unrelated subject.

Formatting

Business email is more formal than personal email, so even if you're just jotting a quick note to a team member, be aware of formatting and how it affects readability. You stand a good chance of being ignored when you don't observe formatting expectations. In these sample emails, compare the message between friends who are coworkers and the message between Leticia and her boss (see figures 4 and 5 on the next page). What do you notice about the way the email opens, the tone Leticia uses, and the way she closes the email?

You can increase the readability of your email by using shorter block paragraphs separated by white space, as you can see in Leticia's email. Providing a subject line is another way to make sure your message registers as important. If the subject line reads "Info: Report on development progress," the reader knows that this is an update with no need to respond. If the subject reads "IMMEDIATE: Investor meeting agenda for this afternoon," the audience knows they should open the email and review it right away.

If you need to discuss multiple topics, consider including a bullet-point summary at the beginning of your email and use headings to clearly indicate the sections in which each bullet is discussed. This is more common in company-wide emails sent to multiple recipients or updates that can be scanned quickly for relevant information.

From: Jason A. Mendoza <jamendoza@gamingcentral.com>
To: Leticia White <lwhite@gamingcentral.com>
Subject: Character profiles for review
Attachment: characterprofiledraft.doc

Hey LW —

I have some of the first drafts of character profiles for *Alpacas!* See attached. Feedback?

JAM

Figure 4. These colleagues have been working together for a long time on this project, so they've dispensed with some of the formalities expected in a workplace email. This is fine since they know their audience.

> Jason and Leticia have agreed that she will be the main point of contact for their boss, Robert. Leticia copies Jason on the email using the CC: field.

> Your audience prioritizes an email's importance based on the subject line. Leticia's subject line makes it clear what she needs from her boss.

> Keep emails short and about one topic at a time. Mention attachments — some business email systems may not display attachments.

From: Leticia White <lwhite@gamingcentral.com>
To: Robert Ossman <bossman@gamingcentral.com>
CC: Jason A. Mendoza <jamendoza@gamingcentral.com>
BC:
Subject: For Review: Alpacas of Doom proposal
Attachment: Alpacas_proposal_final.doc

Dear Mr. Ossman:

My creative partner Jason Mendoza and I have completed the *Alpacas of Doom!* game proposal for your review. Please see the attached file. It includes an overview of the game, gameplay, basic and advanced features, and an update on the development process.

We believe the target audience is ready for a game featuring these furry Peruvian villains. Jason and I are available to meet with you in person or by web conference to answer any additional questions you might have about the game. We are excited to hear your feedback on our proposal.

Sincerely,

Leticia White
Senior Game Designer
Gaming Central, Inc.
lwhite@gamingcentral.com
(541) 555-5555

Figure 5. The email is brief, to the point, and contains all the information the boss needs to respond to the request.

Phone Calls

If you find yourself going back and forth by text or email, you may save some time by picking up the phone. You can get more context out of a phone conversation than you can out of an email or text thread. Unlike those modes, you can discern mood and tone of voice. This is one of the synchronous styles of communication that works better when you need to have a real-time conversation with someone.

Professional Use

Phone calls are like texts without the permanent record. You can use them to discuss sensitive project information, brainstorm complicated subjects, and outline plans before committing anything to a permanent file or database. They are also a better option for working through complex issues with colleagues or clients. As a form of communication, phone calls are multimodal and incorporate aural and linguistic modes in real-time to help the user better understand the message.

See **Chapter 4** for more on multimodal communication.

Formatting

How do you format a phone call, anyway? It's similar to writing an email with a salutation, the body of the conversation, and a closing.

Generally, you greet the caller and say who you are and why you're calling. When speaking to a client, an employer, or a colleague, it can be helpful to schedule the call in advance so you know that the person has time to speak. Sometimes there's small talk if you know the person, but generally, you just want to get to the subject of the call. When you're done exchanging the needed information, be sure to say good-bye.

If you make a phone call and don't reach the individual, you'll normally be greeted by a recorded voice asking you to leave a message. Consider this voicemail message as a document that you're leaving behind. Like all the documents discussed in this textbook, it should communicate effectively. Here's an example of what not to do:

> *Hey, just returning your call. Call me back.*

This caller assumes that the person on the receiving end recognizes his or her voice. Don't assume that the caller ID will provide your name and callback number. Instead, try this:

> *Hello, Ron. This is Stephanie. I'm returning your call about the agenda for tomorrow's meeting. I'll be at my desk for the rest of the day. Please call me back at extension 1234 when you get this message. Bye.*

This voicemail identifies the caller, explains the purpose of the call, and provides call-back information and a time when the caller can be reached.

Memos

The **memo**, short for "memorandum," is a single sheet of information distributed in print or by email. Often it is displayed internally within a workplace or other closed group.

Professional Use

The purpose of a memo is to communicate in brief to a specific audience. The information should be easily and quickly understood. The subject of the memo—however you choose to format it—should not be something of world-changing importance. A change in parking protocol, a policy change announcement, or a reminder to remove your rotting takeout from the shared refrigerator on Fridays are appropriate subjects for a memo. Using a memo to announce the decision to lay off all part-time employees, on the other hand, would not be a wise use of this document.

Whatever your subject, the language should be plain and transparent, and the meaning should be clear. Just like any professional communication, memos are an efficient way to communicate simple messages but not the ideal mode for navigating complex problems or dealing with topics that may be emotional in nature. For example, a **directive** is a type of memo that issues an order to staff. If the order is complicated, or might present an undue burden on staff, an opportunity for a meeting or a procedure for airing concerns and asking questions should be included.

Formatting

Your workplace may have its own letterhead on which it prints memos, but other than that the formatting is simple. The memo format is the predecessor of the email. Memos have a standard format that includes the elements shown in this model (figure 6).

HERRERA, LINDSAY & ORLOV

Memorandum

To: All Employees
From: Patricia Good, Assistant Manager *PG*
Date: November 1, 2019
Subject: International Client Communication

Herrera, Lindsay, & Orlov is excited to announce the acquisition of several new international accounts. This expansion brings the need for updated policies covering client communication to promote healthy working relationships. Several informational sessions and trainings will be offered before putting new policies in place.

Informational Sessions

Informational sessions will be held beginning Friday, November 2, from 3:30 to 4:30 pm in the staff lounge to discuss policy changes.

Trainings

- International Client Communication
  December 1, 9 am to noon
- Cultural Competency and Client Relations
  December 15, noon to 5 pm

Timeline

After collecting employee feedback during the informational sessions, we will establish a committee to revise the current policy.

4001 LANCASTER DR NE, SALEM, OR 97309
T 541-555-5555 U WWW.HLO.COM

Printed memos are often signed with the initials of the authorizing party.

This memo begins with a summary and breaks down information using headings for ease of reading.

This is just the first page of a two-page memo. Patsy will email this out to all employees as well as place a printed copy in their mailboxes.

Figure 6. Memos are often printed on letterhead because they are official forms of business communication. Memos open with these elements: To, From, Date, and Subject.

Meeting Agendas

Sometimes, the best way to adequately convey a message, brainstorm a project, or consume birthday cupcakes is in a standard face-to-face meeting. You can make sure you're all on the same page because everyone is in the same room holding a *copy* of that page. An agenda, like the one shown in figure 7, will provide an outline for the topics for discussion.

HERRERA, LINDSAY & ORLOV

Cultural Competency Committee Meeting Agenda

Location: Orlov Board Room
Date: November 15, 2019
Time: 10 a.m.

Welcome

Approval of Minutes

Vote on Chair for the Cultural Competency Committee

Report on Training Sessions

- International Client Communication
  December 1, 9 am to noon
- Cultural Competency and Client Relations
  December 15, noon to 5 pm

New Business

- Review of employee feedback
- Draft of new client communication policy

Next Meeting

- Decide on date

Meeting Close

4001 LANCASTER DR NE, SALEM, OR 97309
T 541-555-5555 U WWW.HLO.COM

Figure 7. The agenda creates an outline and plan for the meeting.

Professional Use

Efficient meetings make use of a guiding document that is preferably distributed ahead of time. The **agenda** is a piece of paper that outlines the topics of discussion for a meeting. Think of it like a table of contents for the next hour or so. A meeting without an agenda can get off topic. If you need to hold a meeting, make sure the agenda states the purpose, topics for discussion, and the order in which presenters will take turns speaking.

Meeting Minutes

Typically, one person facilitates the meeting. Another person takes notes during the meeting, which can be distributed later to participants and people who couldn't make it to the actual meeting. These notes, called **minutes**, are often kept as a permanent record, sometimes by legal requirement (figure 8). Meeting minutes are not a detailed description of the meeting itself, but instead log the meeting's outcome. If people disagree with one another during a meeting, but reach a conclusion, the disagreement is not included in the minutes, only the result.

Formatting

Often there are rules and technicalities that determine the format of a meeting. If you are in a meeting and hear phrases like "I move to table this topic" or "I move to adjourn," you are taking part in an eighteenth-century tradition defined in *Robert's Rules of Order*. You are most likely to encounter this meeting format in government or corporate board meetings. The order of these meetings follow this general format:

- **Call to Order:** The person holding the meeting gets everyone's attention to begin.
- **Roll Call:** The person taking the minutes records who is in attendance.
- **Approval of Minutes:** If this is a recurring meeting, the notes from the last meeting will be reviewed, approved, or corrected.
- **Agenda Items:** The topics listed in the agenda provide the structure for the meeting.
- **Adjournment:** The person running the meeting announces the official end of the meeting.

Robert's Rules doesn't mention cupcakes, although some of us consider them the most important part. The agenda is the plan for the meeting, and the minutes are the written record of what actually happened.

Business Letters

Business letters are formal documents that are a significant part of the professional world. They are the letters you use to gain employment, build professional

---

HERRERA, LINDSAY & ORLOV

Cultural Competency Committee Meeting Minutes

Location: Orlov Board Room
Date: November 15, 2019
Time: 10–11 a.m.

Attendance: Patricia Good, Jaime Herrera, Ralph Lindsay, Jodie Orlov, Astrid Middlestadt, Richard Carlin, Matthias Chekov

Item #1 – Vote on Chair

- Patricia was unanimously voted to be the chair for the Cultural Competency Committee. She will serve a 2-year term.

Item #2 – Report on Training Sessions

- Both training sessions have open spots. Astrid will send out a company-wide email by November 21 to encourage signups

Item #3 – Review of Employee Feedback

- Employee response rate to the survey sent November 1 is 45 percent. Matthias will send a follow-up to non-responders.

Item #4 – New Client Communication Policy Draft

- See attached.

Item #5 – Next Meeting

- December 15, 2019, 10 a.m. in Orlov Board Room

4001 LANCASTER DR NE, SALEM, OR 97309
T 541-555-5555 WWW.HLO.COM

Figure 8. Minutes record the decisions made during the meeting.

relationships, and create opportunities. That's a ton of pressure to place on a page or two of text, but the fundamentals of technical communication can guide you in creating a message and purpose that are clear for your audience.

Professional Use

Business letters are a more formal type of workplace communication that requires following formatting conventions and finding the appropriate tone for communicating with an audience that is, more often than not, external. This model shows the basic arrangement of elements in a business letter (figure 9).

```
COMPANY LETTERHEAD

Date

Recipient's Full Name
Company Name
Company Address
City, State Zip Code

Dear Name of Recipient:

This is the first paragraph where you identify the purpose of the
letter. The content of your letter should be governed by its purpose.
Most business letters are about a page long, but sometimes they
are much longer depending on the complexity or importance of the
subject.

Most business letters will use the company's letterhead for the first
page. For all other pages after that, a standard piece of paper
similar in weight to the letterhead can be used.

End your letter with a clear and specific call to action. This is
what you want the recipient of this letter to do with the
information you've provided.

Sincerely,

<Sign here>

Your Name
```

- **Salutation:** How you address a business letter often sets the tone for the entire communication.
- **Body:** This is the content of your business letter.
- **Closing:** Choose an appropriate phrase to end your letter.
- **Signature Line:** Type out your full name so it is clear who sent the letter.

Figure 9. Business letters are generally created for an external audience, and because of this they tend to be the most formal of all workplace documents.

Formality	Salutations	Closings
Very Formal	Dear Senator Andrea Jensen-Joli:	Cordially yours, Kind regards
Formal	Dear Ms. Jensen-Joli:	Respectfully, Sincerely
Informal	Dear Andrea,	Best, Thanks, Warmly
Very Informal	Andrea,	Cheers, Later

Figure 10. Notice the levels of formality in these salutations and closings. The use of the term "dear" may seem like a term of endearment, but it is simply a convention used in business writing.

Business letters are often printed on company letterhead. The paper is usually higher quality with features meant to impress the audience and represent the company's brand.

Formatting

Just like the other workplace formats, a business letter has a handful of simple expectations. You are probably already familiar with some of them. For example, most business letters use a standard opening (salutation) and closing (figure 10). The beginning of the letter signals the level of formality between the sender and the recipient.

There isn't one "true" way to format a business letter: just use the style set by the employer or use the style that you like when you're writing your own. Here are the most common formats you will encounter in the workplace (figure 11):

- The block format refers to a letter that aligns all text to the left-hand margin and leaves a space between paragraphs.
- The modified block formats the opening address and the closing along the letter's center line to distinguish them from the body of the letter.
- The indented letter format is similar to the block letter format, except it uses indentation to signal the start of a new paragraph instead of an extra space between paragraphs.

Figure 11. Consistency and alignment are important to consider when formatting your business letter. Pick one format, and stick with it.

Communicating Professionally

How you choose to communicate in the workplace influences how you are perceived by coworkers, your bosses, and customers. You want to make a good impression, so think carefully about the key factors in this section. These factors include using the appropriate tool, using the appropriate tone, evaluating content, prioritizing information, considering audience, and being persuasive.

Use the Appropriate Tool

You need to communicate with a coworker, so what tool do you choose? Should you send an email, compose a text, or pick up the phone? Those methods have been around for a while. But today's workplaces have even more options as a result of web-based communication apps. Tools like Basecamp, Slack, and Trello are common communication management systems you might encounter. Some workplaces have their own communication platform created for that specific workplace. Given all of these different methods of communicating, how do you pick?

The first thing to remember about choosing a communication tool is that many workplaces have specific rules or guidelines about this. If you haven't reviewed the employee handbook to confirm, you might want to check it. Beyond a written policy, most businesses have unspoken expectations about communication. If you're new to a place of work, check with a coworker or even a manager to determine the preferred communication methods.

The purpose of these apps is to improve the efficiency of workplace communication with a dedicated channel that isn't cluttered by distractions and outside requests. But sometimes a tool designed to create focus can cause distraction. Learn how to operate the apps efficiently, including when and how to turn off the alerts that interrupt you every five seconds. Like all other forms of workplace communication, this tool requires you to understand your audience's expectations — in this case, your coworkers and business partners.

Use the Appropriate Tone

You know this by now, but we're going to remind you again: do not communicate in a professional setting the same way you communicate with your friends. You need to sound friendly without being overly familiar. But you also need to sound like a human, not a robot. How do you strike the right balance?

Tone is communicated by the words you choose and by your attitude toward the topic or audience. If you've ever been told as a child to "watch your tone," you know it means to adjust your attitude. The same happens in writing. It's easy to slip up and use a tone that doesn't suit the message. Whether it's exhaustion, indifference, or frustration bordering on hostility, allowing these feelings to seep into workplace communication will eventually cause problems. Take a look at the different ways tone becomes clear in these examples (figure 12).

Exclamation points are another way that tone can be expressed in writing. This flamboyant punctuation adds punch to strong, emotion-filled statements, so it's rare that you would need it in more formal workplace communication. However, less formal modes of communication might benefit from the occasional exclamation. For example, you text your boss to let her know you've got the flu and won't be able to make it in. You receive her response: "Oh no." Without an exclamation point, her message might come across as flat, almost deadpan. The key is to make conscious choices in your writing to create a tone that helps you get your message across with the least potential for confusion.

Confident	Uncertain
This project is moving in the wrong direction.	I just think that maybe this project is moving in the wrong direction.
Respectful	**Rude**
Please sign the form and return it to me by Friday.	It's imperative that you get the form back to me ASAP. And don't forget to sign it!
Objective	**Biased**
Your paperwork is incomplete.	Your paperwork is a mess.
Direct	**Round-about**
I received your recommendation and will contact you next week to discuss the next steps.	Your recommendation has been received. You will be contacted about the next steps soon.
Positive	**Negative**
Thank you for telling me this now.	I wish you would have told me sooner.

Figure 12. Small changes in word choice can affect the tone of your communication.

Evaluate Content

Your workplace communication tools are not where you have personal conversations. It's not considered "personal" to email your colleagues about getting together after the end of a hard project, but use your best judgment when sending a message that will be out there *forever*. Ask yourself two questions before you hit send: Is this work-related? If not, should I be using my personal device instead?

In the summer of 2018, the United States witnessed FBI agent Peter Strzok get grilled by members of Congress. Why? He sent texts to a friend (and colleague) making fun of the president. This isn't typically a big deal: a quick look through history shows that making fun of presidents is a bit of an American pastime. The problem — at least one among many — is that he was using his work system to make some of the jokes. If you want to stay away from a congressional committee, we recommend you keep the jokes off your work email.

A sense of humor is a good, healthy thing. However, it's useful to note that jokes do not always translate well into print—especially if they require a solid grasp of tone. If you send a joke via text or email, remember that the receiver can't see your face or hear your voice. Does the joke work without you there? If the answer is no, maybe don't send it. Would you tell the joke in front of some children? No? Maybe rethink your options. We'd like you to keep your job.

Prioritize Information

Before you give a speech, send an email, or ask for a raise, it's a good idea to identify your top two or three main ideas. For example, if you create an email announcing an upcoming event at your workplace, but you fail to mention the date, time, or location of the event, you have a problem. Be sure to give your audience the information they need. In this case, your email should not only mention this crucial information, but it should include it in such a way that it is impossible to miss. As often as possible, lead with the most important information in a workplace document and follow with any other useful details.

When you're working fast and have multiple projects you're responsible for, you might find it challenging to identify your priorities. That's why it's best to think strategically when you compose a memo, email, business letter, or any other professional communication. In general, you should keep your writing focused on a single point, organize your information clearly, and avoid unnecessary information.

Here are some guidelines to help you figure out what's most important to communicate to your audience:

- Recognize the limits of your document and your audience's attention.
- Identify the key take-away, the one thing your audience needs to know.
- List the information that supports this main idea.
- Organize this list by importance, sequence, or chronology.
- Keep it short, but provide a way (a link to a website or your contact information) for the audience to obtain more information if needed.

This is not to say that you can never include interesting side information in your documents or presentations—just make sure it's not interrupting or distracting from the main flow of crucial information.

Consider Audience

Make sure you take the time to get to know the audience you will address. Are there any cultural factors, such as expectations of formality, that you need to observe in order to make the message successful? What about addressing the person at the beginning of your message? For example, when someone earns the title "Doctor," they tend to want that title observed.

There are other factors to consider as well, such as whether or not you are making assumptions about a person's identity based on missing gender markers. Take a look at the signature field example, which is one way to glean useful information about a potential client or colleague (figure 13). What do you know about their identity? If J. didn't indicate any preference for pronouns, what mistake might you make?

A significant part of avoiding mistakes when it comes to addressing audience is considering your own biases. Do you communicate differently to someone simply because of their name, gender, or race? Be honest in evaluating yourself regarding bias. You may be surprised — after all, many people have biases of which they aren't even aware. If you genuinely aren't sure about the appropriateness of a piece of communication, consider asking a trusted coworker for their opinion. Just getting an outside opinion can make a difference.

```
J. Doe
Regional Representative
People with Anonymous Names (PAN), Inc.
j.doe@paninc.org
(541) 555-5555
Pronouns: They/Them/Their
```

Figure 13. Using a person's preferred pronoun is a way of showing respect. When in doubt, use the person's full name.

Checklist for Business Etiquette

Many technical communicators create documents and deliverables for global audiences. In order to be competitive in the workplace, you must prepare for different styles and approaches to business etiquette. Here's a brief list of business etiquette to get you started:

- ☐ **Arrival Time:** Punctuality is a priority in the US and Germany, but other countries may have a more casual relationship with time. To be safe, show up on time but be patient if you're kept waiting.

- ☐ **Names and Honorifics:** Naming conventions differ around the world. For example, workers in the US generally prefer a more casual address with the use of first names. Many other countries, however, favor the formal equivalent of "Mr." or "Ms." accompanied by a surname. Don't make assumptions about gender or marital status. Ask people what they prefer to be called.

- ☐ **Greetings:** A firm handshake is appropriate in the US, but not in France. In Europe and the Americas, it's standard to present a business card with one hand. But people from the Far East, Southeast Asia, or the Indian subcontinent tend to offer business cards with two hands extended. Watch and mirror the exchanges of others if you're not sure.

- ☐ **Meeting Protocol:** In some parts of the world, people like to get business transactions out of the way before socializing. Other areas place importance on socializing and getting to know a person before conducting business. Research will help you find out if chitchat, interruptions, or following an agenda are customary for the business culture of that area.

- ☐ **Correspondence:** It's worth taking your time when you're communicating with a global audience. Nothing says lack of professionalism more than an ill-prepared email. The preferred communication style might be direct or indirect, casual or formal, concise or chatty, but it takes time to figure this out. Also, be mindful of time zones and when the recipient will likely receive your message.

Conclusion

When it comes to workplace communication, a lot is at stake. Your ability to communicate with your colleagues or clients significantly impacts your role. While a lack of skill in workplace communication could be detrimental to your reputation, excelling in this area can distinguish you as a valued contributor.

Fortunately, you can gain confidence in workplace communication if you focus on meeting the expectations of your work environment and following established communication formats. This chapter gives you a start by pointing out common expectations for most work environments. You'll need to continue to evaluate the expectations for your specific workplace. In addition, you'll want to stay informed about the current state of preferred workplace tools as they change over time. If you stay focused on those expectations and formats, you'll be in an excellent position to master workplace communication.

Chapter 8
Technical Definitions and Descriptions

Abstract: Technical definitions and descriptions give meaning to a process or procedure and can be found in a variety of technical documents. Technical communicators generally use three types of definitions: parenthetical, sentence, and extended definitions. The type of definition is determined by the context of a document and the audience. Descriptions act as a longer definition and require precision. In order to create a useable definition or description, you must know who is going to use it, when they're likely to use it, what they need to know, and what they already know. Nowhere else does audience play a bigger role in determining the amount of information you will need to communicate effectively.

Looking Ahead

1. Why Definitions and Descriptions Matter

2. Creating Definitions and Descriptions

3. Parenthetical Definitions

4. Sentence Definitions

5. Extended Definitions

6. Descriptions

7. Known-New Contract

8. Legal and Ethical Implications

Why Definitions and Descriptions Matter

When you were in grade school and didn't know the meaning of a word, your teacher most likely told you to look it up. Now, as a technical communicator, it's your job to know the terminology of your specific field, to use it accurately, and to be able to explain it precisely to someone else. You can't tell your audience to grab a dictionary. You *are* the dictionary.

The good news is that you don't have to know everything. But you do need to know how to use your expertise to define terms that are unfamiliar to your user. Definitions on their own are not an actual document, but you will find definitions in just about any type of technical document. Though the specific words you need to create a definition will depend on your audience and your industry, the way you create definitions follows a fairly predictable pattern, which we'll cover in this chapter. Figure 1 shows how the Problem-Solution Framework adapts to the task of creating technical descriptions and definitions.

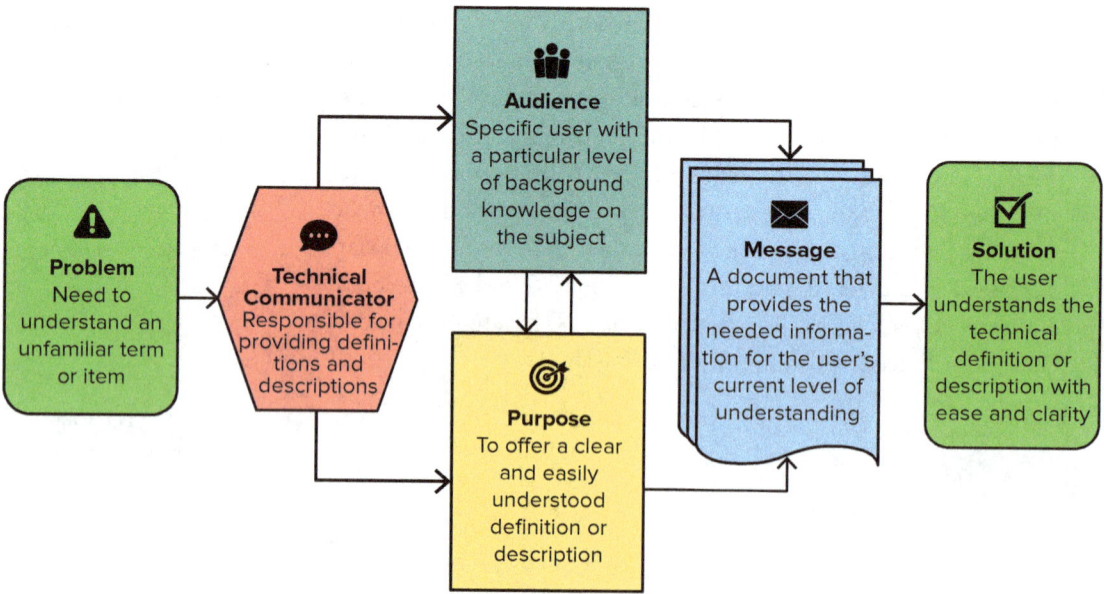

Figure 1. The Problem-Solution Framework can help you think about what your audience knows and does not know in order to provide more effective definitions and descriptions.

As an expert (or expert-in-training), you need to determine how and when to provide definitions to your audience. Never assume that a user knows everything you know. Keep in mind that your background and education have acquainted you with a specialized language. When you understand a subject thoroughly, it can be difficult to imagine what someone new to the subject knows or doesn't know. To combat this tendency, return to the Problem-Solution Framework with these questions in mind:

- What does my audience need to know?
- How much detail does my audience need to know?
- How will my audience use this information?

In your own projects, your job is to determine if the user needs a quick reminder of a term's meaning or extensive description of an object's parts, purpose, and function. To illustrate this, we'll revisit Leticia and Jason's board game project *Alpacas of Doom!* from Chapter 7. Their game uses a variety of familiar concepts (dice, alpacas) with adjustments for gaming purposes. To communicate these new ideas to their boss and potential funders, they need to define how and when these modified elements are used. Documents that alter familiar items and introduce new concepts present an ideal opportunity for exploring definitions.

Creating Definitions and Descriptions

Definitions and descriptions help make a document useable. Both create a mutual understanding between communicator and user. Defining specialized terminologies, describing methods, and clarifying concepts using specific language are important benchmarks for effective communication.

In Chapter 1, we introduced four guidelines to help your technical documents become more useable:

- Be clear
- Be precise
- Be concise
- Be accurate

Think of these concepts as points on a compass. Taken together, they will orient your users and get them where you want them to go. As you create content, it's wise to look up every so often and orient yourself, too.

Definitions and description often go hand in hand. Clear definitions require some description to be effective, though they may also rely on explanation and context. **Description** uses the language of the senses to "show" the user, through writing, what you are talking about. Description focuses on the physical characteristics of an object, its size, weight, shape, color, material, use, and so on.

Explanations provide reasons that help users understand the word and its usage. **Context** is the setting in which the word appears. For example, in a technical document, the word "screw" likely refers to a small, spiral-shaped metal piece used to attach two or more solid pieces together. In a text message from your angry friend ("screw you!"), the word is used in a different context and has a completely different meaning.

If the user has the potential to interpret words in too many ways, your document won't succeed. In the worst-case scenario, a failed communication can have severe consequences.

Be Precise

See **Chapter 1** for more about precision.

Beware of revolving door definitions, such as this one, "Precision means to be precise." Using a term or a variation of a term to define the term itself sends your user in a confusing circle. Your goal should be to explain the new term precisely using words that the user is already familiar with. But what precisely does "precision" mean?

The following chart defines "precision" using different definition strategies (figure 2). In some cases, a term or concept may require an extended, multi-paragraph definition that includes deep research. For example, we took a little more time to define "precision" here because it's a word that many people think they already know. In technical fields, precision is essential and has a specific meaning that's different from its common usage. We break the term down for you in this example to demonstrate its importance. Additionally, we use this term to show how you can begin making your definitions more precise.

For example, *Alpacas of Doom!* players use 3d6 to determine game effects. This language only feels precise to people who already know what 3d6 means. A *more precise* description would recognize that most board game enthusiasts know that 3d6 refers to a set of three six-sided dice, but newer players might need the additional description provided in this sentence. This is why games

Definition Strategy	Example
Comparison/ Negation	Precision is not the same thing as accuracy. While accuracy measures how close something is to being true or meeting a standard, precision measures the degree of exactness with which an operation is performed.
Examples	A precision instrument is a tool that can be controlled with exactness to produce a specific result.
Analogy	Precision is the ability to hit the bull's-eye on a target again and again.
Image	

Figure 2. To define a term, break it down into its simplest parts. What is it made of? How is it used? What is it like? Answering these questions will steer you toward a definition strategy.

that have been around for decades still include glossaries and descriptions — it's no fun if you don't know what they're talking about.

Target Your Audience

How can you be sure you're hitting the mark? In technical documents, your audience is the bull's-eye, the center of your communication target. Always make sure your definitions answer the questions "What is it?" or "What does it involve?" in ways that make sense for your audience. As mentioned earlier, you might need to include analogies, examples, or comparisons to clarify meaning.

A user profile is one way to get a better understanding of your audience. A **user profile** is a collection of information about your potential audience that is usually assembled through interviews, surveys, reports, or

See **Chapter 1** for more information about creating a user profile.

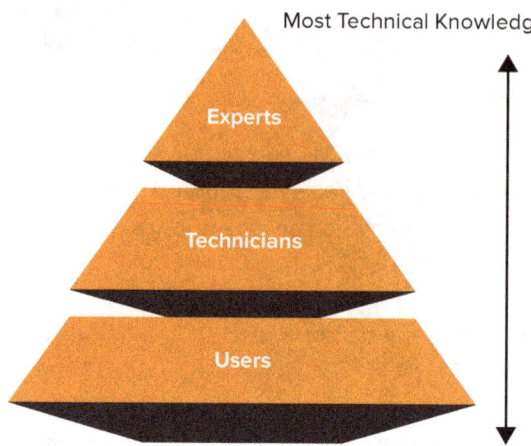

Figure 3. Some technical documents may require you to translate information from one audience segment to another.

in conversation with your client. The more you get to know about your audience, the easier it will be to decide what level of detail to use, what you need to define, and what can be left unsaid.

When your technical document has more than one audience segment, definitions can help you bridge the gap (figure 3). For example, in an audience assessment report for investors, Jason and Leticia identify that *Alpacas of Doom!* will most likely appeal to gaming enthusiasts who enjoy themed resource collection games. They are the same crowd that is likely to already own games such as *Settlers of Catan* or *Zombicide*. To guarantee their document's usefulness, they will have to take this audience's experience into account, while also recognizing they may have audience members who are new to independent board games.

How and What to Define

You should develop the habit of providing your own definitions instead of relying on dictionary definitions, which may not be specific enough for your communication needs. For example, if you're writing a technical report on nanotechnology, you'll find *Oxford's Dictionary of Mechanical Engineering* more useful than *Dictionary.com*.

Industry-specific terminology, or **jargon**, requires definition when communicating with an audience outside your field. You also need to define words that have multiple potential meanings or acronyms. Take the word "heap." To a computer scientist, it indicates a type of data structure, but to a layperson, it could mean a big pile. Be specific and determine what needs to be defined for understanding.

Try another word on for size: "hood." Without a definition, this word could mean anything. Is it part of a ventilation system? Does it cover the engine of a car? Is it the part of a jacket or sweatshirt you wear on your head? In a professional kitchen, the hood is the ventilation and fire suppression system placed above cooking surfaces that draws smoke out and away from the kitchen and dining area. In a document discussing the legal and safety requirements for opening a restaurant, users need a specific definition to make sure they understand.

When to Provide a Definition

The best time for a definition is immediately before or after the first use of the term. Whether or not you need to provide a definition depends on your audience. When you communicate with other experts in your field or employees in the same company, you can assume they know the same words and concepts as you and can choose to leave out the definition to save space. If you have any reason to believe someone may not be familiar with the term, you should provide the definition. Three types of definition we'll cover in this chapter, in order of complexity, are parenthetical, sentence, and extended definitions.

Parenthetical Definitions

When someone needs just enough added information to understand a term or acronym, a **parenthetical definition** is the best choice. A parenthetical definition provides an explanation of a term immediately after its first use, typically enclosed in commas or parentheses. For example, documents that deal with health concerns for a large audience may refer to "seasonal influenza, commonly known as the flu," or simply "seasonal influenza (flu)." When a parenthetical definition is provided immediately after a long name, as in the "National Institutes for Health (NIH)," the acronym is typically used later on in place of the full name to save space.

Parenthetical definitions often provide a synonym, a word or phrase that means the same thing, as an alternative enclosed in commas or parenthesis, as this sentence demonstrates with its parenthetical definition of "synonym." Parenthetical definitions allow specific terms (and their more general forms) to coexist within a document for the purpose of reaching a wider audience.

One way to think about parenthetical definitions is to see them as handrails that guide the user (figure 4). Your goal is to get your user from point A to point B, from the unfamiliar to the

Figure 4. Think of definitions as safety features, such as handrails, that help the user make the climb toward new information.

known. Parenthetical definitions can help you get there without having to explain too much and risk getting off topic. Parenthetical definitions are intended to interrupt the flow of a sentence as little as possible. Users familiar with the term can skip over them. But users who need a little extra assistance will appreciate that the definitions are there for them.

When to Use

A common use for a parenthetical definition is to introduce an acronym for the first time. The usual practice is to spell out the term in full and follow immediately with the acronym. Afterward, users will understand the acronym when they see it. For example, if you use meta-analysis from the National Institute of Mental Health (NIMH), you can introduce the institute followed by the acronym as you see in this sentence. In subsequent reference, you only need to use NIMH.

Textbooks often use parenthetical definitions to make sure the user has quick access to important vocabulary. Acronyms (abbreviations) or specialized terms are defined parenthetically (in passing) when the audience includes people who might not be familiar with these terms. Parenthetical definitions are also used to make sure the audience is guided toward the correct understanding of a term in order to avoid misinterpretation.

How to Use

Parenthetical definitions are best used where the audience needs just a little more clarification or when space constraints make longer definitions impractical. Keeping a parenthetical definition near or below five words is a good guideline. This isn't a hard and fast rule, meaning it isn't an absolute requirement. However, if you need more than five words, you may want to use a sentence definition instead.

Sentence Definitions

A **sentence definition** provides an explanation of a term within a complete grammatical unit, as you can see in this sentence. Sometimes the term is *italicized* or **bold** to indicate to users that a definition is embedded within the sentence. With bold text, the user can scan the document easily for terms they need to know. If the user needs a definition more comprehensive than the parenthetical but won't need the deep dive information provided in an extended definition, a sentence definition is ideal.

When to Use

Sentence definitions are often a good choice for a **glossary**, which is the list of terms used in a publication located near the end. Similarly, this variety of definition is useful any time readers need a moderate amount of explanation. Many paragraphs begin with a sentence definition of the term that the entire paragraph discusses. Avoid using a sentence definition when a parenthetical definition would be adequate. Often a communicator needs to offer a sentence definition before continuing with a technical document.

See the **glossary** located at the end of this book.

How to Use

In architecture, a cornerstone is a block placed at the corner of a building. Conceptually, a cornerstone is a building block around and upon which other ideas are stacked to make meaning. If definitions are the foundation of a technical document, the sentence definition is the cornerstone on which you build other definitions.

Definitions often use a pattern that involves identifying the name, class, and characteristics of your term. You can think of these as another set of building blocks. **Name** refers to the specific term, thing, or concept you are defining. Consider the alpaca from *Alpacas of Doom!* "Alpaca" describes a specific animal name, but what makes it different from, say, a llama? To answer this, you need to move on to the next category.

Class is the more specific category for the word. It does not simply name the object but provides additional details to help us classify it. For example, an alpaca is a mammal that belongs to the camel family. Llamas, camels, and alpacas are all part of the same family though clearly different at the species level.

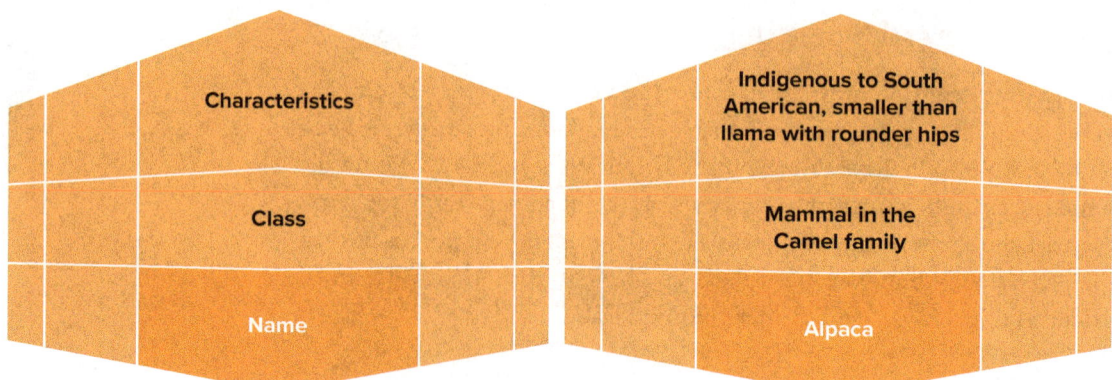

Figure 5. A solid definition can be built by identifying the name, class, and characteristics of the unfamiliar term. Each category becomes progressively more specific, which leads to a clearer understanding.

Characteristics are the unique traits that make the term or thing stand out from other terms in its category (figure 5).

It's useful to set up a table, like the one in figure 6, to help you craft a clear definition for your audience. You can use it to map out the parts of sentence definitions you need in your project. After you've mapped out the definitions, you are ready to craft them into complete sentences.

After Jason and Leticia build their grid, they write the appropriate terms into sentence definitions: "Alpacas are small, determined, civilized explorers who venture into the wasteland to find valuable lost technologies that will help their families and friends."

One example of useful definitions are the glossaries that are often placed at the end of documents. They offer easy-to-find definitions for terms within the document. They help maintain consistency of style, voice, and use of terms throughout a document. This is especially useful if a document is

Name	Class	Characteristics
Alpacas	Wasteland denizen	Civilized, explorers, small but determined, seeking tech/treasure, social
Eagle	Unmanned aerial vehicle	Used for surveillance missions
Blaster	High-tech weapon	Leaks radiation when used, but delivers high damage
D6	Type of dice	Standard, six-sided

Figure 6. In this table, game designers Leticia and Jason generate definitions for terms they used in their game. The categories of name, class, and characteristics assist in the creation of definitions.

> **Alpaca:** clever, techno-savvy, Andean relative of the llama that enjoy going on adventures in search of lost technologies from ancient civilizations.
> **Blaster:** powerful radioactive energy weapon.
> **D6:** six-sided die.
> **Eagle:** a type of unmanned aerial vehicle used for reconnaissance missions.
> **Quetzalcoatl:** the feathered serpent from Mesoamerican myth and the final challenge in *Alpacas of Doom!*
> **Tripalpaca:** this is what you call all three dice in one roll showing the alpaca image.

The colon replaces the phrase "is a." The complete sentence would read, "Blaster is a powerful radioactive energy weapon." Check for parallelism in your definitions by reading in this phrase in place of the colon.

This phrase breaks the pattern of parallelism in this glossary entry. Remove "this is" to make the entry follow the pattern in the other definitions.

Figure 7. Notice the format and organization for glossary definitions do not require you to write in complete sentences. However, the definitions should follow the same pattern and use parallel language to introduce the terms.

translated into other languages. They usually serve as a backup resource for in-text definitions you provide and are written in the style of a dictionary entry (figure 7).

Extended Definitions

The **extended definition** provides an explanation over multiple sentences. For example, this paragraph is an extended definition of the extended definition. Extended definitions provide the most context to the user and help solidify the document's purpose. This kind of definition goes beyond the sentence level by presenting clear facts, examples, and anecdotes the user will understand. It's important to meet users at their level of understanding before introducing new concepts.

When to Use

Save your use of the extended definition for situations that really call for an in-depth approach. In general, users don't want to read an extended definition if they don't have to, so save them for when they really count. Recall that conciseness is one of the key characteristics of effective communication.

A technical report is an appropriate place to make frequent use of extended definitions. The purpose of a technical report is to inform an audience and make recommendations based on the findings. The audience of a technical report expects to see a good amount of granular information on the report's topic. This level of detail helps the audience feel confident that they are getting a good recommendation and that they will make an informed decision based on the report.

How to Use

Here are two examples of extended definitions from students (figure 8).

An extended definition usually starts with a standard sentence definition followed by supplementary information and ends with a discussion of the term, phrase, or concept. If you go back to the process for developing sentence

> The TI-Nspire Touchpad calculator from Texas Instruments is a handheld algebraic graphing calculator that has programmable software capable of solving a wide range of equations. This calculator can perform many different types of equations such as Factor and expand variables, compute limits and give exact solutions, and is solving graphic equation symbolically.

This student model begins with a strong sentence definition.

The next sentence expands on the types of equations but the list gets confusing as it goes due to lack of parallelism.

> A foil cutter is a small, serrated knife attached to a wine key (a wine and bottle opener that resembles a Swiss Army knife). Its purpose is to provide a clean and safe cut while removing the foil at the lip of a wine bottle. In homes, a foil cutter removes the risk of potential harm when individuals try to use a knife (or some other kind of sharp object) to cut away the foil. In a business setting, foil cutters increase efficiency, increase professionalism, and reduce risk of potential harm to employees.

This student model begins with a basic sentence definition. It extends this definition by anticipating the user's questions.

Figure 8. Both students begin with a sentence definition. The second extended definition stays on track by answering these questions: What is it? How is it used? Why is it used?

definitions, you will notice that you can use the same process for building the first sentence for your extended definition.

The next step in writing an extended definition is determining what is in the first sentence that may need further context and explanation. Often you may realize that examples of the concept are useful. After adding more explanation to the sentence definition, you can develop the definition by discussing its position in the broader context. You may want to consider including information about the origins of a word or phrase. Or you may need to include background information. Sometimes it is useful to explain what the term does not mean, referred to as **negation**. At other times, it may be useful to provide a visual to extend your explanation.

Descriptions

Think of descriptions as an extreme version of the extended definition. They go beyond the initial questions of "What is it?" and "What does it entail?" to include other questions, such as:

- What are its parts?
- What does it do?
- How does it work?

Descriptions are used in a variety of documents. In the workplace, you might find them included in purchase orders and as parts of a longer technical document, such as manuals, reports, and instructions. A description will focus on specific details like background, features, physical attributes, function, qualities, and visuals. Like definitions, descriptions use specific, accurate, and concise language to help the user better grasp the concepts in the document. Also, building a bank of descriptive phrases will help you and your collaborators provide accurate, consistent information.

When to Use

Descriptions are best used when you need to define a process or make the user aware of the parts they need. In most cases, visual aids like photos and diagrams are used with descriptions so the user will know what they're looking at and visualize how to interact with the described item or process. Even without images to help, description is the tool we use to help someone else "see" the thing we're describing when they haven't encountered the item or concept before.

Think of technology that didn't exist ten years ago, such as ride-sharing apps, the iPad, or 4G networks. Imagine explaining these technologies to people who have never used a smartphone. To define these terms, you may need to define other terms along the way. For example, to define 4G network, you would need to explain that it is a form of broadband mobile communication that is wireless and allows the transfer of data from one mobile device to another at a rate faster than 3G. From there, you would need to define broadband, wireless, and 3G. Writing definitions requires you to use your imagination and try to imagine what it is like to hear about something for the first time.

Here's another example from *Alpacas of Doom!* The game uses "regular" six-sided dice with images on four sides and two blank sides. This definition helps the user make a distinction between regular dice with pips (dots) and the dice used for this game. The next description tells you how to use them and for what purpose — otherwise you'd have no idea how to play.

How to Use

When crafting descriptions, it's a good idea to use concrete language. **Concrete language** is sensory, tangible, and mostly nouns and verbs. You can use adjectives or adverbs, but sparingly.

Too many adjectives, especially in a continuous string, can cause confusion in surprising ways. It might seem like you're being specific when you use multiple adjectives, as in "4G broadband wireless mobile communication network." But this mouthful description will only make sense to people who already know what you're talking about.

To develop descriptions, ask questions that help you focus on elements that you can see or touch. Depending on what you are describing, you may end up relying on spatial and visual description, temporal and action descriptions, or any number of similar combinations. For example, describing features of a device will reasonably require focus on spatial relationships, shapes, or color, while process descriptions need more attention on timing, movement, and necessary tools.

Examples of questions you might ask when writing a product description start simple and become more granular as you dive deeper into the product. For example, you might start with the question: "What is the first thing I notice about this product?" Chances are that this part will catch other people's attention in a similar way, which gives you a place to start when you organize your thoughts and draft your description. Other questions to ask yourself include:

- What are its distinguishing characteristics?
- What are the primary uses of this product?
- How is this product activated?
- Are there any clear dangers with using this product?
- What are the primary and secondary colors of this product?

In *Alpacas of Doom!*, Jason and Leticia want to use a simple dice system to add an element of chance. They asked themselves questions to figure out how they'd describe the dice to investors and manufacturers. This description is necessary for product development and will also help them understand game mechanics. They want to get the description right because it's not cheap to create and manufacture specialized dice (figure 9).

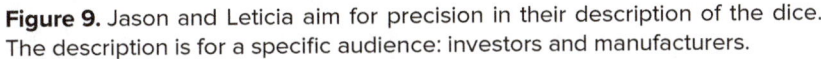

Planning questions
- What are the dice used for?
- What shape are the dice?
- How many will we use?
- What images are on the dice?
- What color will they be?

Final description

The game contains one set of three six-sided dice for each player, up to the maximum number of players. The colors are white, green, yellow, orange, purple, and red. On each die, there are two blank sides, two sides with stylized alpacas, and two sides marked with X. The dice are used to resolve encounters and determine outcomes during gameplay.

Figure 9. Jason and Leticia aim for precision in their description of the dice. The description is for a specific audience: investors and manufacturers.

Process descriptions explain how complex events occur. Here are some questions you could ask when developing a process description:

- What equipment is needed?
- Do users need to set up a space?
- What is the chronological order of each step in the process?
- What are the outcomes of each step?

Since we just received Jason and Leticia's description of the dice their game uses, let's see a process in which these unusual dice are used (figure 10).

> In *Alpacas of Doom!*, dice are used to resolve conflict. Players roll dice to determine the outcome of fights with monsters, haggling with wasteland denizens, and searches for resources and technology. When one player fights a monster or haggles with a denizen, that player chooses another player to roll the dice to represent the opposition. Alpacas are civilized — they engage in friendly competition, but they don't fight one another. Each die that rolls an alpaca is counted as success. Blank results are "no effect" and X results cancel an opposing success. The player with the highest number of successes wins the encounter.

- The most important information comes first.
- The description moves into a narration of the process.
- The results are defined and explained.

Figure 10. The goal of this description is to make sure players can easily understand how to use the game's specialized dice. Simple, descriptive language helps players get to the fun part faster.

In the above examples, Leticia and Jason answer questions to develop equipment for *Alpacas of Doom!* and consider further questions to determine how the equipment is used. These descriptions are important to players' understanding of gameplay as well as the overall theme of the game.

The Known-New Contract

Effective definitions and descriptions depend on the Known-New Contract. **The Known-New Contract** is a basic principle of communication where you start with what your user already knows and then introduce new information. The next sentence begins with the new information you just introduced and adds to it with even newer information. By doing this, you can create a logical and easy-to-follow progression from sentence to sentence.

When to Use

Technical communicators frequently employ the Known-New Contract in all kinds of technical communication, but this principle is especially useful when writing definitions and descriptions.

When offering a definition, it's important to begin with simple, broad ideas that the reader is likely to know. If, on the other hand, you begin with complex terms and higher-level concepts, it's unlikely that your reader will grasp the overall concept that you are defining. You must start with commonly known things to help the user understand the more advanced concept.

For example, when Steve Jobs introduced the iPad in 2010, he explained that it was "way better than a laptop, way better than a smartphone." Jobs built on his audience's knowledge of the laptop and smartphone to sell his new idea.

How to Use

Begin with what you can confidently assume your reader knows. This is your starting point. Don't begin with new, complex concepts, or you'll risk losing the user's attention. For example, Leticia and Jason will need to introduce the users of their game to original concepts. They should begin by reminding the user of familiar things and then relate those familiar things to unfamiliar things found in the game. A logical decision for Leticia and Jason would be to relate the concepts of the game to other games. This strategy will work for both kinds of players: gaming enthusiasts and people who want a break from the family fights caused by *Monopoly*.

Legal and Ethical Implications

Clear and accurate definitions help users navigate challenging technical issues. As a result, definitions carry legal and ethical implications for you as a technical communicator and the organization you work for.

The user of your document doesn't have access to your thought process. They can't see what you think, and they don't necessarily know what you know. Definitions help narrow the space in which users might misinterpret language in a document and make mistakes based on this misinterpretation.

Although there is such a thing as user error, it's a good idea as a designer to assume that misunderstandings or confusion are not the user's fault. This assumption will help you stay sharp while drafting important documents that carry real consequences.

Conveying an accurate interpretation of facts is not only an ethical issue, but also one of safety. If procedures and important terms in your deliverable are vague or incomplete and you work in a potentially dangerous environment, the consequences could be injury or death. That may seem scary right now, but it's a reminder to get a handle on writing clearly and accurately so that you are prepared if you ever need to take on a project with this level of responsibility.

Conclusion

Throughout this chapter, we've used analogies to help you visualize the ways that definitions and descriptions work in technical communication. The parenthetical definition is like a handrail guiding users. The sentence definition is like a cornerstone that brings together two separate ideas and allows you to build upon them. The extended definition is like a bridge that takes the users to a place of understanding. The Known-New contract underlies all of these concepts. Each sentence is a link in the chain that binds you, the technical communicator, to the user at the other end.

Chapter 9
Instructions and Procedures

Abstract: Some people mistakenly think that instructions and procedures are the same. Though these technical documents have similar parts, they have important differences too. Instructions provide a series of detailed steps that define how to complete a task. Instructions exist so that the same actions can be repeated in the same order with the same result. Procedures, on the other hand, provide an overview of the best methods to accomplish a complex process. For both, technical communicators can benefit by using the Problem-Solution Framework, which focuses on how audience, message, and purpose interact. An essential step in creating effective instructions and procedures is usability testing. When you test a technical document, you can see how much the user understands, where you can make changes for greater usefulness, and how to avoid potential problems.

Looking Ahead

1. Why Instructions an Procedures Matter

2. Instructions

3. Procedures

4. Usability Testing

5. Legal and Ethical Concerns

Why Instructions and Procedures Matter

Do you remember starting a new job? If you're like most people, when you showed up for your first day of work, you didn't know what to do. To whom do you report? What are you expected to know already? How do you record your hours? When is lunch? And most importantly, where is the bathroom? You didn't walk through the door knowing all this. Someone had to teach you.

It's normal to feel nervous about doing something unfamiliar, whether it's starting a new job or using a new piece of technology. This is where the technical communicator can help. Technical communicators create instructions and procedures to guide people through a range of actions, from individual tasks such as assembling a bicycle to complex, large-scale projects, such as the crew procedures for a rocket launch. Both document types require intense focus on the end users so they can carry out a task with confidence.

Instructions and Procedures Defined

Instructions explain the *how* of doing something. Typically, instructions are written for an individual person to complete a short task. Instructions use short, simple sentences with lots of action verbs that tell a person exactly what to do one step at a time (figure 1). Often instructions feature detailed images. Consider a piece of furniture that requires assembly. You need instructions to know what tools to use, what parts are required, and what pieces to assemble in what order. Ideally, instructions take you from a pile of screws and boards to a finished nightstand with a minimal amount of frustration or smashed fingers.

Procedures differ from instructions because they focus on the bigger picture and define roles and responsibilities (see figure 2). While instructions deal with how to accomplish a specific task, a procedure considers the larger questions of *who* needs to do the task and *why* they need to do it. For example, many businesses have a procedure for reviewing employee performance. Such a procedure typically establishes how often an employee will be reviewed (annually, every six months, or every quarter), who will do the reviewing (the business owner or a department manager), the nature of the review (a test or an observation), the standard of assessment (points or pass/

Chapter 9: Instructions and Procedures 199

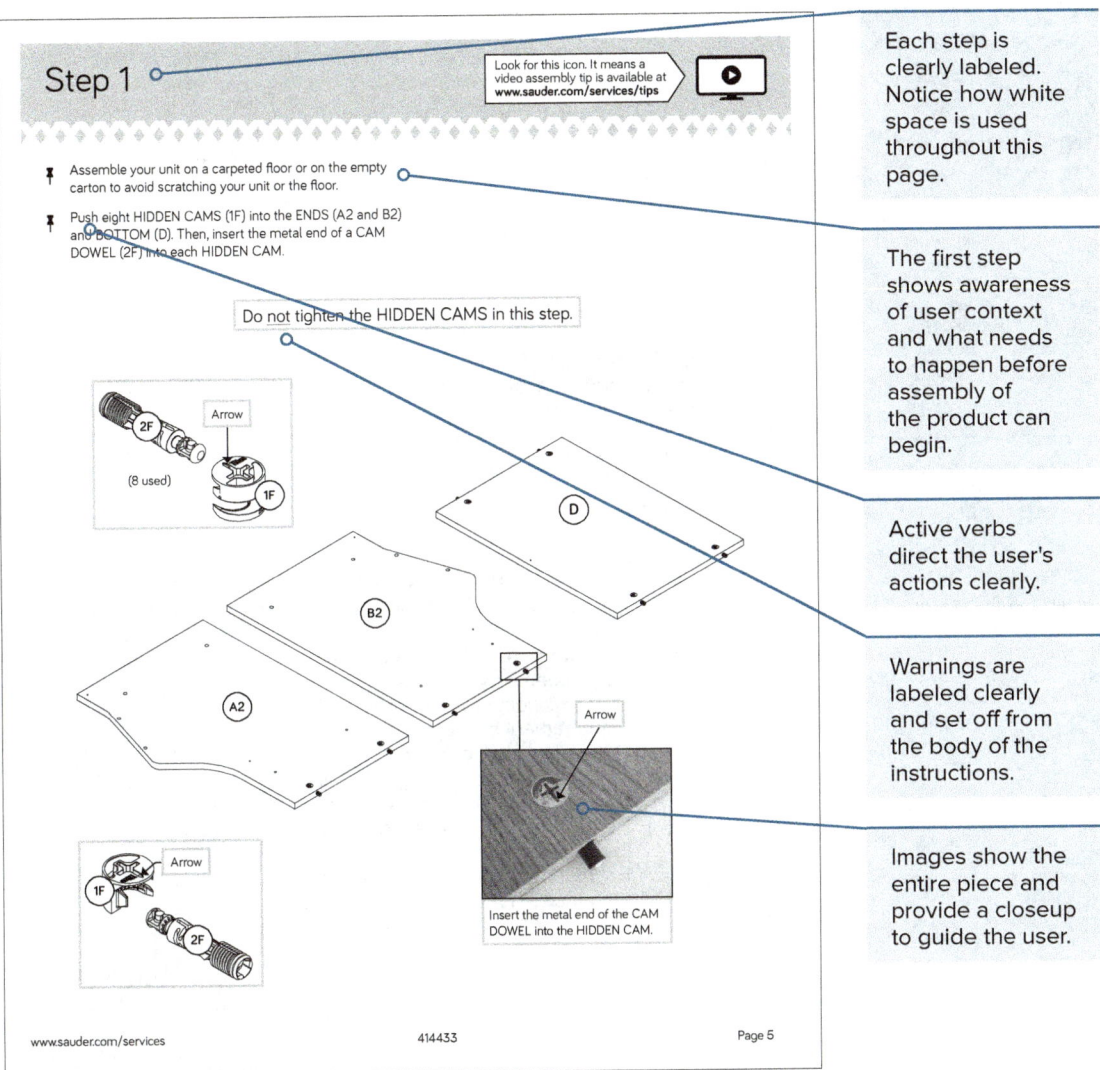

Figure 1. This set of instructions tells the user what to do and what not to do.

> Headings separate the parts of the procedure and show their hierarchical relationship.

LOCAL GOVERNMENT ABC

Accounting Policies and Procedures Manual
Policy #: PC-1
Last Revised: October 19, 2016
Policy Name: Petty Cash

1.0 Policy

Local Government ABC requires all departments to follow the below procedures establishing, overseeing, and closing out petty cash accounts.

Use of petty cash accounts is encouraged for purchasing of low-cost items from local vendors. Petty cash accounts will not exceed $1,000.

2.0 Procedures

The following procedures are designed to guide departments in establishing, overseeing, and closing out petty cash accounts.

2.1 Establishing a Petty Cash Account

- 2.1.1 Departments must complete the *Petty Cash Authorization* form and submit it to the Cash Management manager.
- 2.1.2 Once approved, department managers will be responsible for acquiring a lockable cash box. Contact the business services office for the box.
- 2.1.3 Funds and a transaction log will be provided once the lockable cash box has been obtained.
- 2.1.4 Each department will designate one employee to be responsible for the petty cash account.

> Many documents contain both policy (written rule) and procedures (how the rule is carried out).

Figure 2. This model shows the first page of a multipage procedural document.

fail), and what will happen after the review (promotion, layoff, or continuing education). Procedures are often collected into a manual or standard operating procedures (SOP).

In many ways, procedures help with decision-making, whereas instructions tell someone exactly what to do. While instructions are typically written for a single person, procedures are usually written for departments or even entire companies. Many procedures contain sets of instructions within them

Instructions	Procedures
Describe shorter tasks that are completed in one session	Describe longer processes that often involve multiple tasks in succession
Describe only what the user needs to do	Describe both what the user needs to do and why they need to do it
Focus on individual steps	Focus on an overall objective
Emphasize actions	Emphasize decisions
Involve an individual	Involve more than one person

Figure 3. This table shows the differences between instructions and procedures.

because an involved procedure often has multiple starting and stopping points. Take a look at this table that shows the main differences between instructions and procedures (figure 3).

Instructions and Procedures at Work

Consider the following workplace scenario that involves both types of documents. Rosario is the safety manager at Wrecking Ball Demolitions. This role puts Rosario in charge of reducing the number of injuries, co-planning safe work practices with crew leaders in the field, and ensuring that the company's safety equipment is complete and in good condition. In addition, Rosario occasionally writes documentation explaining how employees should do certain tasks to ensure a safe work environment.

Recently Rosario noted the increase of reported injuries involving reciprocating saws in the field. When she examined the incident reports, she realized that employees weren't following standard safety procedures. While it's common knowledge that the company expects employees to report their injuries in a standardized fashion, this expectation isn't written down anywhere. Rosario knows that writing a procedure will help make the reporting of injuries more consistent.

In a situation like Rosario's, you need to balance the technical nature of your document with what you know about your user. This means that you must communicate accurately about your topic, but you must do this in a way that users understand. For example, Rosario doesn't describe tools to the field workers at Wrecking Ball Demolitions in the same way that she would a homeowner. An employee at a demolition company already has familiarity with the tools. On the other hand, she won't write about injury reporting for these same field employees the way she would for someone working in Human Resources. Her employees need to know what to do when they get hurt. HR staff, instead, need to know about the risks and liability to facilitate a worker's injury claim. For both types of technical documents, your awareness of the audience is crucial.

Instructions

Users turn to instructions when they need to complete a specific task. This might be something as simple as operating a coffee machine or something as complex as disassembling an engine. Regardless of the level of complexity, instructions need certain elements to be effective. Technical communicators must consider elements of effective organization, language, design, and visuals as they create instructions. As with all technical documents, instructions should be written to solve a specific problem for specific users.

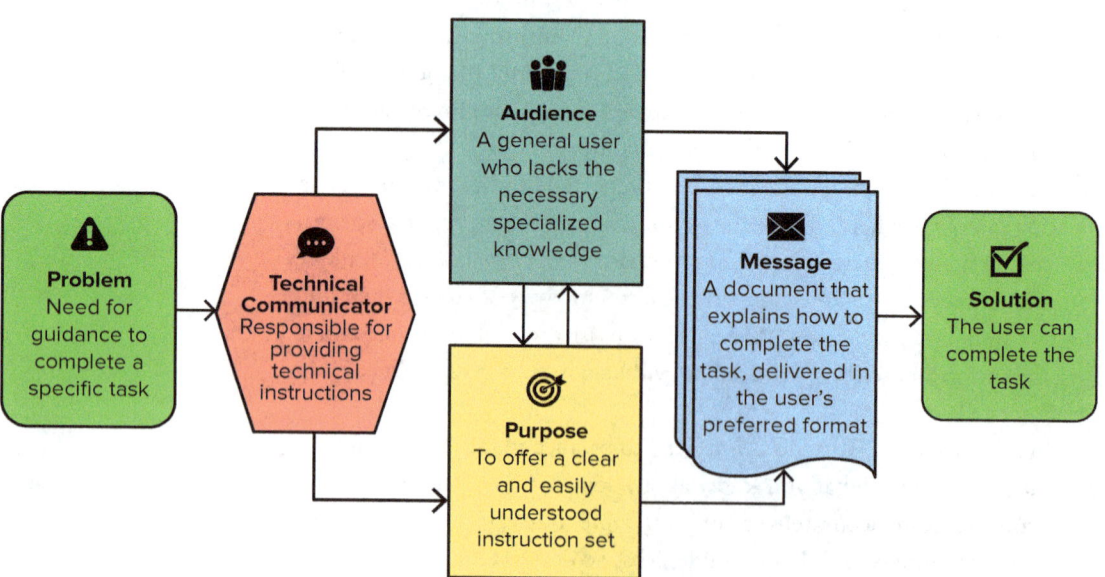

Figure 4. The Problem-Solution Framework can help you think about what your audience needs in order to provide more effective instructions.

Problem-Solution Framework for Instructions

Think back to the Problem-Solution Framework. Instructions are clearly designed to solve a problem, so take note of how the framework adapts to accomplish this end (figure 4).

Keep in mind when a user is likely to encounter your instructions. Users tend to consult instructions only when they can't figure something out on their own or when something isn't working as expected. Talk about a tough audience. Your user is likely to be frustrated, impatient, or, in Rosario's workplace, injured. They don't want to ask themselves, "Why am I doing this? Is this really the best approach?" Your job is to have already thought of those questions and to find the best answer.

Remember the situation and the needs of your user when you begin writing instructions. One of your challenges will be to remember that the audience hasn't thought about the topic as much as you have, particularly if the instructions are about an area in which you have significant experience. You may need to think back to the first time you attempted the task you are writing about. What did you need to know to complete the task? If you haven't completed the task, go try it and see what you learn. How would the activity be best explained? The ideal instruction set uses precise, brief language to save the user time and effort.

Don't forget to consider a range of circumstances that could impact the user. Answering a few common questions helps you decide how to approach your document:

- How will users receive your instructions — in print, online, by mail, in person, cell phone, tablet, or computer?
- What types of visuals will enhance communication for users — photos, screenshots, clipart, drawings, diagrams, tables, charts, graphics, videos?

Best Practices for Instructions

Follow standard practices to make your instructions clear and easy to follow. Best practices include logical organization, standard and consistent language, clarity and accuracy, scannable design, and the effective use of visuals.

Organization

Every set of instructions describes a series of specific actions that must occur in a particular order. For example, "Insert bolt #1 into hole A." The user assumes that following the instructions in the order presented will result in a successfully completed task.

To assist in this goal, you need to make sure your instructions follow a logical sequence. Like a story, most projects have a beginning, middle, and end. Decide where to begin, and then break each part of the task into distinct steps. Describe the steps in order using short, simple directions. One way to prepare to write instructions is to use a template such as the one provided here to organize your steps (figure 5). This document works like an outline that you can expand to fit the needs of any instruction set.

Standard and Consistent Language

Have you ever read instructions that were so easy to follow that you wondered if you even needed them? Your response is a sign that the technical communicator has done an excellent job with word choice. In particular, instructions need to use language that is standard and consistent. This means that the language of the instructions matches what the user is familiar with and expects. For example, you should avoid technical jargon in instructions meant for a general audience. If a specialized term is needed for accuracy, then define the term right away with words or an image to help the user understand.

Consistency of language means keeping the same level of word choice and style throughout the document. Typical factors include verb tense, verb mood, and parallelism.

- **Verb tense:** Keep your verbs in present tense — describe things in the now. For example, "Assemble your unit on a carpeted floor" not, "It will be a good idea to assemble your unit on a carpeted floor."
- **Verb mood:** Use what is called the "imperative" mood — tell people what to do directly. For example, the sentences "Open the door," "stop the car," and "pass the salt" include verbs in the imperative mood.
- **Parallelism:** Keep words and phrases consistent. For example, "This installation requires a hammer, pliers, and a flathead screwdriver" not, "This installation requires a hammer, pliers, and you'll need a flathead screwdriver, too."

Title

Introduction

Use an action-oriented title, such as "How to Write Instructions."

Describe the task and the end result.

Required Materials
-
-
-

List what is needed to complete the task.

Warning!

Heading: Part One

1. Do this.
2. Do this.
3. Do this other thing before moving on to part two.

Inform the user of potential problems, if any.

Heading: Part Two

4. Do this.
5. Do this.
6. Do this other thing before moving on to part three.

Supply headings to show the beginning and end of each part of the task, if needed.

Heading: Part Three

7. Do this.
8. Do this.
9. Do this other thing before finishing.

Conclusion

Write in simple, directive statements that begin with an action.

Figure 5. This template can be adapted to just about any set of instructions.

Clarity and Accuracy

See **Chapter 1** for more on clarity and accuracy.

Along with the importance of using language that is standard and consistent, you need to keep your writing clear and accurate. If you can recall an occasion when you struggled to understand a set of instructions, the problem likely originated with a lack of clarity.

Describe what users need to do precisely and when they need to do it. Avoid vague language. As you'll see in this chapter, pairing text with clear visuals can help with this, but the writing must first be understandable. Don't just say, "Use a computer to go to our website." Be clear — give the exact URL to the specific web page.

The accuracy of your language is also important. Usability testing, a process you'll learn about later in this chapter, will help make sure your word choice

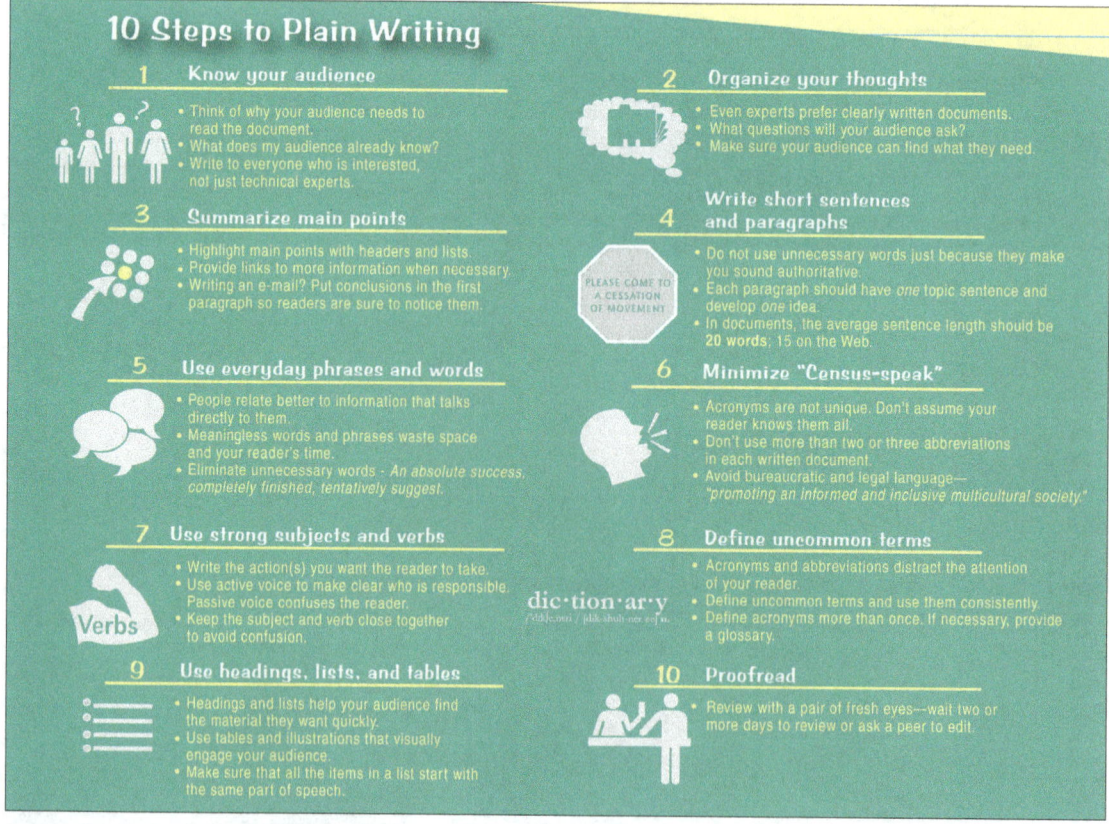

Figure 6. Like many government agencies, the US Census Bureau is committed to using plain language in its communications. Courtesy of the US Census Bureau.

Chapter 9: Instructions and Procedures

is accurate. If your user needs to use a Phillips screwdriver, for example, does it need to be a specific size, such as a No. 2 Phillips? If you're describing how to complete a keyboard shortcut in a computer program, does the shortcut work on both Windows-based computers and Macs? Anticipate the user's unique situation when analyzing your document for accuracy. Recognize that your experience with the task may not reflect the experience of the user.

Using plain language is one way to make your instructions accessible to the largest possible audience. The federal government and many state governments, including Oregon, have adopted plain language policies that promote the use of clear communication in all government documents. The Plain Writing Act of 2010 defines plain language as "writing that is clear, concise, well-organized, and follows other best practices appropriate to the subject of field and intended audience." Not only is clear writing more understandable, but it saves time and money. Writing in this way takes practice, as this document from the US Census Bureau shows (figure 6).

Scannable Design

Think back to the last time you needed to use instructions. Did you read them from beginning to end like a chapter in a novel? Of course not. Reading instructions happens in small steps that accompany each stage of the task. Users move back and forth between the instructions and the actual task. For this reason, instructions need to be broken up into sections that can be located easily by scanning the document.

A scannable design is always important in technical communication, but this factor is particularly important when creating instructions. Notice how you can scan this flyer about the DASH Eating Plan to quickly identify its tips for reducing salt and sodium (figure 7).

Headings are one way to make a document more scannable. Headings show the structure of the document and come in three general categories: question headings, statement headings, and topic headings. The more specific your headings

Figure 7. Effective use of images and headings allows helpful information to fit this single page. Courtesy of the National Heart, Lung, and Blood Institute.

Heading	Example
Question	How do I use headings effectively in instructions?
Statement	Use Headings Effectively in Instructions
Topic	Headings in Instructions

Figure 8. This table includes three kinds of headings: question, statement, and topic. Notice how the level of formality changes slightly with each heading.

See **Chapter 3** for more on headings.

See **Chapter 1** for more on scannability.

are, the easier it is for users to scan for the information they need (figure 8). As you can see, question headings are more conversational, while topic headings are more formal. It's up to you to decide which kind of heading is best for your audience and the purpose of your document.

Headings are only useful when they are distinct from the rest of the document. That often means using a different style font, a different font size, or white space to draw attention to the heading. Heading titles should be chosen carefully. Think about the keywords or phrases users will be looking for when they scan the document. Guide the user by providing similar words and phrases from one heading to the next, as in these headings for fence construction: "building your fence," "installing your fence," and "fixing your fence." Keep the headings as short as possible while still being specific.

Here are some important design techniques to increase the scannability of your document:

- Use plenty of white space.
- Emphasize key ideas or warnings with color, icons, or all caps.
- Enlarge and make clear headlines with your headings.
- Bold important terms.
- Set up bulleted and numbered lists for easy access.

Effective Use of Visuals

Visuals can greatly improve a set of instructions and provide users with extra guidance for a complex process. In figure 7, images enable helpful information to fit onto a single page. Notice the way the images support the text and the text reinforces the visuals. When using visuals, it's important to make sure the relationship between the text and image is clear.

Visuals can also create concise documents. As the saying goes, a picture is worth one thousand words. Graphics, diagrams, illustrations, and charts can show plenty of information all at once and reduce the need for written description. You can see this principle at work in the before and after example from the National Highway Traffic Safety Administration (figure 9).

Another benefit of using visuals is recognition: even if users aren't familiar with the terms the writer is using (such as a specific tool or part), they might recognize a visual representation. Also, some tasks are so complex that trying to write how to complete them (or read such a description) can be challenging. For example, look on the next page at how the exploded diagram in figure 10 allows the user to see all the parts and how they fit together.

Visuals show how the steps connect to each other and fit into a larger process. When thinking about how to use visuals in your instructions, consider the following questions:

- Which type of visual will work best for your instructions?
- Which color theme will you choose for your visuals?
- How much white space is needed to make them easier to read?

Figure 9. Images can communicate complex ideas quickly. Courtesy of the National Highway Traffic Safety Administration and Plainlanguage.gov.

Creating a consistent theme and style makes your instructions uniform, as when you use similar formatting and color schemes for both tables and figures, for instance.

Many technical communicators borrow visuals rather than create them. This can be a way to save time, but as with all forms of borrowing, using visuals created by others means checking for the right to use and giving credit. Just because you find the perfect visual for your document online doesn't mean you have the right to use it. If the owner of the image has given permission for its use, either in writing or with an open license, be sure to recognize the source either with a credit line beneath the image or at the end of your document.

See **Chapter 5** for more on copyright and citing sources for images.

Procedures

Procedures establish rules or methods for complex processes. These typically require approval by an authority, such as a department head at a company. Most of the time, companies develop procedures to streamline or standardize a process. For example, a business might give new cashiers a cash handling

210 — *Practical Models for Technical Communication*

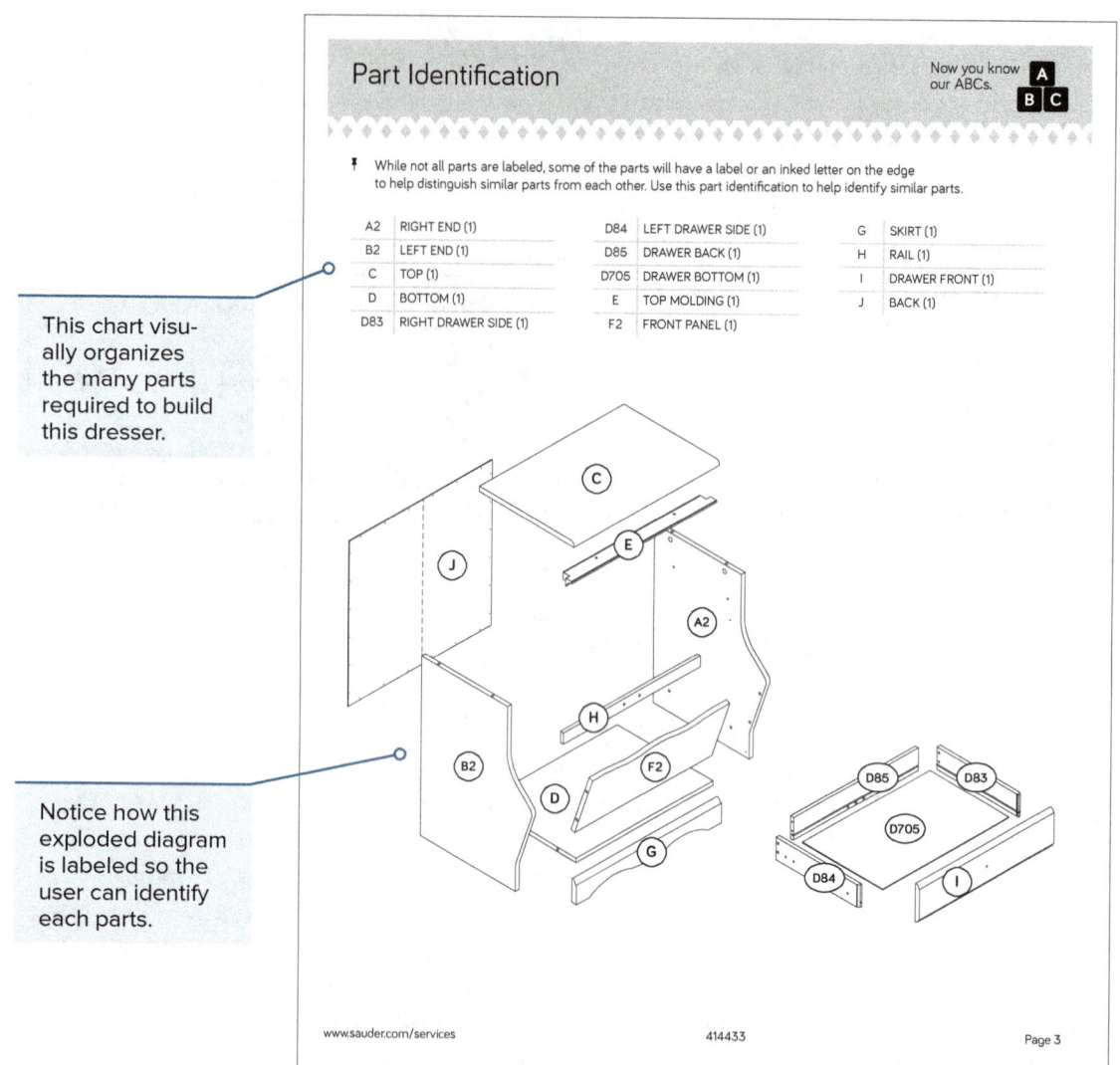

This chart visually organizes the many parts required to build this dresser.

Notice how this exploded diagram is labeled so the user can identify each parts.

Figure 10. This page from an assembly manual uses several strategies for organizing information, including an exploded diagram that shows where all the parts will eventually go and a table of parts listed in alphabetical order. Courtesy of Sauder.

procedure. This document makes sure that the training is consistent, accessible, and covers the same content regardless of who gives the training.

Back at Wrecking Ball Demolitions, Rosario begins working on a new set of procedures for reporting injuries. Employees at the company are regularly getting hurt, but they are not dealing with the injuries according to company policy. Rosario realizes that part of the problem is that no official document exists to guide employees when an injury occurs. She begins creating a procedure. Even more so than when she created the instructions for operating a reciprocating saw, Rosario must carefully analyze her target audience. A procedure is about a more complex situation with multiple decisions, phases, and sometimes even multiple instruction sets.

Problem-Solution Framework for Procedures

Procedures help users make choices as they move through complex situations rather than telling them exactly what to do step by step. The success of your procedure relies on how well you guide users through the decision-making process, which is illustrated here with the Problem-Solution Framework (figure 11).

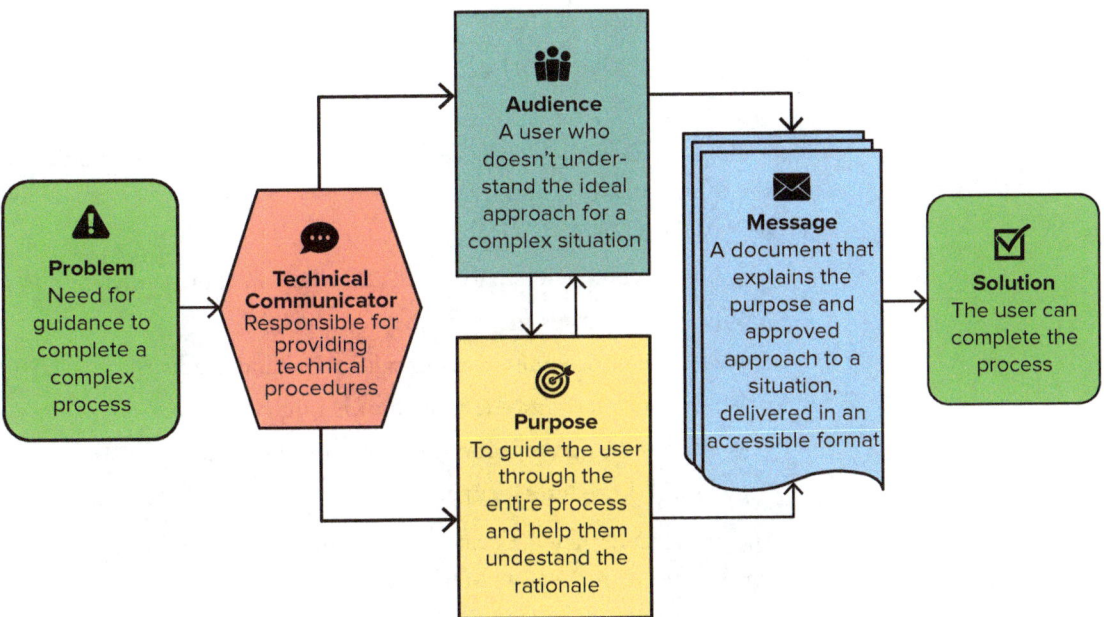

Figure 11. The Problem-Solution Framework can help you prepare procedures for multiple users.

Businesses often create a procedure to ensure consistency among employees when dealing with particular scenarios. For example, suppose a retail business needs to train its managers on how to deal with difficult customers. Creating a set of instructions would be impractical: no instruction set could anticipate the complexity of dealing with every situation involving a difficult customer. A procedure, on the other hand, could give employees guidance to make the best decision in those situations.

Purpose

Here are some examples of procedural documents that many companies create:

- How to use a company vehicle
- How to seek grant funding
- How to write appropriate workplace emails
- How to apply for family leave

Notice that the topics in this list couldn't be dealt with in a set of instructions. Instead, a procedure needs to outline the best way to make decisions about these topics. Remember, procedures are typically about situations that require the user to understand the *what* and the *why* of the situation, rather than the precise method of *how*.

Audience

When thinking about the audience for a procedure, consider the conditions and the impact of the process. Evaluate the who, what, when, where, why, and how of the activities:

- Who will complete the practices, and who will approve them?
- What will the steps cost in money and effort?
- Where will procedures intersect with safety and productivity?
- When will a new procedure be most helpful?
- Why does the current procedure work or not work?
- How will procedures be updated?

Success depends on your keeping procedures current, uniform in design, and simple enough for anyone to understand.

Best Practices for Procedures

A few key principles can make a big difference in the effectiveness of your procedures. As you write, think about the importance of user context, the key steps of the procedure, and useful design.

User Context

Procedures deal with the big picture, so it's important to give the user an understanding of the context. Often a procedure is created in response to past events. For example, a business that has dealt with embezzlement from a former employee might create a hiring procedure that involves a background check. To help future managers understand the purpose of this procedure, the document should explain that the policy of background checks stems from the possibility of employee misconduct. This background information is the context for the procedure and part of what makes it relevant to the user.

Procedures should provide clear definitions so that users know who should be involved and why. For instance, notice how this document created for a lab is specific about who is qualified to carry out the procedure and the required training (see figure 12 on the next page).

Key Steps

A typical procedure includes a description of key steps. These steps are the actions required by the process in order for it to be completed properly. For example, refer to the scenario of the hiring procedure mentioned earlier. An overview of the key steps for this procedure might look like this:

- Review job applications.
- Conduct hiring interview.
- Perform background checks.
- Make hiring offer to prospective employee.
- Complete hiring paperwork.
- Schedule employee's start day.
- Conduct employee orientation.

These steps may look like instructions, but they are more of an outline that guides the user toward the end result. Within each step is a number of decisions that are not spelled out.

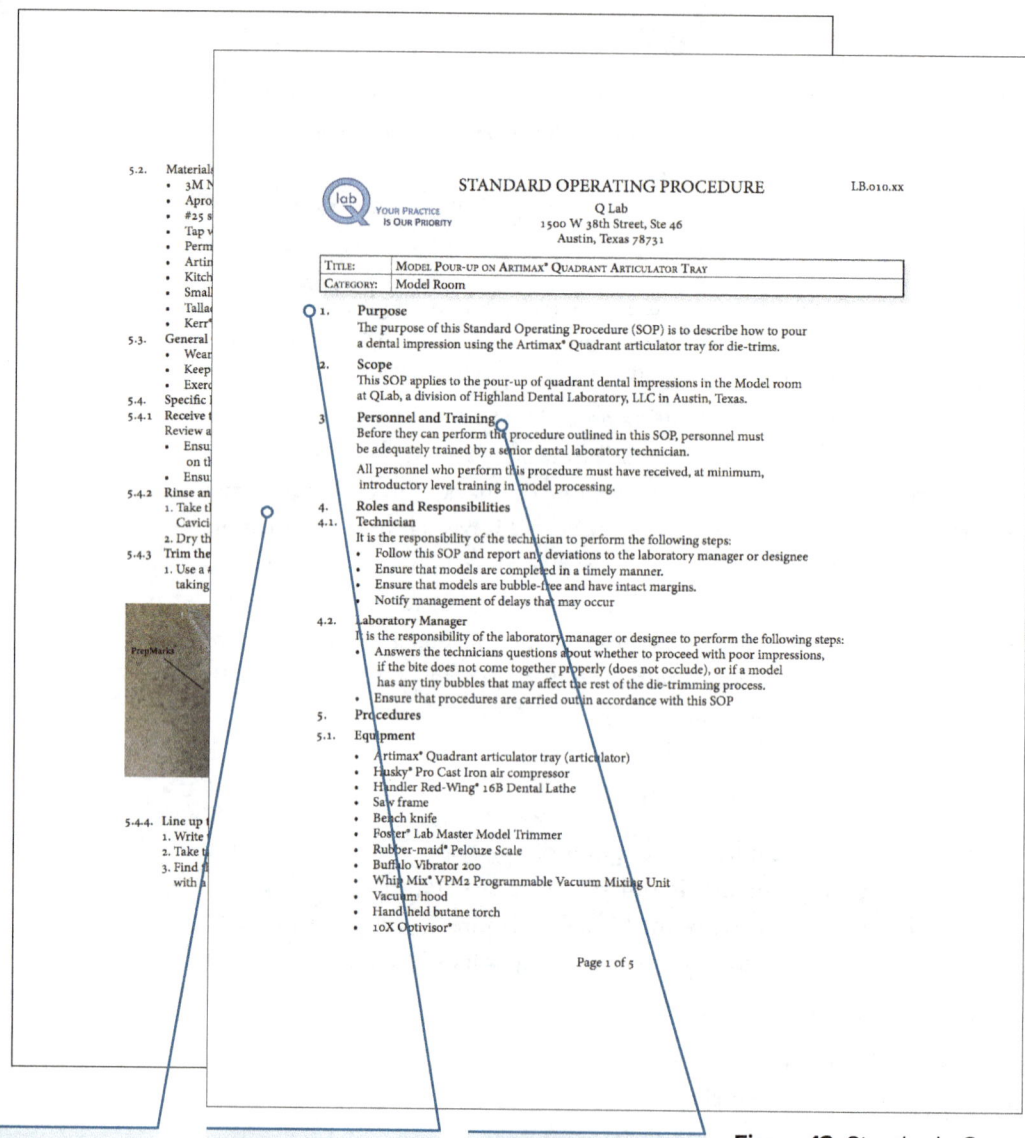

Figure 12. Standard Operating Procedures (SOPs) create a reference for how to complete a complex yet routine task.

Notice that much of this procedure looks like a set of instructions. This is common when part of a procedure involves a detailed, specific task.

Purpose describes what the procedure aims to do. Scope defines the specific use for this document.

The SOP defines who is qualified to carry out this task.

Useful Design

As with instructions, procedures need thoughtful design, including clear organization, headings, and visuals. Flowcharts are a good example of a visual that is often incorporated into a procedure. Often a busy employee can determine the correct course of action simply by referring to a quality flowchart. As the creator of a procedure, you should check that the design makes the procedure easy to understand and follow.

The design of the procedure should aid the user in making the correct choices and quickly. The following model shows a standard operating procedure for NASA (see figure 13 on the next page). This document does not leave room for interpretation. Note how this document is structured and how it uses tables to make a complex process more accessible. A functional and consistent design is an important component of procedures, especially if they involve the level of technical skills described here.

*See **Chapter 3** for more on flowcharts.*

Usability Testing

Usability testing allows the technical communicator to test out a document to determine its effectiveness. Any technical document can benefit from usability testing, but it's especially important in the case of instructions and procedures. If a technical document does not meet the needs of its user, or only half meets those needs, there can be serious consequences.

During the usability testing stage, technical communicators try out their document in a low-risk environment to catch errors. Don't assume that just because something makes sense to you, it will make sense to everyone. Even highly experienced technical communicators need to test their instructions and procedures with potential users.

The US Department of Health and Human Services (HHS) offers suggestions for usability testing on its website, www.usability.gov, a site designed to help students and practitioners focus on the user experience in government and the private sector. Their site sorts testing into four categories: concurrent think aloud, retrospective think aloud, concurrent probing, or retrospective probing. Each method obtains feedback through a slightly different means, and each has positives and drawbacks to consider before you decide which one to use (see figure 14).

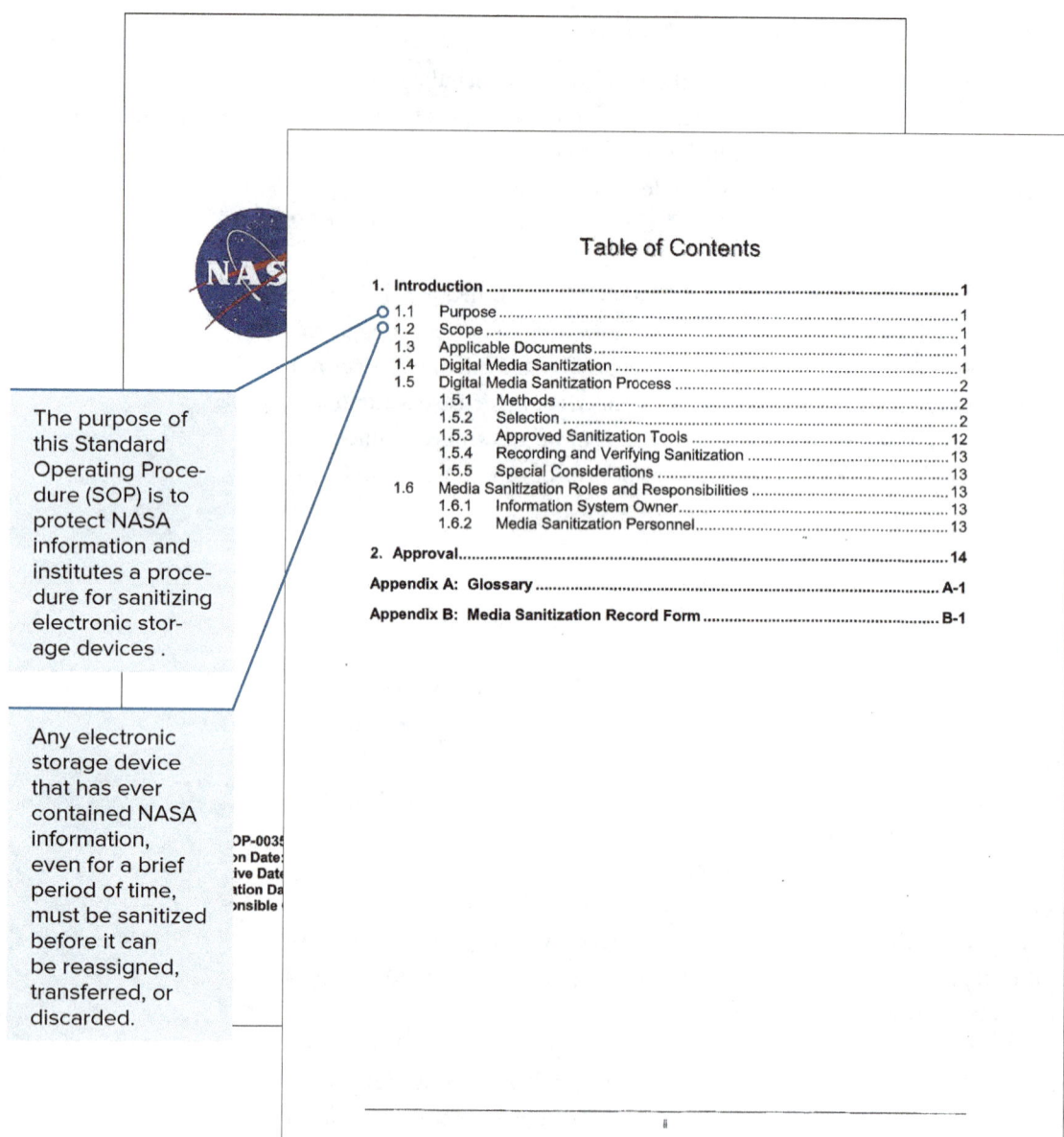

Figure 13. NASA uses best practices for the organization and design of its SOP. Courtesy of NASA.

Technique	Pros	Cons
Concurrent Think Aloud (CTA)	▸ Understand participants' thoughts as they occur and as they attempt to work through issues they encounter ▸ Ellicit real-time feedback and emotional responses	▸ Can interfere with usability metrics such as accuracy and time on task
Retrospective Think Alound (RTA)	▸ Does not interfere with usability mechanics	▸ Overall session length increases ▸ Difficulty remembering thoughts from up to an hour before = poor data
Concurrent Probing (CP)	▸ Understanding participants' thoughts as they attempt to work through a task	▸ Interferes with natural thought process and progression that participants would make on their own if uninterrupted
Retrospective Probing (RP)	▸ Does not interfere with usability metrics	▸ Difficulty in remembering = poor data

Figure 14. This table provides pros and cons for the four categories of usability testing. Courtesy of US Department of Health and Human Services.

Usability Testing Best Practices

The following tips can help make your usability test more successful. These guidelines will help your test maintain objectivity, accessibility, flexibility, and repeatability.

Avoid Anchoring

Beware of influencing your test-takers. The psychological term **anchoring** refers to the way outside questions and comments can influence the thinking and responses of study participants. This is a common pitfall. When handing your document to a tester for review, don't explain: "So, what I'm trying to do here is . . ." or "The point of this document is to. . . ." With just one sentence, you have biased their views, changed their understanding, and disrupted the possibility of actual feedback. Resist this temptation. You won't be there when users are using your document in the future.

Design for Accessibility

Test from people who represent your target audience. If you are designing a technical document for people with disabilities, then don't test the document on people who don't have disabilities. If you are designing a document for English language learners, then test it on people who speak multiple languages. Be mindful of accessibility in both your text and design.

Consider testing the document with people who often lack access, such as visually-impaired participants or participants who do not have access to technology. Keep in mind that color blindness, low vision, hearing impairments, learning disabilities, and any number of temporary disabilities may impact how the user interacts with your document. Test with participants from diverse backgrounds, cultures, and experiences to ensure inclusivity. Think about who you are selecting to test your document. Testers are usually a small group, so make sure they are as representative as possible.

Be Flexible

Be prepared to adjust your usability test and the document itself. Testers will do things you don't expect. This is because they didn't design the document. You need this feedback to improve your document, even if it's unexpected.

Repeat as Needed

When you set deadlines for your projects, make sure that you include time for multiple rounds of usability testing. The best development process has multiple versions of a document, as well as multiple tests.

Considerations in Usability Testing

When you conduct usability testing, look for these four principles as users interact with your document. Technical communicators need to listen and watch carefully to understand the audience's needs and where the document may send them in the wrong direction. Before you begin, consider how you will determine ease of performance, efficiency of performance, measurement of error, and measurement of aesthetics.

- **Ease of Performance:** How easily can users accomplish what is needed on their first use of your document? How intuitive is your design? How accessible is your content?
- **Efficiency of Performance:** How quickly can users accomplish what is needed as they interact with your document?
- **Measurement of Error:** How often and how many errors do users make during the testing? How severe are the errors? What kind of recovery do they make after their errors?
- **Measurement of Aesthetics:** How pleasing is the design to users? Is encountering your document a pleasant experience? Are there aspects that are off-putting?

Checklist for Usability Testing

Usability testing requires you to keep track of many factors, so use this checklist as you prepare to test your document:

Plan the Test

- ☐ **Identify scope and purpose:** How large is the test? What are you trying to determine?
- ☐ **Schedule a time, location, and equipment**: When and where will the test happen? How long will it be? What equipment (if any) is necessary?
- ☐ **Plan scenarios:** Do you need to design a situation in which to test the document?
- ☐ **Determine metrics:** How will you measure the reaction of test takers? How will you collect feedback?

Recruit for and Give the Test

- ☐ **Research:** Who is your target participant?
- ☐ **Recruit:** How will you find willing test-takers who accurately represent your target user?
- ☐ **Moderate:** How will you administer the test?

Assess the Results

- [ ] **Evaluate:** Does anything in the document need to change based on the test results?
- [ ] **Refine document:** What changes in the document will produce better results?
- [ ] **Repeat testing:** What happens when the refined document is tested again?

Legal and Ethical Concerns

With both instructions and procedures, it's important to think about potential liabilities. Instruction sets, for example, might involve the use of tools, which can cause bodily harm if not used properly. The writer of instructions can't assume that the user will know how to use a tool safely. For this reason, many instruction sets will include warnings (figure 15). Warnings should be given before the user begins the task, and the warning should be accompanied by some kind of visual marker, such as an icon, contrasting color, white space, or large text to set it apart from the rest of the document.

Always consider safety when writing instructions. Do you need to remind the user about safe practices? If the task involves using tools, for example, does the user need to wear eye protection? If the task involves handling chemicals, is ventilation important? Some instruction sets will include broad statements about the user taking full responsibility for any activities involved in the instructions. Technical communicators should consult with their company's legal department to discuss how to approach possible liability.

Unclear wording can be a problem with instructions or procedures. If a user misunderstands instructions due to poor wording, the result could be damage to property or bodily harm. If a procedure is unclear due to language, the result could be the loss of company profits, damage to a business' reputation, or employee dissatisfaction. Technical communicators are responsible for testing instructions and procedures by submitting them for review. This means you must budget additional time to allow for conducting usability tests and revising the document based on those results.

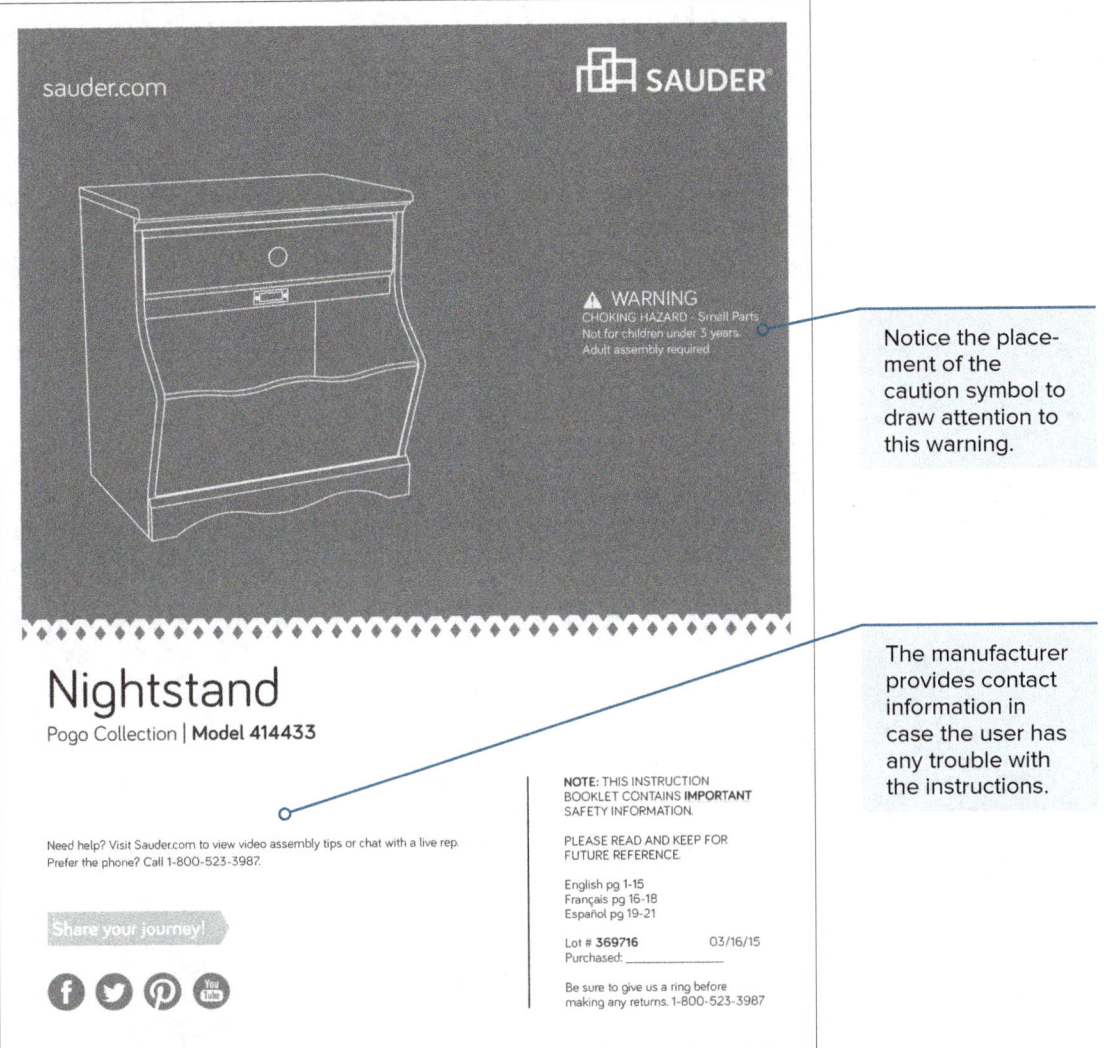

Figure 15. This assembly manual places warnings and important information prominently on the front cover. Courtesy of Sauder.

Conclusion

Once more, think back to your first job and the uncertainty that you might have felt. You needed information and the confidence that you could complete new tasks well. The situation is similar for users of instructions and procedures. By creating accurate, clear instructions, you make it possible for your audience to complete their tasks safely and efficiently. By developing procedures that answer questions and direct decision-making, you can prevent wasted time and effort.

Remember that your task is to understand the situation of your audience and help them with information that is reliable and easy to understand. Give users a simple and well-designed document so they can complete their task with ease. When creating a procedure, demonstrate that you understand why the procedure is needed and how it will be applied so that users will use it with confidence. By anticipating needs, testing your documents, and revising to make your communication as useful as possible, you can save users frustration and enable them to succeed.

Chapter 10
Proposals and Short Reports

Abstract: A technical proposal involves making a persuasive argument for an idea that needs approval in order to move forward. Technical proposals can be written for internal or external audiences and can be requested by a company (solicited) or offered to a company by an individual (unsolicited). The variety of proposal types requires the technical communicator to carefully consider the purpose, message, and audience for the document. Short reports often follow on the heels of proposals that have been accepted. Reports provide information, analysis, or recommendations to solve problems. They can also monitor or document progress, clarify policies, and guide change. Both document types require communication that is succinct, specific, objective, and ethical. Ultimately, these versatile documents bring together many of the key principles of technical communication.

Looking Ahead

1. Why Proposals and Short Reports Matter
2. Proposals Defined
3. Types of Proposals
4. Typical Elements of Proposals
5. Short Reports Defined
6. Steps for Writing Proposals and Short Reports
7. Principles for Proposals and Short Reports

Why Proposals and Short Reports Matter

Suppose you land your dream job and the next day your boss asks you to write a proposal or a short report. Would you know what to do? Could you write with confidence and in a format that your boss would recognize?

Many employees have no idea how to create these documents, yet proposals and short reports are two of the most frequently used documents in the professional world. Knowing how to write in these formats will help you to communicate persuasively and effectively. They will also make you a valuable asset in the workplace. Master proposals and short reports and you'll have an excellent foundation for professional communication.

Proposals Defined

Proposals are persuasive documents written for decision-makers. A proposal convinces the audience to choose a specific course of action. You've probably written persuasive essays in composition classes. Imagine that you are writing another persuasive essay, but this one is for your boss at your dream job. How would you go about convincing your boss to make a particular decision? To write a successful proposal, you must do two things:

- Inform the decision-maker about the pertinent data or issue.
- Suggest a course of action.

Shorter proposals are often presented in a business email or memo format with headings. Longer proposals, which can contain as many as ten sections, will likely have a cover letter and be submitted as a separate document, either electronically or in print. A basic format like the one included in this chapter can help you get started (figure 1).

Proposals at Work

Roy is the IT manager at Widget World, a midsize computer parts company. Part of Roy's job is recommending changes that will benefit the company's bottom line or increase productivity. Roy discovers that his workplace spends a large portion of their money every year buying and maintaining desktop

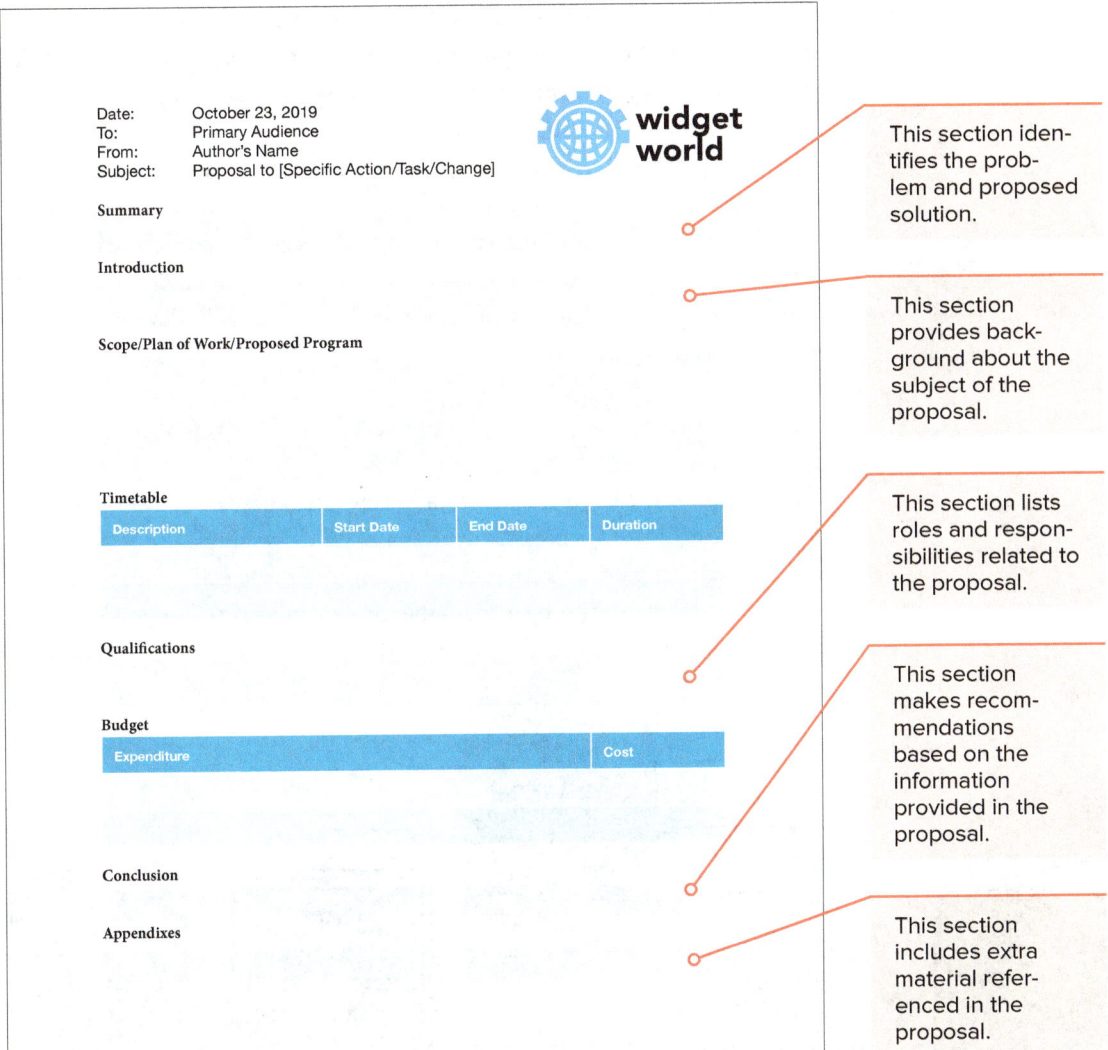

Figure 1. Many organizations and businesses have their own proposal format. This basic format can be adapted to fit almost any project.

computers. Roy believes that an alternate technology to personal desktops could save the company money. He knows that many offices are converting to a virtual machine system (VM) in lieu of traditional PCs for every employee. The new system will require an initial investment. How will he convince his boss that the expense of the new system is needed?

While writing his proposal, Roy keeps his audience's needs in mind. He suspects his boss will be cautious at best and skeptical at worst, so he collects an abundance of data to support his proposal. He researches the cost of the current systems, the cost of buying the new system, and the long-term net savings. Roy also researches the current annual cost of buying and maintaining desktop computers at his company. He projects that cost into the future and compares it with the likely cost of purchasing and maintaining the virtual machine system. In addition to crunching numbers, Roy surveys his coworkers and administrators to determine current attitudes and habits of computer usage. The blend of hard data and personal opinions will play a big part in whether his proposal is agreeable to his boss.

Proposals and the Problem-Solution Framework

Think back to the Problem-Solution Framework. Once again, this concept will help you create a successful document. When writing a proposal, always consider the problem and solution in relation to the specific situation.

In a proposal, the problem takes the form of an issue that needs resolution or an opportunity that could to be realized (figure 2). After clearly establishing

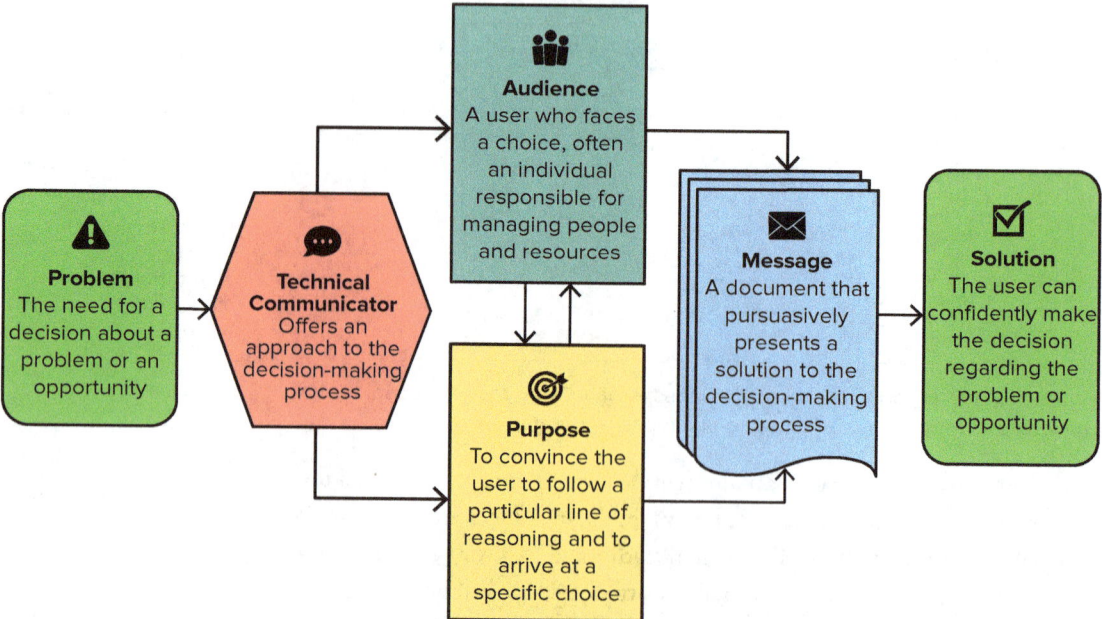

Figure 2. The purpose of a proposal is to point out a problem in the form of an issue or opportunity. An effective proposal shows how the issue can be resolved or the opportunity can be realized.

the problem, you must present a solution in the form of a message. To be convincing, your solution must be realistic and rooted in evidence (rather than guesswork). As with all documents, consider how your audience and purpose contribute to your message.

Audience

A successful proposal carefully considers the user's situation and other factors that impact decision-making. The user of a proposal is typically a manager. One common reason a proposal fails is that it does not accurately or honestly recognize the context for the situation, which includes both the user's and the company's needs *at the moment*.

See **Chapter 1** for more on creating a user profile.

Timing is an important part of whether or not a proposal will be accepted. Because of this, we recommend that you engage directly with your audience during the research phase whenever possible. Conduct interviews, send emails, or administer surveys to collect information from others to find out whether the time is right and the audience is receptive. Even though Roy is working on an unsolicited proposal, he can still meet with his boss and get her perspective so he can better address her concerns.

Here are a few questions to ask that could help you determine how a proposal may affect your audience:

- Is there a limited budget or a tight schedule?
- Does this proposal align with other goals?
- How will the proposal be shared and distributed?
- Who makes the final decision?
- Are there any regional, cultural, or linguistic factors to consider?

In Roy's case, he must keep in mind that his boss, Carmen, is not a technology expert. As a result, Roy must explain the technical side of the proposal in a way that won't frustrate his boss. He needs to use plain language and avoid technical jargon that he and his fellow IT professionals like to toss around. Roy also needs to consider that, like most bosses, Carmen is sensitive to any expenses associated with the proposal. He needs to make a case for why the project will be worth the associated costs. Even if Carmen agrees with his proposal, she will need to take it to the board, which consists of a multinational group of stakeholders. Roy's proposal must be clear and convincing enough to make Carmen want to take that next step.

Purpose

Your purpose is to persuade the user to make a specific decision. Remembering this goal as you write your proposal will impact your choices of what information to include. Remember that decision-makers who read proposals are busy people. You can make them happy by keeping your document simple, short, and focused. Avoid the temptation to overwhelm the user with information. This is not a situation where more is better. Instead, be selective and share only the best information.

Roy's purpose is to convince his boss that the hardware upgrade will benefit the company in spite of the expense. He explains this purpose by showing Carmen that the current setup is hurting the company's bottom line by generating unnecessary long-term maintenance costs. He must show that his proposed hardware upgrade is feasible, realistic, and will save the business money in the long run.

Message

The nature of your message will depend on the type of proposal you choose. Several proposal types are discussed later in the chapter. Keep your message in line with the document type. For example, you don't write a planning proposal the same way you write a sales proposal. It's important that you recognize the intent of your specific proposal type and the needs of the user when creating your message. Many organizations have established standards for proposals, so find and follow these guidelines to make your proposal more attractive.

Roy's proposal is unsolicited, so he must convince Carmen that the project is worthwhile. As a result, his tone must be persuasive while also rooted in factual information. Roy's proposal is also internal because he's presenting it to his own company. His format is similar to a typical goods and services proposal that includes cost-savings resulting from a proposed purchase. While he's not offering a good or service to a customer, his approach will be similar because he must show his boss that the benefits of the project outweigh the investment.

Types of Proposals

There are four main types of proposals: internal or external and solicited or unsolicited (figure 3). The specific approach for writing a proposal will vary depending on the topic and desired outcome. Proposals can be about company policy or sales goals, for example. Or they might be written in response to a request for proposals (RFP). They might be written by an individual or by an entire department. Identifying the type of proposal can help you make important decisions about the document's audience, purpose, and message as you can see here in this table of proposals (figure 4).

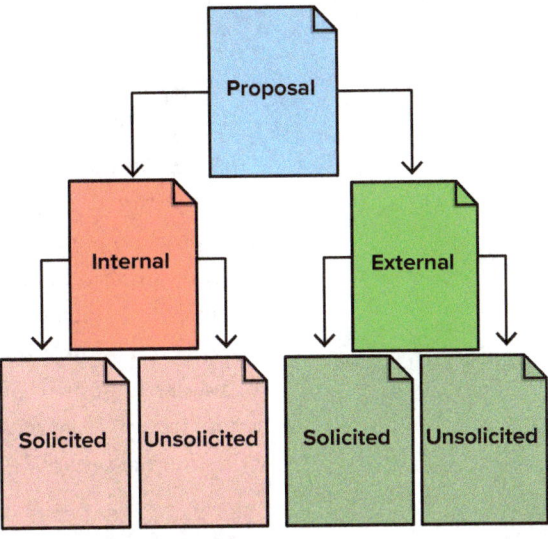

Figure 3. This chart shows the four categories of proposals: solicited/unsolicited and external/internal.

Type	Audience	Purpose	Message	Example
Grant Proposal	Government agency or nonprofit	To obtain funds	"Support our viable project."	A lab applies for funding to expand its research capacity.
Planning Proposal	Decision-maker who can approve a project	To justify a plan of action	"Here is our offer to bid or complete a project."	A business proposes that annexing land will benefit the city in spite of potential complications.
Research Proposal	Decision-maker for a business, organization, or company	To provide evidence to support a change	"We want to gather information for a project."	An engineering firm proposes a seismic study for an at-risk structure in response to an RFP.
Sales Proposal	Contractor, business, company, or organization	To offer goods or services	"Buy our product or service."	An insurance company proposes a detailed alternative to another business's existing employee health plan.

Figure 4. This table lists some of the most common types of proposals and shows how audience, purpose, message differ for each.

Internal / External

One category among proposals is the difference between internal and external proposals. This has to do with who is writing the proposal and how they're connected to the decision-maker who will receive the proposal.

An **internal proposal** happens *inside* a specific business or organization. Roy's proposal is internal because he's writing it for his boss. Often companies will have an established procedure that is required for an internal proposal to be successfully pitched.

An **external proposal** is completed when an *outside* party writes a proposal for a different business or organization, typically as a profitable business transaction. If Roy were a freelancer instead of a Widget World employee, he could write external proposals for potential clients in other businesses.

Solicited / Unsolicited

Another category of proposals has to do with whether the document is in response to a direct request or whether it is independently initiated.

A **solicited proposal** is specifically requested by the audience (typically a business). In this case, one business has approached another business (or sometimes an individual) about a possible project. Often the first business does this by issuing an RFP. This means that they are asking potential business partners to write and deliver a proposal. For example, a business in need of a new building might issue an RFP to multiple architects as a way of getting multiple suggestions.

An **unsolicited proposal** is more speculative because the party writing the document is not responding to a direct request. In this case, the business or individual writing the proposal hopes that the proposal will be attractive to the recipient. Most of the time, the business or individual writing an unsolicited proposal has already done a significant amount of research to determine the likelihood of the proposal being accepted.

Typical Elements of a Proposal

Proposals tend to all follow a similar structure, which typically includes several (if not all) of the following sections.

Summary

While a short proposal might omit this section, longer proposals of more than a few pages will include a summary. Summaries are also called executive summaries or abstracts in some cases. Often this section is included on the title page, and sometimes it is limited to a specific word count. The summary's purpose is to provide a quick rundown of the proposal, as you can see here with Roy's summary (figure 5).

In some cases, a user may review only the summary before making a decision. As a result, it's wise to think of a summary as a short sales pitch. Write the summary so the audience will want to keep going. When writing a proposal summary, present the key information in an abbreviated format. The user wants to know what the proposal covers. If they find something useful in the summary, they'll have a reason to keep turning pages. The abstracts at the beginning of each chapter in this textbook function in a similar way.

Date: October 23, 2019

To: Carmen Lopez

From: Roy Moss

Subject: Proposal for IT Department Cost Savings/VM Integration

Summary

The current cost of replacement and maintenance for physical hardware could be reduced. We spend over 40 percent of the department's budget every year purchasing new desktops and servers, and additional money maintaining the existing physical hardware. The IT department seeks approval to convert to a Virtual Machines (VM) system that will reduce costs due to the elimination of hardware replacement and employee time spent in maintenance. The conversion will only take two months. While the initial cost of moving to the new system would be around $6000, the estimated annual savings for the company will be around $4000.

> Roy is specific and shows what percentage of the department budget is allocated to this type of expense.

> The projected cost-savings of this change is what people really want to know.

Figure 5. This model shows the opening of Roy's proposal to his boss.

Practical Models for Technical Communication

Introduction

This section sets the stage for the body of the proposal. This is where you provide background context, an overview of key ideas in the proposal, and a preview of the document's organization. The introduction is different from a summary. While the summary condenses the entire proposal into a smaller package, an introduction smoothly leads into the main content of the document. In Roy's introduction, he links his proposal with the company's "ongoing goal of reducing technology expenses" in order to show how this idea aligns with other priorities (figure 6).

> ### Introduction
> In keeping with the ongoing goal of reducing technology expenses at Widget World, I've been examining our physical hardware costs. It turns out we spend over 40 percent of the department's budget every year purchasing and maintaining physical hardware. We spend an additional 25 percent of the budget on desktop computers and servers every year. Research shows that we could operate with fewer physical servers and maintain productivity. In addition, we could replace our physical desktop hardware with alternative equipment to save additional money.

- Roy uses targeted language and avoids personal opinion.
- Using evidence is more convincing than vague statements.

Figure 6. This model shows the introduction of Roy's proposal to his boss.

Scope

Here is where you explain the suggested course of action. This is the heart of the proposal. In this section, you must provide convincing evidence that your recommendation is the best choice. This needs to be achieved through persuasive use of data obtained through research. Your research will come from talking to experts, consulting appropriate sources, and possibly doing original experimentation. This section is sometimes referred to as a proposed program or a plan of work. Roy's scope includes multiple steps (figure 7).

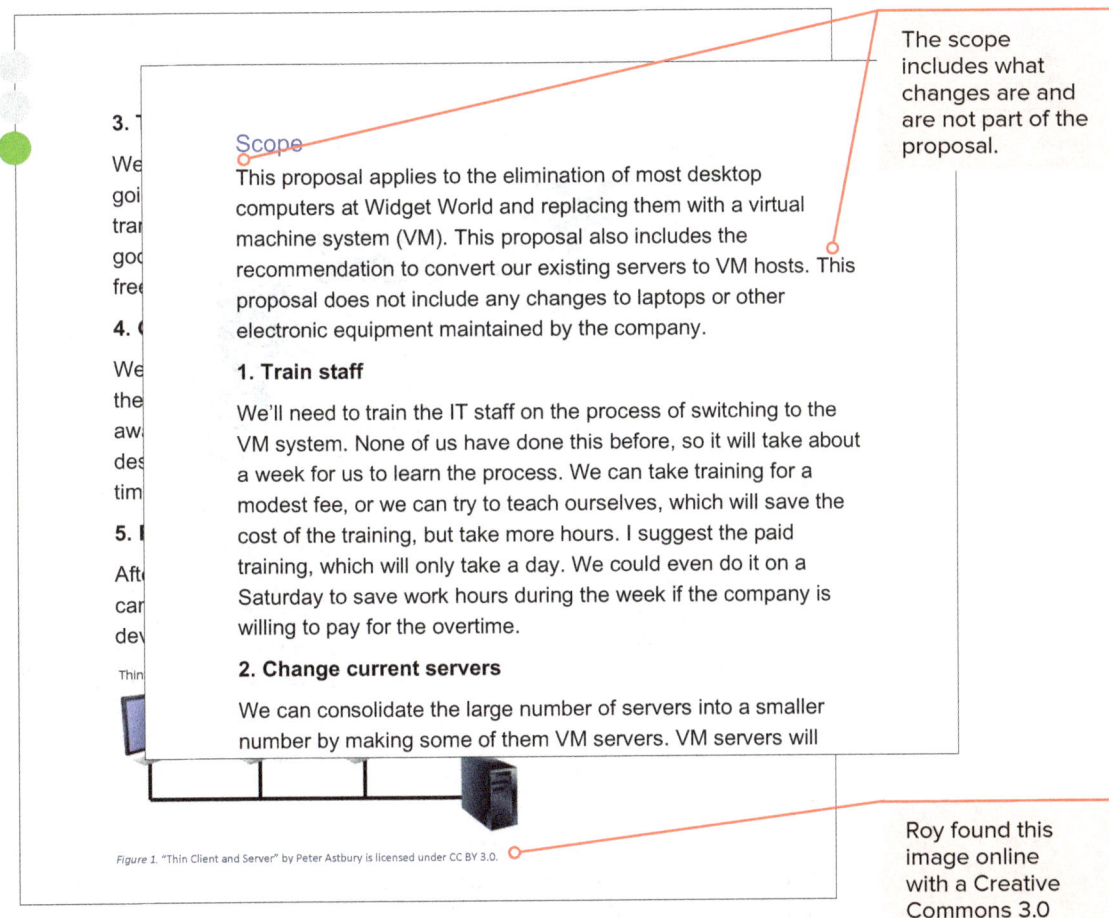

Figure 7. This model shows the scope of Roy's proposal to his boss.

Timetable

Include a well-researched timeframe to give the audience a realistic sense of how long the project will take. This is an important consideration for decision-makers. An accurate timetable that is easy to interpret will make your proposal more valuable. Roy uses a Gantt chart to help his boss see the various stages of this project (figure 8).

> The Gantt graph, also known as a bar graph, is a useful visual to show the timeline of multiple stages of a project at once.

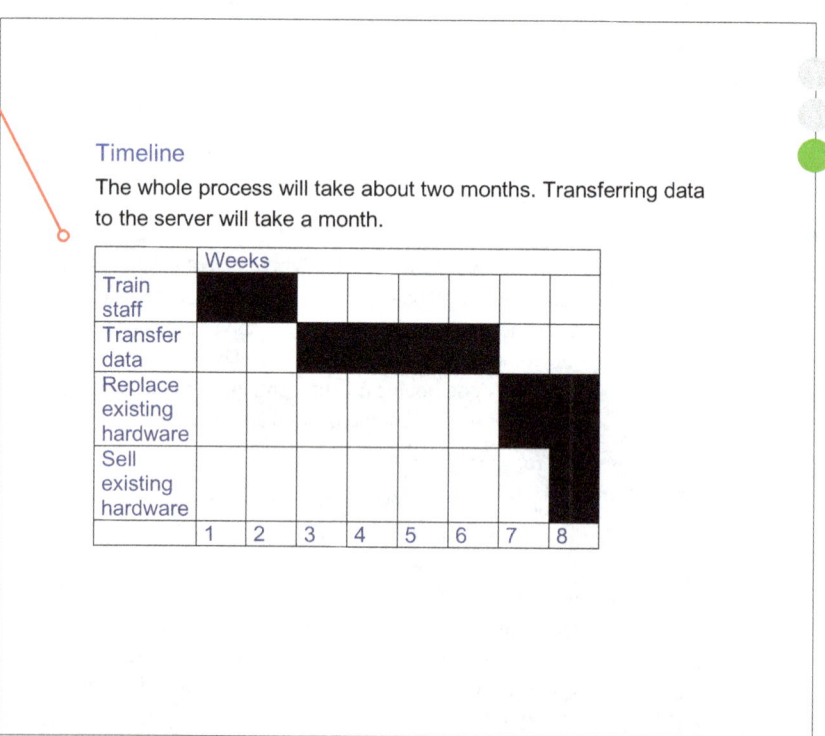

Figure 8. This model shows the timeline of Roy's proposal to his boss.

Qualifications and Experience

You need to convince the audience that you are the best person for the job. Making a clear proposal backed with solid research is one crucial part of showing that you have the ability to carry out the proposal successfully. Do you have specialized knowledge or skills that single you out as the ideal candidate to do this work? If so, state this explicitly.

Budget

Decision-makers are typically concerned about the cost of undertaking new projects. The budget section needs to provide realistic estimates of what the plan will cost. As always, the numbers you use here need to be based on accurate research.

Conclusion

Smoothly bring the document to an end with a clear transition. Be sure to review the persuasive goal of the proposal. In other words, remind the audience of what you are asking them to approve. Always recap the main points of the proposal in a short format. Leave the audience with something to think about in your closing statement, something that highlights the lasting benefits of the proposed solution.

Appendixes

Any supporting information, in the form of graphs, charts, or background readings, typically goes into an appendix. This section isn't mandatory, but it is commonplace in proposals.

Short Reports Defined

Short reports take many forms, but they are always brief documents that provide information about a specific objective, event, or ongoing issue. When you write a short report, your goal is to inform clearly and simply. Ideally you should save your audience time and effort by putting yourself in their shoes. What would you need to know? What would be unnecessary?

In many ways, short reports are similar to a formal report. The difference lies in the level of detail or complexity. While formal reports tend to be long, contain multiple sections, and frequently involve significant expense for a business, a short report deals with a single issue that may be less complex.

See **Chapter 11** for more about formal reports.

Short Reports at Work

Back at Widget World, Roy presents his finished proposal to his boss Carmen. After receiving approval from the board of directors, Carmen tells Roy to begin the project and submit a status report after two weeks. The **status report** is a short document that provides an update about an ongoing situation. It delivers necessary information to Roy's boss in a simple format that can be quickly digested.

Just like when he wrote the proposal, Roy should follow the steps of planning, researching, drafting, revising, and editing. He should carefully consider the needs of his audience as he makes progress. What does his boss need to know? Better yet, Roy can ask Carmen directly what kind of update she would like to receive. Roy should write as simply and clearly as possible and avoid providing more information than Carmen wants.

Short Reports and the Problem-Solution Framework

As you can see in the Problem-Solution Framework, the problem in a short report originates with a lack of information (figure 9). Consider the amount and detail of information the user will need. Fit the information being presented and the method of presentation in the short report to the exact needs of your audience. The information could be data, description, evaluation, or another mode that aids understanding. Your success in writing a short report hinges on how easily and accurately users can gain the knowledge they need.

Audience

The audience for a short report is typically a manager, such as a department manager or the head of a business or organization. Respect their time by keeping your reports focused and as brief as possible. Remember that a decision-maker will likely approach your document with a critical mindset. They won't necessarily take your word for it when you make an assertion. It is your job to convince them. You can do this by anticipating and addressing the questions that they'll most likely ask.

In Roy's case, his document is a status report going to his boss who wants updates on his project. Carmen has made it clear to Roy that his report is

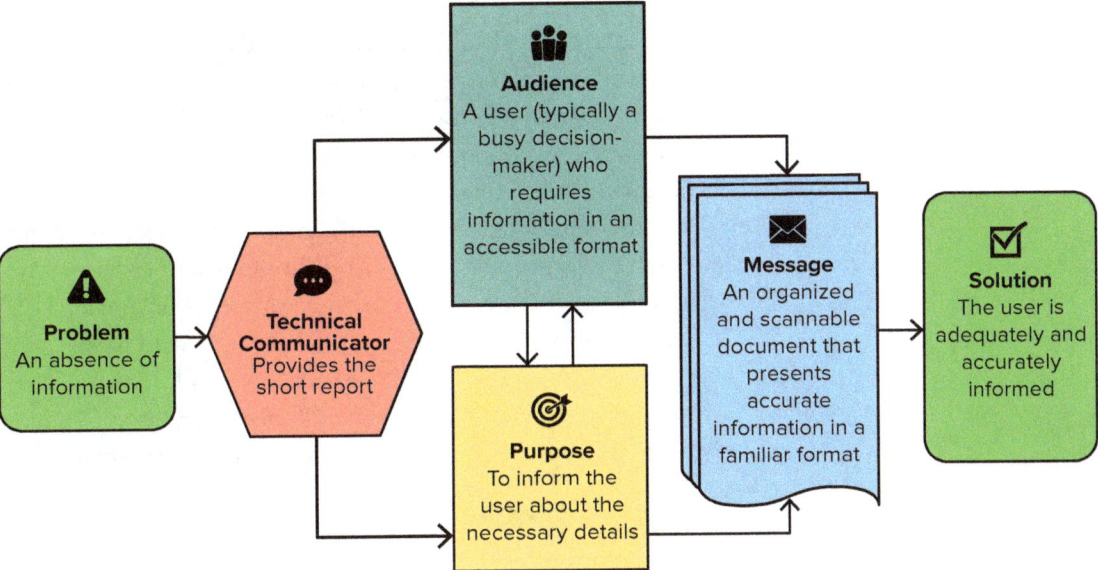

Figure 9. The purpose of a short report is to provide information that moves the user closer to a solution.

important, but she also wants something that she can quickly review to get a sense of how the project is going. Roy must be careful to stay on target.

Purpose

When writing a short report, your purpose is to inform the user about specific data, decisions, or policies, among other possibilities. The success of your short report depends on how easily and accurately the audience understands the content. Be clear and eliminate anything that distracts from the key details. Be objective and represent information accurately.

When Roy composes the status report, his purpose is to give accurate and timely information. This means that he must relate updates regardless of whether the project goes according to plan. Sometimes, progress reports must relate bad news. If the project falls behind schedule, for example, Roy needs to explain why in the report. Typically, a status report also offers solutions to problems that happen along the way. If Roy discovers an unexpected expense, he needs to report this to his boss. Ideally, he'll find a way to offset this extra cost and include a plan for this in his report as well.

Message

The message in a short report should match an expected format. Decision-makers are familiar with a range of report formats, but they expect you to be efficient and select the appropriate type. Familiarize yourself with the best report varieties. If the user's organization has established standards for the specific type of document you're creating, be sure to follow them.

Roy has a responsibility to be honest and accurate with his report. In spite of his desire to make the project look as successful as possible, he has an obligation to keep his boss informed of the specifics, whether good or bad. Additionally, Carmen expects the status report to follow a standard format. Roy also needs to review company policy to determine if any additional requirements have been established for status reports at Widget World. For his project to succeed, he needs to adhere to company standards for all project updates.

Types of Short Reports

Short reports fall into many different categories, but the common objective is to present information in a clear, digestible format. Some of the possible goals of a short report are as follows:

- To collect data
- To evaluate
- To provide a progress update
- To announce an executive decision

The goal of the report plus the topic will determine the exact type of report. Three of the most common types of short report are status reports, research reports, and sales reports.

Status reports update an authority on the progress of a project. Often, status reports are required on some kind of recurring schedule, such as biweekly. The purpose of a status report is to give specific details that help an authority follow the progress of a project, to confirm that the project is in good shape, and to anticipate or deal with problems.

Research reports present data about a specific topic. If an employee or a business has done a study about a particular topic, that employee or business can present their findings (typically to a boss or a customer) in the form of a short research report. This kind of report has similarities to a formal report, but it will typically omit some of the additional sections found in a formal report, such as the front matter and back matter. The goal of a short research report is to consolidate the data into a simple format. Succeeding with this kind of report means being selective about which figures are being shared, without distorting the information. As the writer, you must understand which findings from the research are truly valuable to the audience.

Sales reports present findings about product sales. These kinds of reports are crucial for businesses to maintain an accurate sense of how they are doing financially. Typically, short sales reports are required on a regular schedule, but sometimes they are written under unique circumstances. If a company that sells physical goods launches a new product, for example, it would be valuable for the company to track sales figures and then present those figures in a simple format. The job of the technical communicator in this scenario would be to present key figures in an impactful (typically visual) way. It would also be important to anticipate and answer questions that might arise when the audience peruses the sales report.

Beyond the three most common reports, here are some additional examples and how audience, purpose, message vary for each (figure 10).

Report Type	Topic/Message	Purpose	Audience
Audit	Business finances	To examine data	Owners, governing bodies
Feasibility report	Testing practicality of a project	To evaluate and recommend	Managers, governing bodies
Incident report	Formal explanation of an occurrence	To document	Owners, managers
Manager's memo	Formal statement of executive decision	To announce	Employees
Survey	Data taken via polling	To compile data	Researchers, managers

Figure 10. This table lists additional types of short reports and shows how audience, purpose, message differ for each.

Typical Elements of a Short Report

While the organization of short reports varies according to type, a few basic divisions typically appear.

Introduction

This section at the beginning should explain to the users why the report was written. Sometimes, this section is called "purpose." Be clear about the intent so your users understand how to interpret what follows.

Body

This section may contain a variety of components, including findings from research, summary of activities, potential research or activities in the future, or costs. In the body, share specific information rooted in data and analysis.

Conclusion

Here the technical communicator will remind the user of the overall purpose of the report, review the key findings, and bring the report to a close. Some short reports conclude with a recommendation based on the findings. The recommendation should follow logically from the findings in the body.

Steps for Writing Proposals and Short Reports

Regardless of the particular type of proposal or short report, the basic steps in creating the document remain similar. The longer the proposal or report, the more likely it is that the project will require collaboration. Be sure to plan additional time for coordinating various members of your team.

Plan

Determine a realistic scope before beginning.

Narrow the focus of the topic to make it manageable. If a choice must be made on one side or the other, it's better to make a topic specific rather than broad. When planning, get input from your audience if possible. Talk to your audience directly, but if you can't, find other ways to determine what they want from the document.

Research

Locate convincing and relevant data.

If your document gives the impression that you've partially understood the topic or the audience, it will likely be dismissed. Just like when you write a college essay, outside sources should be included to make a strong case. What are the expert sources of information that you should consult? Who are the experts in the particular field? Are there authoritative sources of data that can be researched? Research thoroughly and present your findings in an accurate and properly cited fashion.

See **Chapter 5** for additional research methods for technical communicators.

Draft

Begin drafting the document once you have an adequate understanding of the topic and the needs of the audience.

Ideally, the first draft should be written quickly. The goal in an initial draft is to get the information out of your head and onto the page. Avoid second-guessing yourself in an initial draft. Aim for a reasonable target word count. You might want to write a little more than you think you need in this stage because some sections will likely be cut during revision and editing.

Revise

Revise the document by focusing on the big picture.

What is the purpose of the document? Look at the draft and determine if your purpose is clear and direct. It's often valuable to get outside feedback at this point, especially from someone who is experienced with the topic. Review the needs of the audience. What do they want to see in the document? What will convince them that your idea is valuable? What will be their likely concerns or interests? Look at the draft as a whole and consider whether you have successfully dealt with these audience needs.

Edit

Edit the document with a focus on precise paragraphs, sentences, and words.

This is where you take care of the details. Your editing should focus on sentence and word level concerns. Any of the typical considerations for grammar, punctuation, or other conventions should be resolved. Remember that a lack of editing reflects poorly on an author and that your document could be rejected based on its presentation. In addition, consider whether your word choice is appropriate for the specific industry. Does your vocabulary reflect an appropriate level of familiarity with the topic and the audience?

Principles for Proposals and Short Reports

You can improve the quality of these documents by following a few basic principles, which include using precise language and an objective tone. With both of these principles, the emphasis lies in accuracy and fairness. The user must feel confident interpreting the meaning of a document. You can make this easier by examining your word choice and presentation of information.

Use Precise Language

The success of a proposal or short report hinges on specificity. Users need to know precise details that inform and (when appropriate) lead them to make a decision.

Be Specific

Avoid making sweeping statements based on insufficient evidence, otherwise known as generalizing. For example, don't say that something is a certainty if data suggests that it's only highly likely. Those are two different things.

Be Accurate

Words such as "always" or "never" can be useful, but they can also be inaccurate. Modify assertions when necessary with words such as "frequently," "seldom," or "almost." If the qualifier makes the statement more precise, use it.

Maintain an Objective Tone

Biased or slanted language can destroy credibility and cause a user to reject a document. Maintain objectivity to build a strong foundation for proposals and short reports. Even when you seek to convince the user in a proposal, your tone should remain objective.

Eliminate Opinion

Phrases such as "in my opinion" or "in our estimation" are overused in short reports and proposals. Instead, state information objectively. When persuading, use facts as a basis for opinions. Instead of stating, "we believe that moving to a virtual machine system is the best decision," use data to demonstrate that it's the best decision: "This graph shows that investing money now in a virtual machine system will save Widget World $50,000 in two years."

Include Experts

Use research to incorporate data and expert opinion to support your idea. Asking the user to trust the information in your proposal or short report based solely on your opinion is usually a mistake. Cite information from quality sources to support your claims and bring objectivity to the project.

Present Information Ethically

Even a hint of unethical practice will hurt your reputation as a reliable source of information. Following the principles of accuracy and objectivity will go a long way to ensure ethical presentation. When Roy gives credit to the creator of the image he uses in his report, he shows that he's paying attention to details and knows how to handle outside information properly.

Never present information obtained from outside sources as your own. Cite sources accurately and consistently. This not only resolves the issue of ethical use of material, but it also presents you as a thorough researcher.

Be Honest and Transparent

Don't cover up negative issues or problems. If a topic deals with a problematic situation, don't ignore the difficulties. Rather, present a realistic solution. This will increase your credibility in the eyes of the user. Also, it's highly likely that the user was already aware of the problem, so not dealing with it would likely be a setback anyway. Transparency is crucial, so always communicate with honesty.

Conclusion

Success in proposals or short reports depends on your ability to persuade or inform. Make communication choices that support your purpose for the particular document type. Study the situation of your user and communicate accordingly. Craft a message that fits within the expected parameters for that type of document so the user can easily understand.

When you effectively create proposals and short reports, you can save users money and demonstrate your expertise. In the case of Roy, he can gain the approval of his boss, help his company, and show that he's motivated and competent at solving problems. You too can demonstrate your ability to solve problems by creating convincing proposals and short reports that make it easier for those in charge to take action.

Chapter 11
Formal Reports

Abstract: Formal reports are multipage documents that collect and interpret data. Formal reports generally contain some variation of these three elements: front matter, body, and end matter. A formal report presents complex information and suggests a solution or makes recommendations. This task frequently involves collaboration and requires that you present your research and recommendations ethically. The creation of a formal report is as much about the process of planning and research as it is about organizing and writing the final product. It may seem like a lot to juggle at first, but don't worry. You have been practicing the elements of effective technical communication throughout this entire book. Now you just need to pull it all together in a formal report. You've got this.

Looking Ahead

1. Why Formal Reports Matter

2. Types of Formal Reports

3. The Steps of a Formal Report

4. Writing the Formal Report

5. Revising the Formal Report

Why Formal Reports Matter

Employers often rely on technical communicators to research complex issues and present their findings in an easy-to-digest format. The result of this process is often a formal report, sometimes called a long report or final report. Technical communicators are well-positioned to produce these reports because of their ability to study a subject and present ideas in a clear, concise, and accurate format.

Decision-makers, such as managers or business owners, can save time by commissioning a technical communicator to do research and present the findings. This frees the decision-maker to do other important work. Even if you are not an expert on the topic of your report, the act of writing the report can make you the resident expert in your workplace.

Formal Reports Defined

Formal reports have similarities to short reports, but formal reports are typically longer and take more time to develop. The purpose of a formal report is to gather and condense information relevant to a specific topic. Sometimes these reports also analyze information and make a recommendation. A typical formal report requires a technical communicator to draw from all of the skills you've encountered in this text.

Creating a formal report involves planning and researching, collaborating with and persuading others, and considering ethical situations related to the topic and your research. You must consider design, the use of multiple modes, and how to acknowledge information from other sources. These reports require you to apply everything you've learned about technical communication, critical thinking, and research.

Here are a few examples from various fields where the formal report might be used:

- An engineering firm needs to determine which buildings are structurally sound. They hire you to offer solutions of structural integrity for buildings on a fault line.
- As a member of the safety committee at your school, you are tasked with completing a report that examines the adequacy of nurse staffing within the school district. You must work with your committee

members to review reports on student care, survey the nursing staff, and compile recent research from educational and medical reports.
- You are an analyst for your state's Health Authority, and you have been asked to compile a report on the opioid epidemic in your state and make recommendations for a new prescription drug monitoring program.

As you can see, formal reports are flexible documents used in many fields. Formal reports identify a problem or examine alternatives and then present the findings at length as a written solution or recommendation.

Formal Reports and the Problem-Solution Framework

The Problem-Solution Framework is fully realized in the formal report (figure 1). In the case of a formal report, the problem typically originates with a lack of information that prevents someone from making a decision. By considering audience and purpose, a technical communicator can create a message in the form of a document. This document should provide a solution to the user's problem.

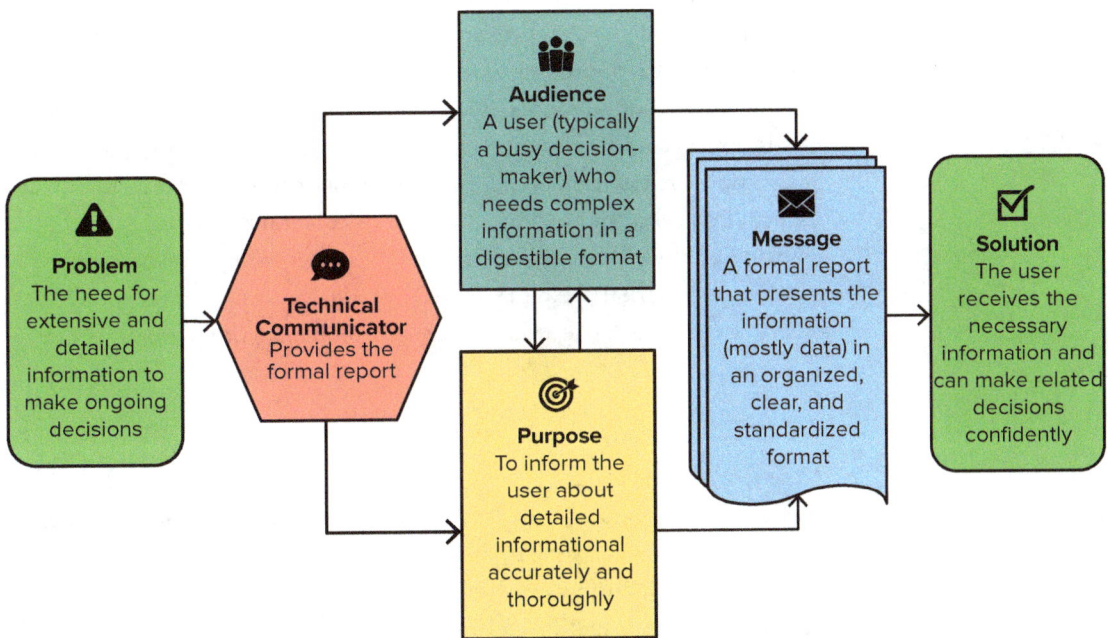

Figure 1. The formal report represents the quintessential example of the Problem-Solution Framework.

Formal Reports at Work

In Chapter 5 you met Jessamyn, the technical communicator who was completing research on electric vehicles for Tomorrow's Taxi Company. In this chapter, she dives into a report that goes a little deeper. At her boss's request, Jessamyn will create a report that explores whether the use of autonomous vehicles is a viable option for their company.

Jessamyn's boss wants to know if adding driverless cars, also referred to as autonomous vehicles (AV), to the company's fleet is a smart move. Notice how the problem (a lack of information) leads to the purpose of the report (to find information). Now Jessamyn needs to identify the report's message, which is what her boss (the audience) wants to know. She could approach this analysis in a variety of ways. Her formal report could be one or a combination of the following forms: a comparative analysis, a causal analysis, or a feasibility analysis. The next section considers each of these at length.

Types of Formal Reports

Formal reports take different forms depending on their purpose, but all require some kind of analysis. **Analysis** means to look at how the individual parts of a complex process or product work together. For example, chemists regularly perform analysis on substances to identify their makeup on a molecular level. As a technical communicator, your analysis will focus on how complex ideas or situations are made up of more specific components. Most technical analysis includes a certain amount of informed speculation about causes and future possibilities as well. Formal reports almost always include analysis, which is why the three varieties explored here have "analysis" in their name. Refer to this table for a quick overview of these common analytical reports (figure 2).

Comparative Analysis

A **comparative analysis** is a formal report that establishes a set of criteria to look at similar items or situations to determine the best choice. Businesses often need a comparative analysis when they are considering a large purchase. For example, if a business wishes to expand to an overseas market but can't decide between two specific locations, they might request a comparative analysis. Or consider an organization that wants better healthcare coverage for its

Analysis Types	Actions
Comparative Analysis	‣ Establish points of comparison (criteria) for the options. ‣ Rank the criteria by importance. ‣ Assess the options using these criteria. ‣ Make a recommendation based on this assessment.
Causal Analysis	‣ Determine if you are looking for the cause or the effect of the problem. ‣ Research the possible causes or effects. ‣ Make a recommendation for a solution based on your research.
Feasibility Analysis	‣ Identify the problem. ‣ Examine the strengths and weaknesses of various solutions. ‣ Recommend a course of action based on your analysis of the solutions.

Figure 2. Use this table as a quick reference for the three main types of analysis reports described in this chapter.

employees. In this case, a comparative analysis could present possibilities and help the organization make the best choice.

If Jessamyn conducts a comparative analysis, she will need to determine how to compare the cars in the company's current fleet to potential autonomous vehicles. Since Jessamyn also researched electric vehicles, she might include them in her comparison as well. Jessamyn must establish points of comparison up-front so that the different vehicle types are compared fairly and consistently. She will likely compare the cost of purchase or replacement, fuel, insurance, maintenance, and labor. She'll determine how much revenue each vehicle generates (or is estimated to generate) and its reliability. Then, in the report, she will clearly explain the criteria she used in the methodology section. In her findings, she will rank the cars according to the criteria, assess their strengths and weaknesses, and end with a recommendation of the best option.

A comparative analysis weighs the evidence between two or more ideas, situations, or products and makes a claim based on evidence about which one is best. What's best for one group may not be best for another, so this is important to define up front. For example, if Jessamyn's research points to autonomous vehicles producing significant cost-savings, the decision to go with AV may be *best* for the company. However, it may not be the *best* for the drivers who would be replaced. In order for a comparative analysis to be effective and ethical, the items or issues under comparison must be measured by the same standards.

Causal Analysis

A **causal analysis** looks at why something happens or could happen. Often this variety of formal report analyzes effects or what might occur if a particular decision is made. In other cases, the causal analysis considers what already took place to help decision-makers understand how to prevent future problems or take advantage of opportunities. For example, if important machinery breaks down in an industrial business, a causal analysis is often conducted to shed light on what happened. The report helps the business determine what to do going forward to protect the machinery and the people who operate it. Such a report might also allow the business to plan for better maintenance or replacement of the machinery.

In Jessamyn's case, a causal analysis might investigate what is causing the current fleet to break down as a part of measuring reliability and revenue. She might also need to look at ethical issues of autonomous cars or liability issues with insurance companies and how these issues might impact the company's bottom line. Other reports may narrow the focus to a central cause, such as why the company loses money every January, why employee turnover is high, or why certain cars contribute more to air pollution.

Determining cause requires careful analysis. There may be direct and indirect causes. There may be one cause or multiple contributing factors. The researcher must consider what is relevant and avoid rushing to judgment. Causality must be clearly demonstrated through cause and effect evidence. Beware of confusing correlation (two things being connected by circumstances) and actual causation (one thing directly impacts something else).

Feasibility Analysis

A **feasibility analysis** helps determine if a strategy, plan, or design is possible. Is it a good idea for a business or client? Is it economically justifiable? Will the strategy, plan, or design produce the desired results? A feasibility analysis can be invaluable for a business that is weighing the possible benefit of a risky decision. In the example of the organization considering the best option for providing healthcare for its employees, a feasibility analysis might determine whether the organization can afford to go with the best provider and package.

Jessamyn's formal report for her boss is primarily a feasibility analysis. Her job is to determine if autonomous cars are a financial, marketable, and operational solution to the fleet's problems. To make a solid recommendation, she will have to look closely and honestly at both the strengths and weaknesses of using autonomous vehicles. On a personal level, Jessamyn finds the idea of driverless vehicles unnerving, but she needs to set aside her opinion as she collects and presents her data.

The technical communicator must objectively assess the possible benefits or drawbacks of a particular course of action, without allowing their personal opinion to cloud the final conclusions. A feasibility analysis considers alternate points of view in the decision-making process. The best feasibility studies will weigh the pros and cons of the collected data before recommending a course of action. Beware of all the ways bias can sneak in when you interpret data or draw conclusions. Analysis requires a steadfast commitment to objectivity.

The Steps of a Formal Report

This section outlines steps to create a report. Familiarize yourself with the different sections so you can be productive during each step.

Develop a Plan

To develop a plan, ask yourself three questions: How much time do I have? Who do I need to talk to? What information do I need first?

Before you dive into the deep work of your report, give yourself ample time to plan. Consider how much time you have and what you need to accomplish. If you don't know, you need to confirm the deadline for the report with your manager.

Often, a formal report will involve multiple contributors. Generate a contact list for others involved in the project, and if necessary, determine what part of the report they will be completing. Formulate a basic outline of how you'll complete the project, even if it may change later. The rest of this section offers more steps that can help you develop a plan that you can customize to the project.

Jessamyn's outline helps determine what steps to take and in what order. She makes a list of everyone she needs to talk to and calculates how much time it will take to gather and analyze the information from various departments. She builds in a little extra time to her total — 20 percent should do it — because she knows that collaborative work takes longer. With this in mind, Jessamyn sets reasonable deadlines for herself and others.

Like Jessamyn, if you want to stay on target, you need to begin with a question. Sometimes your boss determines the question when requesting the report. Other times, you determine the best course of action, beginning with a question of inquiry. Take a moment to consider the main question that you are trying to answer. This typically leads to other smaller questions, which should be addressed in the analytical section of your report.

Jessamyn's main question is whether it is feasible to add autonomous cars to the fleet. As she searches for an answer, many other questions arise:

- How much would a fleet of autonomous cars cost?
- How would they operate? Are they safe?
- Would they save the company money on repairs, insurance, or staffing?
- What type of fuel and maintenance would they require?
- Would the community, their customer base, support the idea?
- Would they be likely to increase company revenue?

The challenge is to determine which questions directly relate to the issue. Jessamyn needs to prioritize her questions. One way to do this is to carefully consider the report's purpose.

Determine Your Purpose and Scope

To determine your purpose and scope, ask yourself: What is my report intended to do? What are the boundaries for my research?

Asking *why* will lead you to the **purpose** of the report. You can think of the purpose as similar to a thesis in your academic essays. Your purpose explains why the report exists and what it's about. Establishing a clear purpose early in the project will help you stay focused and communicate clearly. Often, reports will have a primary purpose and a secondary purpose. For example, if the primary purpose of a comparative analysis is to consider two different building designs for a future business location, a secondary purpose might be to introduce a third design option.

In Jessamyn's case, her boss wants to know if autonomous vehicles are a better option for Tomorrow's Taxi Company. The primary purpose for her report is to determine whether making a change will lead to greater profits. A secondary purpose of the report could be to determine if there are other factors that they need to consider to produce greater profits.

Scope refers to the type and amount of information included in your report. At some point, you will need to decide what belongs in the report and what does not. You can arrive at your project's scope by asking what type of information the end user needs and does not need. Too little information leads to an uninformed decision. Too much information can be overwhelming, unnecessary, and a waste of time.

Identify Your Audience

To determine your audience, ask yourself: Who will be the primary user of this report? Is there a secondary audience?

Your audience determines the tone and language of the report. Use language that is understandable to the majority of your users. If you are using technical terms that are not common in the field in which you are writing, you need to define them. Knowing as much as you can about your audience can also help you determine your tone of voice and word choice. Usually, this means using neutral, unbiased language that is accessible based on your audience's level of technical expertise.

See **Chapter 1** for more on creating a user profile.

Jessamyn's boss or a committee may be the primary audience, but the document might also be read by other departments, such as human resources or finance. Rarely will someone read a report from start to finish. Your audience is likely to read certain sections that are relevant to them, depending on their relationship to the problem and their decision-making responsibilities within the organization.

Most of Jessamyn's audience knows very little about autonomous cars, though many know about traditional ones. Most terms specific to the auto industry will be easily understood while those specific to the new technology will require explanation.

State the Issue

To identify the issue, ask yourself: What is at stake? What problem am I trying to solve?

Stating the issue for yourself can help you stay focused during your project. For your formal report, create a short, specific issue statement to guide you. This statement should result from the steps that came before, so form it after considering your purpose, scope, and audience. For example, if a technical communicator were completing a causal analysis regarding a business's loss of productivity, they might state the issue as follows: "The factors that led to a 15 percent loss of employee productivity during the past fiscal year are reversible by providing additional training for supervisors."

Jessamyn's purpose is to determine the feasibility of autonomous cars. Why? Because the current fleet is becoming expensive, contributing to air pollution, and reducing the company's revenue. As Jessamyn has done here, aim to keep your statement of the issue direct and short. It will help you stay on track as you begin your research.

Conduct Research

To begin conducting research, ask yourself: What sources will reliably give me the information I need?

The type of research will depend upon the type of report and your field, but it generally falls under two categories: primary research and secondary research. **Primary research** is the type that you collect yourself directly from a source, such as through interviews, surveys, or observations. **Secondary research** is the use and synthesis of previously collected data — other people's surveys, studies, opinions, or observations.

Whenever possible, it's important to combine primary and secondary research. Secondary research helps get a full background understanding of your topic. Primary sources help you add to what is already known and build your credibility. Remember to explore the topic from a variety of angles.

Jessamyn thinks her company needs to conduct surveys in the community to see if their customer base will support the idea of autonomous vehicles. This is an example of primary research. A survey would help add validity to Jessamyn's recommendation by bringing in a local voice. Ideally, she examines surveys done by other credible sources and considers them along with the data she collects on her own.

To accompany the community survey responses, Jessamyn needs to gather and organize specific data on the current fleet, so she interviews the Department of Motor Vehicles (primary research). She also gathers financial reports and estimates from other departments, as well as current accident statistics and studies on driverless vehicles, as these are readily available from reliable sources (secondary research).

Quantitative and Qualitative Research

Research is generally organized into two main categories that appeal to different parts of our brains. **Quantitative research** involves objective forms of reasoning, including the use of facts, surveys with yes-no answers, and numerical data. **Qualitative research** examines more subjective forms of reasoning, including the use of opinions, interviews with open-ended questions, and case studies of specific situations. Depending on the issue and the recommendation, one form of research might be better suited for your report. Or you might choose to include both types of research (figure 3).

Jessamyn knows that much of her research will focus on facts and numbers, such as direct cost and accident statistics. Yet there are qualitative elements that are essential to consider. Jessamyn will consider customer satisfaction, expert opinions, and ethical issues of autonomous vehicles, all of which could impact revenue.

Research Types	Characteristics
Qualitative Research	▸ Subjective experience ▸ Based on opinions, observations, case studies ▸ Interview selected individuals
Quantitative Research	▸ Objective evidence ▸ Based on facts, statistics, numbers ▸ Survey random sampling of people

Figure 3. Most reports require a combination of quantitative and qualitative research. Quantitative research aims to measure or prove something. Qualitative research aims to describe or give depth to a topic.

Objectivity and Subjectivity

See **Chapter 5** for more on research methods.

Researchers need to practice objectivity and recognize when they, or the sources they consult, have moved into subjective interpretation. **Objectivity** means to arrive at an understanding of a topic based on external evidence or verifiable facts. **Subjectivity**, on the other hand, means to consider a topic based on personal perceptions and interpretations.

In Jessamyn's case, an objective statement would be "Autonomous vehicles reduce air pollution," which she can back up with fact. A subjective statement would be, "Autonomous vehicles will scare away customers." While that might be a reasonable conclusion, there's no data on that yet. It's easy to cross over from objectivity to subjectivity without realizing it, which is why it is so important to analyze the information you find.

Analyze the Information

To analyze the data, ask yourself: What is this information telling me? What does it mean?

Here are some additional questions to help you consider the information you've gathered:

- Is it thorough enough and consistent with the criteria I've established?
- Does it help answer the focus question?
- Is it enough to draw a conclusion and make recommendations?
- Have I presented the information ethically and without bias?

Once you have considered these questions, you can also consider the levels of evidence (figure 4). **Levels of evidence** (sometimes called a hierarchy of evidence) are assigned to studies based on the quality of their methodology. In other words, studies are evaluated by how rigorous and precise their research methods are. These categories are used in evidence-based medicine, but it can also help you analyze data you're collecting for any kind of evidence-based report.

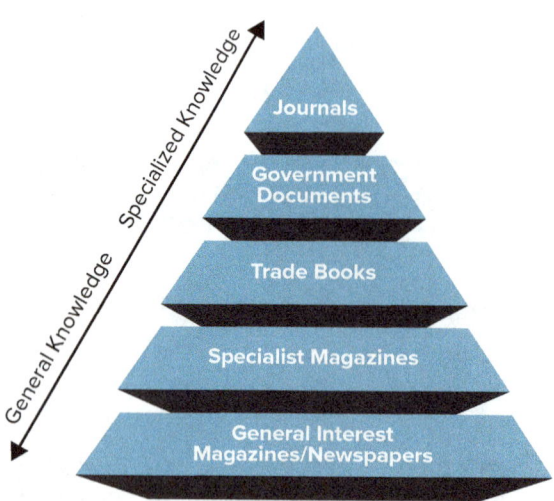

Figure 4. Peer-reviewed academic journals are the highest level of evidence because they are produced by experts in the field and reviewed and evaluated by experts prior to publication.

When considering what information is essential to your report, remember your scope. Information that merely adds to the length or variety of the report is unnecessary. After spending so much time collecting data for this report, Jessamyn struggles to decide what is relevant and what is not. This struggle is not a sign of failure. At this stage, Jessamyn may need to take a draft of the report to a trusted colleague who can look at it with fresh eyes and provide feedback.

Draw Ethical Conclusions

To draw ethical conclusions, ask yourself: Have I remained objective? Does the research drive my conclusions?

After analyzing your data, it is time to consider what the information tells you about the strengths and weaknesses of the idea or the cause of the concern. Let your research drive the conclusions. It's important to look at the information without bias and to be fair and honest in the treatment of the material, even if it does not align with your preferences or your boss's preferences.

Despite her initial hesitation, Jessamyn recognizes the value of autonomous vehicles and supports the idea of using them to replace the current fleet. However, the evidence doesn't demonstrate their clear advantage. The technology is new and expensive, and the regulations regarding the vehicles are fluid. Essentially, the vehicles are still in the pilot phase. Her job is not to talk her boss into her preference or stack the evidence in favor of it. Instead, she must view and present the information rationally and ethically for the best interest of the company.

Decide on Recommendations

To make a recommendation, ask yourself: What is the best option based on the research?

Most varieties of long reports include a recommendation. Base your suggested course of action on what you've concluded from your analysis. Again, remember your purpose. Form your recommendation on the best option or most reasonable, demonstrable cause. Sometimes you will not be able to make a recommendation due to limited information. Sometimes the study does not yield a definite conclusion. Your recommendation might be conditional or tentative, depending on other factors.

See **Chapter 3** for more on effective visuals.

In order for your recommendations to be convincing, you need to show the connection between your findings and your suggested actions. Don't make recommendations based on your feelings or impressions. Instead, show how your suggestions directly result from your analysis of the data. The users who study your document need you to convince them that your recommendations are reasonable, so highlight the connection between data and recommendations. Be overt, and don't assume that the connection is clear. Often, applying some graphical representation of the data from your research can help to establish your recommendations.

Based on her research, Jessamyn knows now is not the right time to add the high-tech vehicles to the fleet, but she sees the potential in a few years' time. The information suggests that the industry will eventually head in this direction and that the company will need to be ready when the time comes. She decides to recommend that the company begin a slow transition process, but only if the technology continues to improve.

Writing the Formal Report

As you write the report, ask yourself: Do I have all the parts I need and do I have them in the expected order?

The report consists of front matter, the body, and end matter. The following example provides an outline that can be adapted for just about any formal report (figure 5). Even though the sections may be called different names depending on the type of report or the field you're working in, they serve similar purposes.

Outline for Formal Report

1. Front Matter
    a. Cover letter or letter of transmittal
    b. Title page or cover page
    c. Abstract or executive summary
    d. Table of contents

2. Body
    a. Introduction
    b. Background and definitions
    c. Purpose and target audience
    d. Methodology
    e. Scope
    f. Findings
    g. Interpretations of findings
    h. Summary
    i. Evaluation of findings
    j. Recommendations
    k. Conclusion

3. End Matter
    a. Bibliography/references/works cited
    b. Appendix
    c. Glossary
    d. Index

Figure 5. This outline shows the most common sections in formal reports. This chapter will explore each in more detail.

Front Matter

Front matter introduces the report's contents. It also helps guide users to relevant information in the report. Since most users will be looking for specific information, they need to be able to locate it easily. Front matter can consist of the letter of transmittal, title page, table of contents, and abstract.

- The **letter of transmittal** is written to the user or users who requested the information (figure 6).
- The **title page** includes the title of the report, the authors and their organization or department, the person or organization for which it was prepared, and the date.
- The **table of contents** lists the various sections of the report and their page numbers.
- The **abstract**, or executive summary, is a brief summary of the report that includes the problem, method of analysis, results, and conclusion or recommendation.

Jessamyn has a draft of her front matter, but her table of contents needs a little work. Take a look at the model that follows to see if you notice what needs improvement before this goes to her boss (figure 7). In addition to the annotations on the model, you may have noticed some consistency issues in the headings. The subheading "Safety Concerns and Controversies" is under the "Safety" heading, so the repetition of "safety" is unnecessary. Jessamyn should aim to keep her headings as concise as possible. Turn to the end of the chapter to see how she revises her table of contents.

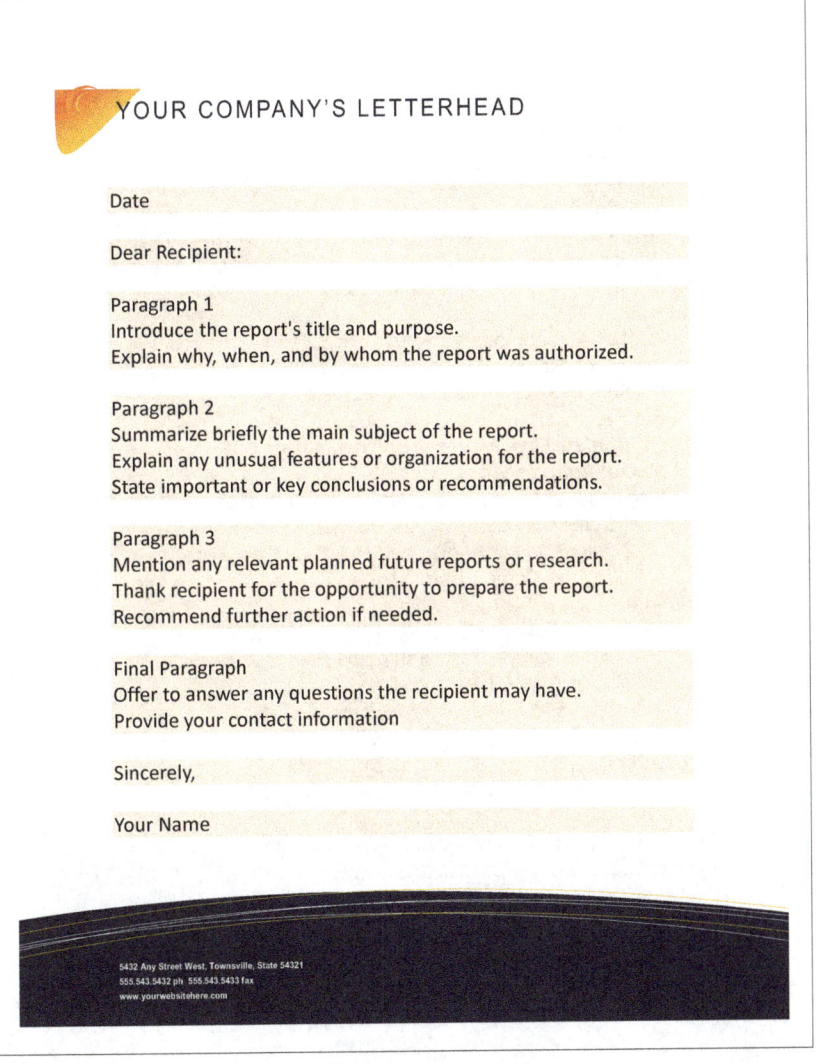

Figure 6. This model provides guidelines for a standard letter of transmittal.

Practical Models for Technical Communication

The page numbers are not properly aligned.

The three recommendation options use faulty parallelism. The options are formatted and punctuated differently from each other and are not italicized like others of the same heading level.

The bold text makes the table and figure look like sections of the report. The font and spacing of the table of contents is large and forces the list of tables and figures to be too close to the other material.

TABLE OF CONTENTS
Executive Summary……………………………iii
Introduction………………………………………………1
    Methodology……………………………………1
        Limitations……………………………………1
Background………………………………………………1
    What is an Autonomous Vehicle?…………………………………………2
Findings………………………………………………..3
    Cost of Autonomous Vehicles……….3
    Insurance Rates…………………….3
    Maintenance……………………………….3
    Safety……………………………………….4
        Safety Concerns and Controversies…….4
    Market Analysis……………………………….4
    Regulations…………………………………….5
    Cost Comparison…………………………6
        Discussion of Known and Unknown Cost Factors Affecting the Comparison……….7
Conclusion……………………………………….7
    Recommendations……………………….8
        Option One – Partnership and Pilot……..8
        Option Two: Test Vehicles…………..8
        Option #3 – Partial Replacement……8
Works Cited……………………………….10
Appendix A……………………………………12
Table 1: Estimated Revenue for an Autonomous Vehicle Fleet…………………………..…………………..6
Figure 1: Society of Automotive Engineers Automation Levels………………………..…………12

Figure 7. To avoid errors on your table of contents, use the automatic table of contents feature in Word. The mistakes you see here are a result of manually typing the table of contents.

Body of Report

The report consists of an **introduction** that describes the problem and defines the purpose, scope, background for the topic, and methods of analysis. If terms require definition, they will be included in the introduction. If there are five or more terms, these will be included in a glossary instead, which is located in the end matter.

Methodology explains how you gathered data, including what tools you used, what sources you consulted, and what research strategies you defined. This section is where you explain how you went about assembling your report. Establishing your method does two things. First, it helps you control the scope of the analysis. Second, it helps the user to understand the process used to arrive at conclusions in the report. This is important because users often want to consider the value of data and analysis in light of the methodology.

You can see how Jessamyn begins her report with a draft of the methodology section (figure 8). Note how the design makes it easy to scan the areas to be evaluated, as well as the limitations for the report. Jessamyn's introductory statement helps the user understand how she is connecting the purpose of the report to the specific areas of evaluation. This is her first draft of the section, though. She still needs to polish it up a little more. Turn to the end of the chapter to see how she revises her entire report.

The introduction is followed by the **main body**, which includes the collected data, analysis of the findings, or results (figure 9). This section is followed by a conclusion.

The **conclusion** ties the results together and can continue at length if it includes steps for implementation or a proposed plan. When requested or appropriate, recommendations are made as part of the conclusion. Results include background on the issue, data, expert opinions, and an interpretation of the material. Essentially, this section presents what you learned that will help the end user make a decision. The specifics of the results will vary depending on the type of report.

Jessamyn's report ends with recommendations (figure 10). She describes three possible options and then concludes with an evaluation of these options.

> While the bullets do break up the material visually, nine bullets are a bit much for the reader to absorb. Jessamyn should consider limiting her list to seven items or fewer.

> Parallelism in lists is another way to increase readability. Jessamyn should revise to make sure every bullet begins with a similar part of speech.

Methodology

To weigh actual costs vs. benefit(s) of this option, the following areas must be considered:

- The annual cost of the current fleet in routine maintenance, repairs, insurance, and fuel
- The annual cost of labor to drive and maintain the current fleet, as well as train new drivers
- Estimated opportunity losses (lost revenue) for downed vehicles
- The initial cost of replacing the current vehicles with autonomous ones
- The estimated annual cost of the autonomous fleet in routine maintenance, repairs, insurance, fuel/energy, and operation
- The safety risks and benefits to clients
- Market reaction
- Potential regulatory changes or restrictions within the city and state
- The estimated gross revenues of the autonomous fleet vs. the known revenues of the current fleet

Limitations

This technology is new and while several companies are working to produce these vehicles, many are still in the development phase. There are few vendors for driverless vehicles at this time and the estimated costs to purchase, insure, and maintain them are estimated or theoretical.

Figure 8. Jessamyn has determined criteria for her methodology, but she needs to shorten her bulleted list for readability. Her inclusion of limitations, however, is a good move. It shows her awareness of the complexity of the topic.

for the vehicle are similar to what we see now, with the notable exception of the hardware and software specific to the driverless package. Other

Findings

Cost of Autonomous Vehicles

Today, the cost of driverless vehicles is significant, ranging from $225,000 to $1,000,000. The software and hardware packages are the costly portion, ranging from $70,000 to $150,000 (Lienert). According to Kevin Clark, the CEO of Delphi Technologies, "the cost of that autonomous driving stack by 2025 will come down to about $5,000 because of technology developments and (higher) volume" (as cited in Lienert, 2017).

The cost of LIDAR is already declining. Velodyne, the primary producer of this technology, indicates that it will cut the $8000 cost of its most popular sensor in half. Given that one vehicle likely has more than one sensor, the cost reduction is significant (Davies, 2018). This is due, in large part, to investments from automotive leaders like Ford. Many companies, such as Tesla, are busy designing their own sensors or finding ways to adapt without the LIDAR to cut costs, driving Velodyne to solve the cost issue. The industry is aware that the high prices are a significant barrier to advancement (Davies, 2018).

Insurance Rates

At this time, insurance rates are higher than expected, largely due to liability in the event of an accident with this unknown, high profile technology, as well as the replacement cost of the vehicle. As AV's become common, the rates are expected to drop dramatically since over 90% of accidents are the result of human error. In time, liability insurance may be the only need for most drivers. Laurence Burns, a retired executive for General Motors, now advises insurance companies like Allstate. He indicates that driverless cars could be the "demise of the car insurance industry." This is because the cars will not experience the same frequency or severity of accidents (McMahon, 2018).

Maintenance

Many of the vehicles are current models that have been modified, such as the Toyota Prius, Lexus RX450H, and Chrysler Pacifica. The sensors and parts to make it autonomous are developed by and purchased from various tech companies. With a modified vehicle, the parts and repairs

Annotations:
- Heading 1 is used for main sections of the report.
- Heading 2 is used for subsections under the main section.
- Jessamyn may want to consider using heading styles that are more distinct from each other to help the reader scan for important information.

Figure 9. The results section of a formal report is often labeled as "Findings."

conservative and will yield the lowest revenue while allowing the community time to adjust and time to retrain or reallocate drivers. The third

Recommendations

The following options are the most feasible at this time:

Option One – Partnership and Pilot

"Corporation X" seems to be the U.S. automotive company most eager to release a fleet of AV's. They've developed partnerships with a few other companies in order to pilot their vehicles and are interested in using Tomorrow's Taxi Company as well. For the first year, they would provide the thirty-eight vehicles. Tomorrow's Taxi Company would be responsible for maintenance and energy costs, insurance, as well as monitoring staff. They would oversee any issues with the vehicles, make changes and upgrades, provide parts, and train our staff. They would receive .5% of fare profits for this period for the use of the vehicles. At the end of the contract period, it could be renegotiated for another year if the technology is still needing improvement (which would likely be the case) or Tomorrow's Taxi Company would have the option to negotiate a purchase for the vehicles at a discounted rate.

Option Two – Test Vehicles

Under this scenario, Tomorrow's Taxi Company would lease-to-own two driverless vehicles from "Corporation A" at a rate of $20,000 per month for a period of six months. For the first six months, the corporation would handle the monitoring of the vehicles remotely. After the trial period, the company would have the option of extending for another six months or paying the balance on the vehicles and purchasing the monitoring equipment. If leased for an additional six months, then an end-of-term buyout of return of vehicles would be required.

Option Three – Partial Replacement

In this option, Tomorrow's Taxi Company would replace five of its vehicles that have the highest mileage with AV's and purchase the monitoring equipment at an estimated cost of $1,200,000. This would include replacing the two minivans currently used in the hilltop community, as these are experiencing significant wear and tear on brakes. The company would not reap the same benefits as replacing the whole fleet, but would have the opportunity to do a trial run. The first option is the most aggressive. Though the vehicles would not be purchased initially, it does require commitment to the concept. Once the drivers and current vehicles have been reallocated to another division or become unavailable, it will be difficult to return to previous operational systems. The second is the most

Not all feasibility reports will require multiple options.

These paragraphs are getting a little too long. Jessamyn should break these up to make the text more readable.

Figure 10. The recommendations section of the formal report is likely to get a lot of attention. Be sure to provide a clear statement about what should be done.

End Matter

End matter includes anything after the main body of the report. Examples of end matter include some or all of the following items:

- A **bibliography** is a list of the sources used for research in the report. This could be a list of "References," if citing in APA, or "Works Cited," if using MLA. There are many other documentation styles that are industry specific. The title and format will depend upon the citation style.
- An **appendix**, or appendixes if you have more than one, provides information that offers further explanation or reference. Appendixes may include maps, complicated formulas, specific questions and answers in a survey, or reports that were referenced in the body. These extras may be of interest to specific users who want to better understand how you came to your conclusion or to verify your methods. When writing about information that appears in the appendix, be sure to provide a parenthetical reference, like so: (see Appendix A). Be sure each appendix is given a title and, if there is more than one appendix, a letter.
- A **glossary**, an alphabetized list of specific terms with definitions, can be included if your report has more than five terms that need to be defined. Otherwise, the terms can be defined in the introduction.
- An **index** is a list of specific items or terms within the body and the page numbers where these items or terms appear. An index enables users to search the report by topic.

See **Chapter 5** for more on documentation styles.

Checklist for Revision

As a technical communicator, you need to keep your project's scope in mind so that you provide only the most relevant information in the final draft. This is also the time to think carefully about the end users of the report. People are busy, and reports are written in sections to make large amounts of information easy to skim. Fortunately, the report's organization can help you focus during revision.

Where once you saw only the complexity of an issue, now you have that same problem broken down into parts. Revising sections means you can examine small units of information individually rather than the whole, unwieldy beast you wrestled with at the beginning of the project. Large projects will benefit from having a checklist to make sure you have all the parts you need. Try this checklist for revision to get you started:

- ☐ **Title:** Does the working title still reflect the report's revised content?
- ☐ **Table of Contents:** Are all sections in the report listed in the table of contents? In reviewing the table, do you see any sections that should be added, relocated, or removed?
- ☐ **Headings:** Are the headings specific to each section's content and consistently styled using three levels of headings?
- ☐ **Introduction:** Does the introduction set up the context with enough background, discuss any methodology or limitations, and present a guiding purpose statement?
- ☐ **Body:** Does each section in the body stay focused on one relevant topic? Do the recommendations describe the option(s) in enough concise detail so the outcome can be fulfilled in a timely, practical, and efficient way?
- ☐ **Visuals:** Is each visual communicating a key message in the most effective way — bulleted lists, tables, graphics, etc. — and with a consistent visual style?
- ☐ **Citations:** Is every source accounted for in your text, in your visuals, and in your bibliography?

Revised Formal Report

Take a look at the revisions Jessamyn made in her final formal report (figure 11).

Jessamyn Sanchez, Business Development
Tomorrow's Taxi Company
1111 NE Rogers Dr.
Averagton, AZ 62000

November 15, 20XX

Morgan Milford, CEO
Tomorrow's Taxi Company
1111 NE Rogers Dr.
Averagton, AZ 62000

Dear Mr. Milford:

Enclosed is my report, Feasibility of the Implementation of Driverless Vehicles, for your review. As the technology is new and constantly advancing, it has been an interesting subject to explore. Thank you for giving me this opportunity and allowing me to further my knowledge and the knowledge of our organization on this very important issue.

As you will see, some of the information included in this report is theoretical. There are limitations to the analysis in that the vehicles are not yet commonplace and primarily operated by large automotive and technology companies. Taxi companies are just beginning to join these ranks, and I'm confident that the material enclosed will help Tomorrow's Taxi Company decide when to make a similar leap.

I would like to thank our marketing, service, payroll, and human resources departments for contributing to this report. Their knowledge and data are essential to our decision and I'm grateful

Callouts:
- Get straight down to business with the first sentence of your letter of transmittal.
- Acknowledge the limitations as well as the purpose of your report.
- Show that you are a good colleague by naming the individuals and departments that contributed to your report.

Figure 11. Revised Formal Report

for the hard work they put into gathering and analyzing this information.

If you need any additional information, please do not hesitate to contact me. I can be reached at *sanchez.j.@ttc.com* or 555-222-1000, ext. 200. Thank you for your time and consideration in reviewing this proposal.

Sincerely,

Jessamyn Sanchez
Director of Business Development

Running head: FEASIBLITY OF DRIVERLESS VEHICLES   1

Feasibility of the Implementation of Driverless Vehicles

Jessamyn Sanchez

Tomorrow's Taxi Company

Author Note

Funded by and prepared for Tomorrow's Taxi Company

Correspondence related to this report should be addressed to Jessamyn

Sanchez, Business Development

1111 NE Rogers Drive, Averagton, Arizona 62000

Contact: jsanchez@tomorrowstaxi.com

The report's title should convey its purpose and scope. Notice that the first, last, and all other important words are capitalized in this title. This is called headline-style capitalization.

The title page should indicate who prepared the report and provide contact information.

FEASIBLITY OF DRIVERLESS VEHICLES 2

Table of Contents

Abstract 3
Introduction 4
Methodology 5
    Limitations 5
Background 6
    What is an Autonomous Vehicle? 9
Findings 10
    Cost of Autonomous Vehicles 10
    Insurance Rates 10
    Maintenance 11
    Safety 12
        Concerns and Controversies 12
    Market Analysis 14
    Regulations 15
    Cost Comparison 17
        Discussion 19
Conclusion 20
Recommendations 21
    Option One – Partnership and Pilot 22
    Option Two – Test Vehicles 22
    Option Three – Partial Replacement 23
References 25
Figures 28

FEASIBLITY OF DRIVERLESS VEHICLES

Abstract

Due to the age and cost to maintain its current fleet, Tomorrow's Taxi Company looks to determine the feasibility of replacing their current vehicles with autonomous vehicles. The technology is new and still developing but is expected to be safer for customers and more cost effective to operate. Research suggests that these expectations are likely true, but the cars are not yet readily available and affordable.

The primary players in this field are large automotive and technology companies with large amounts of capital and industry support, though they are beginning to offer their vehicles to other companies, such as taxi and delivery services. It is clear, however, that the market is moving quickly in this direction and that costs, which are quite high at this time, will become more accessible within the next few years.

It is recommended that the company begin cautiously transitioning into the driverless market and preparing its business model and employees for this change.

The abstract is sometimes called an executive summary.

The report summary ends with recommendations.

FEASIBLITY OF DRIVERLESS VEHICLES   4

Introduction

Over the past two years, Tomorrow's Taxi Company has been experiencing an increased financial burden arising from the wear and tear on its aging fleet of vehicles. The concerns include an increase in expense for parts and labor, as well as missed opportunities for revenue due to unavailable cars. Employee turnover has added to this cost. Drivers expect a consistent number of work hours and a certain level of tips and many have left to work for other companies, leading Tomorrow's Taxi Company to more frequent hiring and training expenditures. The company is one of many that experience this ongoing issue.

One option that businesses are considering is the addition of driverless vehicles, which are promoted as more cost effective and less prone to many of the issues that result from driving practices. Cities across the world have implemented pilot programs of both semi and completely autonomous fleets with the goal of cutting down on labor expenses, increasing safety (lower liability costs), and promoting a more technologically advanced (and often more environmentally sound) service to its consumers. This report investigates the economic feasibility of replacing Tomorrow's Taxi Company's current vehicles with an autonomous fleet.

FEASIBLITY OF DRIVERLESS VEHICLES 5

Methodology

To weigh the actual costs vs. benefits of this option, the following areas must be considered:

- The annual operational cost of the current fleet in labor, routine maintenance, repairs, insurance, and fuel
- The initial cost of replacing the current vehicles with autonomous ones
- The estimated annual operational cost of the autonomous fleet in labor, routine maintenance, repairs, insurance, and fuel/energy
- The estimated gross revenues of the autonomous fleet vs. the known revenues of the current fleet, including estimated opportunity losses (lost revenue) for downed vehicles
- The safety risks and benefits to clients
- The potential regulatory changes or restrictions within the city and state

Limitations

This technology is new and while several companies are working to produce these vehicles, many are still in the development phase. There are few vendors for driverless vehicles at this time and the estimated cost to purchase, insure, and maintain them are estimated or theoretical.

The methodology section explains what research was used and how the research was conducted.

The methodology section often recognizes the limits of the available research.

Background

According to the National Highway Traffic Safety Administration (NHTSA), in 2016 alone 37,461 people were killed in traffic accidents ("Automated Vehicles," 2019). Ninety-four percent of these crashes were the result of human error. Many companies are hoping to reduce these staggering statistics by shifting the work and responsibility of driving from the driver to the vehicle through an increase in automated features. In theory, fully autonomous vehicles will solve many of the problems that often arise from (or are at least made worse by) human error, such as accidents, traffic congestion, and wear and tear. There is even hope that there will be a decrease in fuel consumption leading to reduced costs and lower greenhouse gas emissions (https://navya.tech/en/).

Most new vehicles already offer options designed to lessen some of the driver's burden. Various sensors, cameras, and other high-tech systems are in place to help the person detect objects in their blind spots, park the vehicle, stay in their driving lane, and are even able to steer and brake in an emergency. The NHTSA highlights six levels of automation as established by the Society of Automotive Engineers, with zero being no automation and five being fully automated (see Figure 1). In general, the automotive industry has progressed to a level three, conditional

FEASIBLITY OF DRIVERLESS VEHICLES 7

automation, meaning a driver is necessary but not required to monitor the environment.

    Society still has far to go before driverless cars will be exiting the driveway of the average person. However, technology in this field, as with so many others, is advancing rapidly. Marc Andreessen, a venture capitalist in Silicon Valley, suggests that software is "eating the world" (as cited in Husain, 2017, p. 129). It will continue to get smarter, more capable and adaptive, and more independent because of its ability to "reason through complex processes" and "consume more information than any human could ever conceive of" (Husain, 2017, p. 129). While a fully autonomous vehicle (level five) is not yet commonplace, the NHTSA predicts that the world is heading in that direction and that we will likely see vehicles with automated driving systems (ADS) that are more highly functional (even independent) and more frequently used as early as 2025. Ford is hoping to release one to the market as early as 2021 (Pyzyk, 2018).

    However, quite a few technology companies and auto manufacturers are already piloting level four and five vehicles in cities throughout the country, even the world. Ford, for example, has begun piloting their vehicles by using them as a delivery service. In Florida, the company has partnered with Domino's Pizza. This enables them to see how the vehicles operate in a congested area without the risk of transporting a person

---

This is an example of an indirect citation using APA style.

The first citation is for a print source. The second is for an online source, which is why it does not have a page number included. Both are in APA style.

FEASIBLITY OF DRIVERLESS VEHICLES   8

(Pyzyk, 2018). Google's company Waymo is also moving forward quickly, having begun their "self-driving car project" in 2009 (https://waymo.com/). Pilot programs such as these are popping up all over the globe.

In preparation for the inevitable future of their industry, taxi companies have been among the first to participate in piloting driverless cars in urban areas. One such company is NAVYA, based in France. According to their CEO, Christophe Sapet, people view cars in a different way today, particularly young people, many of whom do not even have a driver's license, let alone a car. "What really interests them," he says, "is having mobility solutions that are operational 24 hours a day, 7 days a week, ensuring their safety and well-being at a reduced cost" (https://navya.tech/en/). Rides are arranged as shared or private and paid through a smart phone app, eliminating the need for a time-consuming middleman. Their cabs provide not only transportation but onboard Wi-Fi, tourist information, and even the ability to buy theater tickets and things of that nature in route. They are currently piloting their program in Las Vegas. Other companies, such as Uber and Lyft, are conducting similar pilot programs on a smaller scale.

FEASIBLITY OF DRIVERLESS VEHICLES   9

What is an Autonomous Vehicle?

An autonomous vehicle (AV), also called driverless, is one that can operate without a driver present (level five). They accomplish this feat through a large array of sensors, cameras, global positioning systems (GPS), and a mix of software and hardware intended to replicate (or improve upon) human drivers.

The most interesting and important features are the sensors. They serve as the eyes and ears of the vehicle, telling the body when and how to react. One of the most commonly used is LIDAR (light detection and ranging). This is a "remote-sensing [method] that can use light in the form of a pulsed laser to measure ranges" (Husain, 2017, p. 33). The sensors and software are "designed to detect and predict the behavior…of all road users," including cyclists and pedestrians (https://waymo.com/). The vehicle is expected to know its exact proximity to any object at any time, the speed limit, where it is and where it's going.

Formal reports define essential terms. Notice how this single-sentence definition expands into a longer definition.

Define unfamiliar terms and acronyms by providing parenthetical definition immediately afterwards.

> Notice the use of headings to organize information. The first is Heading 1. The second is Heading 2.

> Formal reports rely on quantitative research.

Findings

Cost of Autonomous Vehicles

Today, the cost of driverless vehicles is significant, ranging from $225,000 to $1,000,000. The software and hardware packages are the costly portion, ranging from $70,000 to $150,000 (Lienert). According to Kevin Clark, the CEO of Delphi Technologies, "the cost of that autonomous driving stack by 2025 will come down to about $5,000 because of technology developments and (higher) volume" (as cited in Lienert, 2017).

The cost of LIDAR is already declining. Velodyne, the primary producer of this technology, indicates that it will cut the $8000 cost of its most popular sensor in half. Given that one vehicle likely has more than one sensor, the cost reduction is significant (Davies, 2018). This is due, in large part, to investments from automotive leaders like Ford. Many companies, such as Tesla, are busy designing their own sensors or finding ways to adapt without the LIDAR to cut costs, driving Velodyne to solve the cost issue. The industry is aware that the high prices are a significant barrier to advancement (Davies, 2018).

Insurance Rates

At this time, insurance rates are higher than expected, largely due to liability in the event of an accident with this unknown, high profile technology, as well as the replacement cost of the vehicle. As AV's become

FEASIBLITY OF DRIVERLESS VEHICLES   11

common, the rates are expected to drop dramatically since over 90% of accidents are the result of human error. In time, liability insurance may be the only need for most drivers. Laurence Burns, a retired executive for General Motors, now advises insurance companies like Allstate. He indicates that driverless cars could be the "demise of the car insurance industry." This is because the cars will not experience the same frequency or severity of accidents (McMahon, 2018).

Maintenance

    Many of the vehicles are current models that have been modified, such as the Toyota Prius, Lexus RX450H, and Chrysler Pacifica. The sensors and parts to make it autonomous are developed by and purchased from various tech companies. With a modified vehicle, the parts and repairs for the vehicle are similar to what we see now, with the notable exception of the hardware and software specific to the driverless package. Other vehicles that are developed from start to finish primarily by the tech companies will be more unique and access to parts will be more limited.

    The driverless vehicles are expected to save maintenance costs in some ways just by removing the driver. Humans ride their brakes, idle unnecessarily, do not maintain a consistent (or often legal) speed, park too close to their neighbor, etc. These are issues an AV will not experience.

Provide specific details to make your report stronger.

FEASIBLITY OF DRIVERLESS VEHICLES

Safety

> A concrete example helps illustrate the ways that AVs are superior to human drivers.

As previously mentioned, autonomous vehicles are expected to be safer than current vehicles. Humans are prone to distraction and overreaction. They don't react when they should or, in theory, as quickly as a computer. AVs are programmed to follow the rules of the road. They do not speed up when a light turns yellow, cut people off in traffic to make a turn they almost missed, forget to use their blinkers, text or drink and drive, or suffer from road rage. When all of the reasons accidents happen are considered, it is easy to understand the capacity for AV's to reduce accident statistics and save lives.

Concerns and Controversies

> An ethical presentation of data will not ignore potential problems that might result from the proposed solution.

Many people, customers and drivers alike, fear the reliance on software. It's natural to compare personal smart devices and computers to the technology in the vehicle. Think about how often phones or laptops have to be restarted to get them to cooperate. Many companies have had similar concerns that their technology may not yet have "learned" enough to be self-sufficient. They've chosen to keep a driver in the vehicle to take over in an emergency and the technology requires this (level three or four).

This idea to keep the human in the driver's seat misses the main reason for wanting to remove them in the first place. Tesla, one of the companies that has chosen to form their own technology in lieu of LIDAR,

FEASIBLITY OF DRIVERLESS VEHICLES

uses a system they've named "Autopilot." In May 2016, a Tesla sedan ran into the broad side of a tractor trailer while the Autopilot was engaged. "Tesla said that Autopilot didn't register the white side of the trailer against the bright sky" (as cited in Simonite, 2016). Neither Autopilot nor the driver braked.

Uber is testing the waters in the driverless taxi industry in Arizona, California, and Pennsylvania. Their vehicles also have a driver ready to take control of the wheel. In March 2018, one of their vehicles struck and killed a pedestrian in a crosswalk. Its LIDAR sensors apparently detected her at .9 seconds before the impact, which should have been enough time for the machine to react; however, it struck her without slowing down or attempting to maneuver (Kerr, 2018). In theory, the driver should have taken control in both of these scenarios. "The leader of Google's autonomous-car project, Chris Urmson, has said his company's experiments have proved that humans can't be relied on to do that, because they quickly come to trust that the car knows what it's doing. All the same, Tesla CEO Elon Musk has said his company's data suggests Autopilot is twice as safe as human drivers" (Simonite, 2016).

Other companies, like Waymo (Google's company) and NAVYA, have been operating their vehicles without a driver for some time now and have advanced their technology significantly. The cars have been in accidents,

The formal report includes alternate points of view.

FEASIBLITY OF DRIVERLESS VEHICLES   14

though few, but nearly all were the result of cars with drivers who don't follow the rules. As these vehicles become more commonplace, which will be several years yet, these types of accidents should rarely occur.

Market Analysis

Pew Research Center recently surveyed over 4,000 to determine their comfort and concerns with advances in technology, including driverless cars and technologies that would replace human workers. They learned that "Americans are roughly twice as likely to express worry (72%) than enthusiasm (33%) about a future in which robots and computers are capable of doing many jobs that are currently done by humans" (Smith and Anderson, 2017). The majority believe that such advances will create a larger income inequality and that "the economy will not create many new, better-paying jobs for humans if this scenario becomes a reality." With specific regard to autonomous vehicles, 39% expect the roads will be safer while 30% think the vehicles will make them less safe... In fact, 56% indicated that they would not ride in a driverless car (as cited in Smith and Anderson, 2017).

The concerns related to job loss are valid. In many industries, job loss in one area due to automation tends to increase jobs in others. In the taxi industry, this is not necessarily the case. Any revenue growth model must take this factor into consideration, both for the community's positive

---

Annotations:

- Credible research is important. Pew Research Center is well-respected and the sample size is large enough to provide meaningful results.

- Surveys are a good way to quantify the subjective experiences of how people feel about driverless cars.

- An ethical approach to a report like this one will acknowledge the impacts of a decision, whether intended or not.

FEASIBLITY OF DRIVERLESS VEHICLES 15

response and to satisfy the ethical concerns of contributing detrimentally to the economy in the area.

In cities where the vehicles are more common and these issues have already been addressed, the market reaction is more positive. Studies show that 65% say they would ride in an AV and of those that have already ridden in one, 90% were satisfied with the experience (Jones, 2018). Much of this is due not only to the lack of fear but the lower cost. Without tipping a driver, they save a few dollars each trip. It's also an advanced technology, which younger generations find exciting and progressive.

Regulations

The regulations regarding automated driving systems (ADS) are not prohibitive. The NHTSA has established guidelines for states to help them safely integrate these vehicles onto their roadways. Most states require an application process for test vehicles, as well as licensing and registration that includes more detailed information on vehicle ownership.

Regulations will likely adapt on state and federal levels as the technology progresses and as our government begins to realize that auto and tech companies looking at their bottom lines may not always be relied upon to move forward with caution or with the public's safety in mind. There are suspicions that some have moved forward with pilot programs even when they knew of flaws in their systems and that a lack of rules is to

> Be sure to back up claims with research that is cited.

> The formal report does not avoid complexity. The entire purpose of a formal report is to analyze a topic in depth.

FEASIBLITY OF DRIVERLESS VEHICLES 16

blame (Wolverton, 2018). The NHTSA wants this technology to move forward, as many do. Yet it is hard to regulate what is not yet understood, and, in this case, it is hard to fully understand it until tested under true conditions — an interesting conundrum.

    State and federal governments are relying on the private sector to test the waters in this area and seem to be developing regulations in a reactive rather than proactive way. Arizona, for example, did not initially require companies wanting to use AV's on the roads to have any special licensing or permit. After Uber's fatal accident, that changed quickly. Their governor, who had previously seen California as over-regulated and inhibitive for progress, promptly took charge after the incident to pass an executive order requiring special licensing, permits, and safety regulations more closely aligned with the NHTSA's guidelines. One of these regulations is that the vehicle "will stop automatically or take other safety actions in case the self-driving function fails" (Stern, 2018). In general, states are beginning to realize the need to follow NHTSA's guidelines or be more stringent for the time being. The technology has advanced enough and has enough government support that it is not likely to undergo any regulatory changes that would halt the use of the vehicles or make their use significantly prohibitive for companies.

FEASIBLITY OF DRIVERLESS VEHICLES   17

Cost Comparison

If Tomorrow's Taxi Company were to replace all vehicles, the numbers would look tentatively like the following:

	No. Cars	Driver/Operator No.	Driver/Operator Annual Cost	Fuel/Energy	Maintenance	Insurance	Revenue	Net
Current Fleet	40	65	2,710,000	237,104	50,536	151,609	6,551,020	$3,401,771
AV Fleet 20XX	38	10	360,000	94,605	40,858	163,435	7,062,020	$6,403,122
AV Fleet 20XX	38	8	380,000	94,605	34,049	149,815	7,062,020	$6,503,551

Table 1: Estimated Revenue in Dollars for an Autonomous Vehicle Fleet

This would be in addition to the purchase price of a complete fleet of driverless cars, which today would be very costly, approximately $9,400,000 for a fleet equaling the current size, plus the monitoring equipment.

Driver/Operator: Numbers include annual salary, benefits, and worker's compensation insurance for the drivers. Operators will replace the drivers, taking on the role of dispatching and monitoring the fleet remotely.

Fuel/Energy: Tomorrow's Taxi Company's current vehicles are hybrids that average 50 MPG, driving approximately 2,339,000 miles per year, at an average of $2.90 per gallon. The AV fleet is electric and will get the equivalent of 93 MPG at a rate of $3.48 per 100 miles. The electric fleet should be able to drive approximately 2,522,150 miles per year.

Maintenance: Numbers for the current fleet are actual. Numbers for the AV fleet assume 3% of the IRS mileage reimbursement rate. This number reduces to 2.5% in 2021 with the assumption that the cost for

> **Lead into a list with a complete sentence followed by a colon.**

> **Use numbers and bullets to emphasize important information and make it more visually appealing.**

FEASIBLITY OF DRIVERLESS VEHICLES

parts, which are now quite expensive, will drop as mentioned. AV's are also expected to experience less wear and tear in most areas. This assumes the following:

1) Human error causes most accidents that result in repair.
2) Inconsistent driving practices, such as braking patterns, unnecessary idling, and not maintaining speed will be reduced in an AV.

What isn't clear, is the cost for parts and ease of replacement. While they are likely to spend less time in the service bay, they could be costly once there.

Insurance: This number is unknown for the AV fleet. Here it is estimated at the same rate of 12% of the IRS mileage reimbursement rate as it would be for a traditional vehicle. The numbers are expected to be lower as the technology becomes more established.

Revenue: These numbers are based on a rate of $2.80 per mile for both the current and AV fleet.

Net: This number is related to the direct cost of operating the vehicles and does not include numbers for any other operating costs for the company.

FEASIBLITY OF DRIVERLESS VEHICLES   19

Discussion

The largest savings is in operational labor. The company would need to maintain a dispatcher and a small staff to monitor the position and condition of the vehicles. By removing the drivers, the company not only lowers the costs of annual salaries (an average of $34,000 per driver), but also benefits and worker's compensation insurance.

There is also a significant reduction in fuel. On average, drivers spend 30% of their time driving their routes looking for customers. The AV's are accessed via an app, which cuts down our fuel/energy expenses related to non-revenue drive time. The electric vehicles also have a higher MPG equivalent.

The change in labor structure also enables the company to keep the taxis on the road more often. The AV's eliminate downtime from breaks, sickness, and the general inattention humans have that software doesn't. The estimated annual amount of lost revenue from driver-related issues is approximately $30,600.

There is, however, one large ethical concern — what to do with the 65 drivers currently employed. As a small, family-owned business Tomorrow's Taxi Company has prided itself on personalized service to its customers and employee satisfaction. Any changes made will need to include some accountability in this area. Human Resources, Business

> Notice how topic sentences frame and guide the ideas within each paragraph.

> Ethical concerns should be addressed directly in formal reports.

FEASIBLITY OF DRIVERLESS VEHICLES 20

Development, and Marketing departments recommend completing a cost-benefit analysis of the following:

- Early retirement packages for those drivers age 55 and over
- In-house job retraining for 10 current drivers able to assume the role of fleet monitors
- Expansion of personal driver service, catering to the elderly, handicapped, and elite clientele who need or prefer human assistance
- Off-site job retraining in conjunction with both Averagton Community College and City Technical School

Conclusion

The country's leading legal and financial consulting firms, Deloitte, has witnessed changing trends in the automotive industry and sees an expansion in what they call the "mobility ecosystem":

> Across the ecosystem, from auto retailers to insurance to finance, businesses are watching automotive industry trends and realigning to remain competitive and viable as the future of mobility unfolds. Companies that are preparing now—deciding where to play, transforming operations, implementing new technology, refocusing talent and marketing—will be well positioned to win. ("Future of Mobility," 2018)

Annotations:

- Keep bulleted lists short.
- If a direct quote exceeds forty words, it should be formatted as a block quote without quotation marks.

FEASIBLITY OF DRIVERLESS VEHICLES   21

The company will need to be prepared to make the transition to fully autonomous vehicles, likely within the next five years. The companies currently entering this field are large players in the automotive or technology industries, with the knowledge and financial resources to venture into this unchartered territory. Driverless vehicles are still a work in progress, though the progress is impressive. They are a new and exciting technology but also a frightening one for many. For that reason, they are under a microscope with various authorities and the community in general, and a company like Tomorrow's Taxi Company may be highly vulnerable should one of the vehicles have a safety issue. However, the taxi industry will be the first to integrate AV's regardless of such concerns, so it is important that the company move forward proactively but cautiously.

Recommendations

Given the relatively small size of the company, and its financial limitations in comparison to industry leaders, Tomorrow's Taxi Company would need to tread carefully into the area of driverless vehicles. The autonomous projects that require a driver's presence have been excluded from the discussion for safety and cost reasons. The following options are the most feasible at this time:

Even if a topic has many pros and cons, be sure to state the conclusion clearly and confidently.

A recommendations section typically follows the conclusion in a formal report.

A feasibility report ends with an analysis of options.

> This report includes additional research to support each option under Recommendations.

FEASIBLITY OF DRIVERLESS VEHICLES

Option One – Partnership and Pilot

"Corporation X" seems to be the U.S. automotive company most eager to release a fleet of AV's. They've developed partnerships with a few other companies in order to pilot their vehicles and are interested in using Tomorrow's Taxi Company as well. For the first year, they would provide the thirty-eight vehicles. Tomorrow's Taxi Company would be responsible for maintenance and energy costs, insurance, as well as monitoring staff. They would oversee any issues with the vehicles, make changes and upgrades, provide parts, and train our staff. They would receive .5% of fare profits for this period for the use of the vehicles. At the end of the contract period, it could be renegotiated for another year if the technology is still needing improvement (which would likely be the case) or Tomorrow's Taxi Company would have the option to negotiate a purchase for the vehicles at a discounted rate.

Option Two – Test Vehicles

Under this scenario, Tomorrow's Taxi Company would lease-to-own two driverless vehicles from "Corporation A" at a rate of $20,000 per month for a period of six months. For the first six months, the corporation will handle the monitoring of the vehicles remotely. After the trial period, the company would have the option of extending for another six months or paying the balance on the vehicles and purchasing the monitoring

FEASIBLITY OF DRIVERLESS VEHICLES   23

equipment. If leased for an additional six months, then an end-of-term buyout of return of vehicles would be required.

Option Three – Partial Replacement

In this option, Tomorrow's Taxi Company would replace five of its vehicles that have the highest mileage with AV's and purchase the monitoring equipment at an estimated cost of $1,200,000. This would include replacing the two minivans currently used in the hilltop community, as these are experiencing significant wear and tear on brakes. The company would not reap the same benefits as replacing the whole fleet but would have the opportunity to do a trial run.

The first option is the most aggressive. Though the vehicles would not be purchased initially, it does require commitment to the concept. Once the drivers and current vehicles have been reallocated to another division or become unavailable, it will be difficult to return to previous operational systems. The second is the most conservative and will yield the lowest revenue while allowing the community time to adjust and time to retrain or reallocate drivers. The third enables the company to keep 100% of its profits but with less oversight and assistance from the manufacturer, it encompasses higher risk. All three provide the opportunity to test the waters of the industry before fully committing financially.

> This paragraph provides a summary evaluation of all the options.

FEASIBLITY OF DRIVERLESS VEHICLES

The concerns with the technology over safety, regulatory changes, and cost are there; however, at the current pace, these will soon be of little issue. The AV's, though not without their accidents, are still safer than Tomorrow's Taxi Company current vehicles. As the numbers are tracked, studies done, and more people experience the technology, a company with a driverless fleet will find itself well-positioned to succeed.

FEASIBLITY OF DRIVERLESS VEHICLES   27

http://www.phoenixnewtimes.com/news/arizona-governor-doug-ducey-

creates-rules-for-self-driving-cars-10191122

FEASIBLITY OF DRIVERLESS VEHICLES   26

Lienert, Paul. (2017, December 05). Cost of driverless vehicles to drop

dramatically: Delphi CEO. Retrieved from

FEASIBLITY OF DRIVERLESS VEHICLES   25

References

Automated Vehicles for Safety. (2019, June 18). Retrieved from

https://www.nhtsa.gov/technology-innovation/automated-vehicles-safety

Davies, C. (2018, January 02). A key part of many autonomous cars just got a

huge price cut. Retrieved from https://www.slashgear.com/velodyne-lidar-

puck-autonomous-car-more-affordable-02513340/

Future of mobility trends. (2018). Retrieved from

https://www2.deloitte.com/us/en/pages/consulting/solutions/future-of-

mobility-trends-industry-

ecosystem.html?id=us:2ps:3bi:confidence:eng:cons:::na:DUCmzMfu:10777

03201:76690968088885:bb:Future_of_Mobility:Future_of_Mobility_BMM:n

b&msclkid=8b6b23a0a7e81f9f1d7f79664ec6db34

Husain, A. (2017). *The sentient machine: The coming age of artificial*

intelligence. New York, NY: Scribner.

Jones, J. (2018). Driverless vehicles gain support. Retrieved from

https://howardresearch.driverless.vehicles-support*

Kerr, D. (2018, March 23). Was Uber's driverless car crash avoidable?

Experts say yes. Retrieved from https://www.cnet.com/news/was-ubers-

driverless-car-crash-avoidable-some-experts-say-the-self-driving-car-

should-have-braked/

This reference list uses APA style. Information is fictionalized for this example. The costs, unless otherwise cited, are also fictional. Your research, on the other hand, should be real.

This entry shows how to cite an online source in APA style.

This entry shows how to cite a book in APA style.

All information from outside sources, including graphs and visuals, must be cited. Publications from federal agencies such as the National Traffic Safety Administration are in the public domain but should still be cited.

FEASIBLITY OF DRIVERLESS VEHICLES

Figures

Figure 1: Society of Automotive Engineers (SAE) Automation Levels

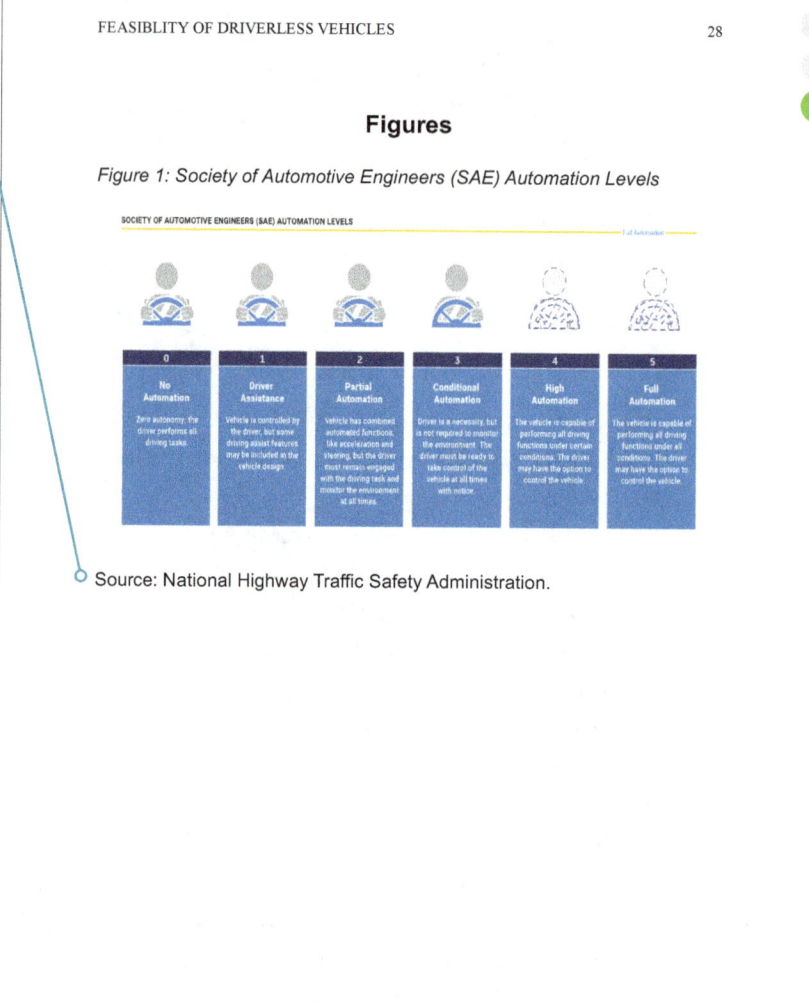

Source: National Highway Traffic Safety Administration.

Conclusion

Formal reports draw on all of the skills that are explored in this text and allow you to bring all of your expertise together to create an impactful finished document. Your use of multimodal strategies, visual elements, effective definitions, concise descriptions, accessible instructions, convincing proposals, and analytical formal reports can get you closer to providing a solution.

Jessamyn's report ultimately led her boss to refrain from the purchase of autonomous vehicles, but it earned her a promotion. She's now known within the company for her capacity to conduct research, analyze information, and clearly communicate complex ideas. Your future is equally bright. Even when cars can drive themselves, technical communication will always need a human touch.

Moving from problem to solution is not a process you'll complete just once. If you're good at it, you'll continue to find communication challenges throughout your career. These challenges are opportunities to deliver helpful messages that will benefit others and bring you satisfaction in your work.

The next chapter explores how technical communication functions in the everyday professional world. The chapter includes a range of professional profiles from people who use technical communication in their work, whether or not they were hired as technical writers. In the final pages of this book, you will learn how professionals develop and apply their skills in technical communication and how you might use your growing technical communication abilities in the future.

Chapter 12
Make Technical Communication Work for You

Abstract: Not everyone becomes a technical writer, but most of you will use technical communication in your chosen fields. At its core, technical communication is a specific message with a clear purpose for a certain audience. Strong communication skills are essential to success in any field you choose. Everything you write is a reflection of you and the company or organization you represent. Learning how to bridge the gap between student and professional work can be useful as you advance your educational pursuits and eventual careers. This chapter explores job postings that require technical communication skills and introduces profiles of professionals who use technical communication in their work. This chapter offers practical advice from a diverse group of professionals who have found ways to make technical communication work for them.

Looking Ahead

1. Bridging the Gap

2. Applying Your Skills

3. Meet the Professionals

4. Tips for Success

Bridging the Gap

Understanding how your undergraduate classes connect to each other and your profession informs your educational path. For example, once you see how this technical communication class helps you write an individualized educational plan (IEP) for one of your future students or how a sociology class helps you become a better manager, then you have begun synthesizing your education with your professional life. While it's true that some elements of your undergraduate work may never apply professionally (and other elements will surprise you with their relevance), strong communication skills are fundamental to all higher wage, postsecondary careers.

From the Classroom

Educational requirements and standards in the classroom are set by your professors. We tell you what to write, how much, and when it's due. We model what to do and ask you to practice it before you prepare it. You're even asked to explain the choices you made and how you got to the answer. If you stumble or fall along the way, we're there to show you the variety of ways to learn from the experience and rise to your feet.

This type of guided instruction prepares you for the workforce because it gives you something to lean into and trust along with the flexibility and curiosity to adapt to new expectations and solve problems. There are many protections put in place to help you achieve success. Worst-case scenario—you don't pass a class. Even with these protections in place, it's important to establish good habits to carry with you beyond the classroom.

To the Professional World

Professional demands vary widely. The principles taught in this book aim to encourage discipline and resourcefulness as you continue to learn skills for technical communication. It's important to tap into and trust your resources because you'll need many of these skills as you train for new positions and accumulate professional experience.

You may have noticed that we focus more on longevity skills like writing with clarity and understanding design instead of using specific software. That's because software advances so quickly and companies often choose different programs. Instead of giving you step-by-step tutorials on how to use specific programs to create documents, we provide you a foundation to work from and build upon.

Some lessons from your technical communication course are universally applied, others will need to be modified to fit the specifics of your workplace, and a few will become surprisingly relevant years from now. Your education enhances your workplace training and gives you the flexibility that comes with having the right tools for the right situations.

Applying Your Skills

The following sections provide sample job descriptions and show how you can communicate your skills to a potential employer.

Technical Communicator

Technical communicator is a specific job that clearly uses the skills from this textbook, along with those you might learn if you major in technical writing. But the places in which you can expect to use technical communication daily might surprise you. Technical communicators are people working in fields where they communicate specialized knowledge. Most did not major in writing or communications, but all use those skills in their fields. For example, the Bureau of Labor Statistics (BLS) shows us that the highest paying postsecondary certificate careers are all jobs that require clear communication:

- Electrical and electronics repairers, powerhouse, substation, and relay
- First-line supervisors of firefighting and prevention workers
- Insurance appraisers, auto damage
- Aircraft mechanics and service technicians

This list shows some of the higher-paying careers you can enter by earning the appropriate certificate. Here is a job posting that requires technical communication, even though that's not the job title (see figure 1).

> Repair and technician work often requires updates, recommendations, estimates, and organizing with coworkers and clients. This is why you typically see communication listed under requirements instead of preferences.

Preferred Attributes and Qualifications
- Years of related experience: Over one year and up to three years of electronics-related experience.
- Degree and or certification from college/technical/vocational school.
- Ability to solder.
- Understanding of static control procedures.

Job Title: Electronic Repair Technician
Location: Portland, OR

Position Summary
Test, modifies, upgrades, performs basic repairs, calibrates, aligns, and burns-in assigned Client computer hardware to the component level following established procedures and guidelines.

Position Responsibilities and Essential Functions
- Tests, repairs, burns-in, and cleans assigned equipment in accordance with policy.
- Interacts on a professional level with associates, participating in Job circles, cross-training, and information sharing.
- Monitors assigned equipment safety stock levels and maintains enough equipment to meet safety stock requirements.
- Maintains work area and assigned test equipment and tools.
- Follows department static control procedures.
- Maintains required paperwork, records, and documentation.
- Performs other related duties as assigned.

Qualifications and Requirements
- Good mechanical skills including soldering skills.
- Ability to use troubleshooting strategies.
- Ability to lift up to fifty pounds.
- Ability to work effectively in a team environment.
- Communicates effectively verbally and in writing.
- Ability to adapt to shifting priorities and be able to handle multiple tasks simultaneously.
- Must be able to demonstrate an understanding of basic electronic theory.

Figure 1. Even though "technical communicator" is nowhere near the job title, notice how communication and technical skills, are part of the job's requirements.

The following list is, according to BLS, associate's degree-level careers with median wages above $70,000 per year, all of which include communication skills as a requirement:

- Dental hygienists
- Radiation therapists
- Diagnostic medical sonographers

The following six-figure careers typically require a bachelor's (or higher) and, you guessed it, require excellent communication skills and, in some cases, the ability to write and publish research:

- Computer and information systems managers
- Architectural and engineering managers
- Petroleum engineers
- Nurse practitioners
- Physician assistants
- Nurse anesthetists
- Psychiatrists

Technical Writer

Technical writers provide instruction manuals, informational reports, and other documents communicating complicated technical information to specific audiences. These are people who have chosen to use their writing skills as technical writers. Most majored in related fields like English, media, or communications. However, enterprising engineering students have learned to minor in technical writing as a strategy to stand out in competitive fields.

You can also choose to major in technical writing itself, with a minor in science, engineering, or other technical fields. Whether or not a technical writer majors (or minors) in a technical field, they mostly write for engineering and computer industries and need to be familiar with these industries.

In this next job posting, notice all the highlighted areas that align with principles from this textbook (figure 2). What other connections do you see with the course material?

Practical Models for Technical Communication

> This is the Problem-Solution Framework all over again.
>
> Revision is not just something you do in school.
>
> This is what technical communication is all about.

written and verbal).

Preferred Qualifications:
- Technical certification(s) in networking area
- Familiarity with XML authoring tools.

About the Position:
The Information Experience (iX) team develops and delivers the content our customers need to install, manage, and configure Juniper products. The iX team strives to deliver the right product information in the appropriate medium to meet customer requirements and exceed their expectations. The iX team is looking for a motivated candidate to create product documentation, including comprehensive concepts, examples, tasks, and reference information for Juniper's routing, switching, and security products.

Responsibilities:
- Work with Engineering, System Test, Program Management, Customer Support, Product Line Marketing, and other key stakeholders to identify requirements and develop best-in-class documentation.
- Incorporate feedback from customers and internal sources to improve existing and future documentation.
- Work with editors and other writers to identify and implement standards and process improvements to enhance product documentation and usability.
- Participate in special projects or initiatives outside the scope of regular tasks.
- Follow established style and process guidelines to provide consistency and completeness.

Minimum Qualifications:
- Bachelor's degree, Entry-level position with 1-2 years of technical writing experience and/or previous internship.
- Knowledge of networking technology areas, such as switching, routing, and security.
- Ability to transform complex technical concepts and specifications into easily understood, clear tasks and concepts.
- Excellent communication and collaboration skills (both

Figure 2. Scan this job description paying special attention to the highlighted portions. Notice how the requirements of this position align with the content covered in this textbook.

Freelance/Contractor

One of the realities of living in the twenty-first century is the rise of the "gig" economy. While the gig economy has a variety of examples, from peer-to-peer ridesharing jobs to listing how much work you'd do for $5, there is one commonality among these jobs: they are all **freelance/contract work**. Temporary, contract, and freelance labor is attractive to organizations because the people filling these posts are less expensive than full-time, permanent workers and, often, aren't even employees. Some people like this style of employment for the flexibility and the chance to work in diverse fields.

While contract or freelance work can be exciting (travel writing, for example, sounds exhilarating), this is a type of work with many feast or famine cycles. A good freelancer knows how to save their money for the inevitable slow period between gigs. Inconsistent employment is the norm for freelancers. Another major factor to consider is that most freelance work requires self-motivation and discipline to find contracts and then to do the work. The ability to realistically assess and communicate the scope of a project is vital to successful freelancing.

Learning more about how to effectively navigate these types of jobs is becoming increasingly important, since the gig economy represents about a third of the job market, according to BLS estimates. However, it's hard to accurately track how many people are contract or freelance because there is so much fluctuation. Additionally, many positions come with a variety of job titles that confuse data collection. For example, your "professor" (a specific job title) might actually be an "adjunct" who is officially titled as "part-time instructor," which is actually a temporary contract position that renews every quarter or semester. On paper, it would look like the college hires a bunch of permanent part-time faculty, but the reality is completely different.

According to BLS, the following types of freelance gigs are more common:

- Arts and design (ranging from graphic design to crafts and fine arts)
- Computer and information technology (web and software designers, programmers)
- Construction and home repair
- Media and communications (tech writers, interpreters, translators, and photographers)
- Transportation (Lyft, delivery drivers)

Even if you decide that freelancing full-time is not for you, short-term contracts and freelance assignments can bring in extra money. The following example is for a graphic design freelance position at a regional radio station (figure 3). Sometimes people are surprised at how much technical communication is expected as part of "non-writing" careers.

> writing skills.
> - Knowledge of digital and print media standards and practices.
> - Ability to work within a budget.
> - A degree in Graphic Design or related field is preferred.

This requires you to be able to adapt your communication style to different types of audiences.

Get ready to write more status reports.

Job Description

All Classical Portland seeks a creative, enterprising graphic designer. The ideal candidate will be part of a collaboration where your creativity, personality, and integrity will help shape the image and branding of a dynamic radio station, helping to carry out All Classical Portland's mission to build cultural community and provide access to the arts for all. This position will conceptualize, design, and layout a wide variety of materials for internal and external use, including promotional materials and multimedia campaigns. You will act as a liaison between internal project managers and external vendors, obtaining quotes and preparing projects for outside printing companies, while keeping the internal project manager apprised of the status throughout the production process. This position is a great opportunity for fun, creative artistry. Candidates should have superior multi-tasking and organizational skills and be able to meet deadlines.

Essential Responsibilities
- Conceptualize, design, and layout a wide variety of materials for internal and external use.
- Collaborate in planning and designing an annual and monthly marketing strategy.
- Work with the Community Engagement and Management teams to create a streamlined brand identity.

Required Qualifications
- At least three to five years of design experience and a strong understanding of design fundamentals, branding, typography, and visual hierarchy in layout.
- Proficient in graphic design and layout; creative in finding solutions to design needs.
- Demonstrated ability to work both independently and collaboratively under deadline pressure.
- Proven intellectual curiosity, creativity, and rigor with strong

Figure 3. Notice how this graphic design job positing requires many of the skills you've learned in this book, and not just in visual design principles.

Meet the Professionals

The following pages are profiles of those who have bridged the gap between their education and their career. We sent out a survey to a variety of professionals who use different types of communication in their field. Note the commonalities and the areas in which flexibility comes into play.

Technical Communicator Profile

These are profiles of people working in fields where technical communication is a significant component of the job duties. Most did not major in writing or communications, but all use those skills in their fields.

Q & A with a Head of Products and Services

Q. *How do you explain your job to someone outside your field?*
A. [I] create and tell the story of our brand through useful products.

Q. *What technical documents do you feel are relevant to educating a future professional in your field?*
A. User story definition, acceptance criteria, Product Requirements Doc (PRD), Marketing Req Doc (MRD), Pitch Decks, term sheets, and machine-readable resumes.

Q. *What do you wish you'd had access to as a student training for your profession?*
A. A clue, some mentorship.

Q. *What's the biggest difference between academic writing and professional communication in your field?*
A. Writing clear, thoughtful narratives are more important in tech writing than was previously taught. The documents of yesteryear (memos, spec docs) have disappeared.

Q & A with a Designer

Q. How do you explain your job to someone outside your field?
A. [I] design underground storm and sanitary sewers.

Q. What technical documents do you feel are relevant to educating a future professional in your field?
A. The Engineers Joint Contract Documents Committee (EJCDC) Contract Documents. Understanding the front-end documents to my project and the contract itself is extremely important to understand construction and the responsibility in construction.

Q. What do you wish you'd had access to as a student training for your profession?
A. Construction Document Technologies (CDT). I have recently completed this and it would have been beneficial in college.

Q. What's the biggest difference between academic writing and professional communication in your field?
A. In college, it was stressed to keep it to the point and technical. I have found that as a professional, you have to adjust your writing to your audience. I have to explain items differently to a homeowner than I do a colleague. They only really teach the technical, but I have found that explaining in everyday terms is just as important.

Technical Writer Profile

These profiles are people who have chosen to use their writing skills as technical writers. Most majored in related fields like English, media, or communications.

Q & A with a Principal Technical Writer

Q. *How do you explain your job to someone outside your field?*
A. [I] write documentation (instruction manuals) for how to use my company's software with multiple audiences in mind.

Q. *What technical documents do you feel are relevant to educating a future professional in your field?*
A. There's so many! *The Product is Docs* [a book by the Splunk documentation team], the *Write the Docs* Slack [an online network of professionals], and *Every Page is Page One* [a book by Mark Baker] for starters.

Q. *What do you wish you'd had access to as a student training for your profession?*
A. Honestly, I wish I'd had a mentor. I probably would have jumped from support into writing sooner.

Q. *What's the biggest difference between academic writing and professional communication in your field?*
A. Having an actual editor, plus the pressure of knowing that if I mess something up, I could partially be responsible for causing a customer issue.

Q & A with a Technical Writing Instructor and Technical Writer

Q. *How do you explain your job to someone outside your field?*
A. Technical writing is clearly explaining literal information in a way that makes it perfectly understandable and usable to its intended audience.

Q. *What technical documents do you feel are relevant to educating a future professional in your field?*
A. Procedures, emails, functional descriptions, technical illustrations, specifications (both "what it is" and "how it should work"), troubleshooting trees, quick reference cards, formal reports, and articles.

Q. *What do you wish you'd had access to as a student training for your profession?*
A. An instructor who had actually done the job! Great examples of good work and explanations of how bad work specifically didn't measure up. Knowledge of word processor features like outlining, automatic table of contents, document element styles (e.g., XML tags) vs. formatting, and a really good peer reviewer.

Q. *What's the biggest difference between academic writing and professional communication in your field?*
A. There should be none, but academic writing tends to be ego-driven in tone: more words, more syllables, longer, more cumbersome sentences, incomprehensible vocabulary, and gibberish titles seems to be the rule. Also, academic work has a much higher emphasis on citing all sources both in-text and in a bibliography; technical work may give an acknowledgment somewhere or do nothing at all.

Unexpected Technical Communicators

These are profiles from others who use technical communication in unexpected ways.

Q & A with a Real Estate Broker

Q. *How do you explain your job to someone outside your field?*
A. I help people buy and sell homes.

Q. *What technical documents do you feel are relevant to educating a future professional in your field?*
A. The online courses for obtaining a license and for continuing education are horribly written. I think they were written by an attorney — very confusing language.

Q. *What do you wish you'd had access to as a student training for your profession?*
A. Maybe more real-world accounts of experiences/scenarios as part of the [real estate] curriculum, written by actual agents (or writers), not attorneys. The material is so dry and hard to get through.

Q. *What's the biggest difference between academic writing and professional communication in your field?*
A. [Real estate] is a people-based one with plenty of face-to-face time and phone interaction, as opposed to academic documents.

> **Q & A** with a **Finance Manager**
>
> **Q.** How do you explain your job to someone outside your field?
> **A.** I take care of financing vehicles for a dealership.
>
> **Q.** What technical documents do you feel are relevant to educating a future professional in your field?
> **A.** Excel [spreadsheets].
>
> **Q.** What's the biggest difference between academic writing and professional communication in your field?
> **A.** My professional communication is much shorter in comparison to academic writing.

Tips for Success

Education is a lifelong pursuit. It gives you the awareness and flexibility to meet changing job markets, technology, and to adapt accordingly. It also exercises your curiosity, which is a fundamental survival skill that keeps you interesting and hirable. Your training shouldn't stop at graduation.

Stay Current

Stay current in your field with continued education. Many careers require you to continue earning credits to maintain licensure. Even if your field doesn't have license requirements, education is a solid investment. You can attend industry conferences. Many of them offer credits for their proceedings. Look into area colleges and see what relevant classes or certifications are offered.

Become a member of industry-related organizations. Most industries have their own organizations. For instance, computer scientists and engineers can join IEEE (https://www.ieee.org). There are also associations for minorities as well. The National Association of Women Business Owners (https://www.nawbo.org) is just one example. You will find the support and resources needed for a long and productive career.

Remember to network and stay connected to other professionals. There is truth to the old adage "it's who you know" when it comes to developing new opportunities. Continued education, trade shows, conferences, organizations, and the like will provide numerous networking opportunities. Just like in college, your best resource may be sitting next to you.

Pay It Forward

In the same way that the people profiled in this chapter took time out of their day to share their experience, you should do the same. There will be times when you have more time than money, so give back your time to future professionals in your field by volunteering to share your knowledge. We learn from those who came before us. Go back to your college or university and speak to a new crop of young professionals—share your experiences. Become a mentor to someone. Sometimes, having one person believe in you can help catapult a career.

Conclusion

Use the skills you learned in this book to apply for jobs, communicate in the workplace, create and design ethical documents, and provide resolutions to problems that need them. Workplaces need employees who can think critically about information and design in this multimodal world.

This book is an introduction to a way of communicating that will serve you well throughout your career. Think of it as a building block and look for other opportunities that will help you build invaluable tools such as communication, design, and innovation. You will learn many more skills on the job. Be open to learning and new encounters. Getting a job is not the end of your journey—it's the beginning.

Be open to innovation and challenges in your careers. Remember what the Problem-Solution Framework has taught you: each of us is made to be a problem solver.

Glossary Index

The glossary index increases the usability of this book by providing definitions and page numbers where extended discussion of important terms can be found. All defined terms below can be found in bold within the text. Additionally, the bold numbers tell you where to find the definition of that term within the text. Additional page numbers direct you to where the term is explained in depth.

The index does not include every mention of a word. If we did that, the entry for technical communication would be almost as long as the book itself. Instead, we have selected the most relevant locations for these terms. Additional page numbers refer to illustrations, models, examples, and extended discussion of these relevant terms. See also directs you to a similar term within the index. See directs you to the full entry for that term.

A

Abstract: a brief summary of the entire report, including the problem, methodology, results, and conclusions.
viii, 1, 231, 260; model of, 273

Accuracy: the use of error-free information.
22, 206

Agenda: an outline of the planned contents of an in-person meeting.
166–68

Alignment: horizontal or vertical connection between separate elements that fall along straight lines.
59–60, 143; center, 60; full justification, 60; left, 59

Ambiguity: the presentation of two meanings at the same time that can lead to uncertainty.
38–9, 41

Analysis: the act of examining an object or idea closely to understand its parts and how they work.
248, 249–51; causal, 250; comparative, 248; feasibility, 250–51

APA Style: a style of writing and documentation defined by the American Psychological Association for behavioral and social sciences.
49, 115; model of, 272–96

Appendix: a section at the end of a report that provides additional information on subjects requiring further explanation or reference.
267; for proposal, 235

Audience: the group of people to whom a document or deliverable is addressed. See also user.
5, 89, 175, 183–84, 212; demographics, 13; for proposals, 227; for short reports, 236; for formal reports, 253

B

Bar Graph: a visual representation of data in horizontal or vertical bars. See also graphs.
71–72, 234

Bibliography: a list of sources used for research in a report.
267; Chicago style, 116, 117, 118, 271

C

Causal Analysis: a type of report that investigates why something happens. See analysis.

Center Alignment: a consistent connection in vertical text along a straight line at the center of a document, creating ragged left and right margins. See alignment.

Characteristics: the unique traits that make a term stand out within its class.
188; of technical communication, 8–12

Chicago/Turabian Style: a style of writing and documentation used within the publishing industry and some business and history courses.
49, 116

Chronological Pattern: a method of organizing information along a time-based progression.
67

Circumlocution: the use of evasive or excessive language to disguise one's meaning.
40

Citation: the academic convention that gives credit to the owner or creator of content and provides an ethical way to use content.
46, 48–50, 113–14; in-text, 115–17

Clarity: the use of understandable words, sentences, and organization to improve content.
15, 140, 206

Class: the category in which a defined word belongs.
187–89

Cliché: a phrase that is overused and shows a lack of originality.
148

Client: a person or organization who commissions work from a technical communicator.
11, 34

Code of Ethics: a documented set of professional or personal values to guide decisions.
27, 32, 35

Code-switching: the act of changing the way you speak to fit a situation.
159

Collaboration: an activity or project where tasks are divided among several individuals who combine their separate efforts into a final product.
73–75

Color: a visual element that results from the perception of light on the surface of an object.
63; designing with, 54; for accessibility, 58, 218

Comparative Analysis: a type of report that identifies criteria for determining the best choice from multiple options. *See analysis.*

Concise: the use of the right amount of detail and information.
20–21

Conclusion: the section of a report that ties the results together and often includes steps for implementing a solution or other recommendations.
263; for proposal, 235; for report, 240; model of, 290

Concrete Language: specific and tangible words with clear, unambiguous meaning.
192; versus abstract language, 21

Confidentiality: the state or quality of keeping information private or secure; one of the six ethical principles embraced by the society for technical communicators.
34–36

Content: the information a technical communicator wishes to transmit to their audience.
15; evaluation of, 173

Context: the setting or situation that gives words additional meaning.
182; for users, 213

Contrast: a way to create emphasis by highlighting differences between elements in a document.
58, 63

Copyright: the legal protection that exists for people who own their content.
46–47; law, 118–20

Creative Commons: an organization that provides legal designations called licenses that allow copyrighted content to be used in an "open-source" style.
47, 119

D

Data: units of information used to create meaning.
23

Definition: a statement that expresses the meaning of a word or group of words.
187–89; extended, 189–91, 192–93; parenthetical, 185–86; sentence, 187–89

Demographics: the group characteristics of an audience.
13

Description: a statement of the physical characteristics of an object.
182, 191–94

Design: the presentation of information to an audience.
52–54, 207, 215, 218; for use, 7; principles of, 55–73

Diagram: a visual representation of how objects or parts of an object fit together.
72; model of, 212

Digital Literacy: a form of technological knowledge that provides essential skills for finding, using, and sharing information.
84–85

Directive: a type of memo that issues an order to staff.
164

Dissimilarity: a visual element that creates emphasis through contrast.
63

E

End Matter: the parts of a formal report that follow the main body, which may include a bibliography, appendix, glossary, and/or index.
267

Ethics: a system of principles or morals that determine the actions of an individual or group.
29; at work, 33; professional codes, 34–37

Euphemism: a word or set of words that replace other words to blunt or soften the intended message.
39–40

Extended Definition: an explanation over multiple sentences. *See definition.*

F

Fact: verifiable information.
23

Fairness: the state or quality of treating people or situations without bias or favoritism; one of the six ethical principles embraced by the society for technical communicators.
36

Fair Use: a narrowly defined legal use of copyrighted content for specific purposes.
119

Feasibility Analysis: a type of report that helps determine if a strategy, plan, or design is a good idea based on finances, outcomes, or possibility. *See analysis.*

Feasibility Report: a technical document that examines whether a proposed idea or product is likely to succeed. *See report.*

Font: the style of a set of characters used in typesetting and design.
57–58; sans serif, 58; serif, 58, simplicity of, 141–42

Formal Report: a long document that presents solutions to complex issues involving research, analysis, methodology, results, and recommendations. *See report, formal.*

Full Justification: a consistent connection in vertical text along a straight line at the left and right margins. *See alignment.*

G

Glossary: a list of terms used in a document, located near the end.
187; model of, 189; in formal reports, 267

Graph: a visual that represents data points and allows the viewer to compare two or more variables.
71–72; bar, 71–72, 234; distorted/mispresented, 37, 44–55; line, 72

Grid: the underlying structure used to help create visual order in documents.
61

Group Work: a type of project work where multiple individuals are given a task or set of tasks to complete regardless of individual strengths and skills.
73–75

H

Heading: a word or phrase used as a title for a section of text.
64–65; Organization of, 142; for scannable design, 207–8; model of, 19, 265, 280; in table of contents, 272

Honesty: the state or quality of sticking to the facts and speaking the truth; one of the six ethical principles embraced by the society for technical communicators. See also ethics.
35

Hypothesis: an "educated guess" that serves as a testing ground for a research process.
100

I

Idiom: a phrase that has a specific meaning in one language that cannot be directly translated into another.
42

IEEE Style: a style of writing and documentation defined by the institute for electrical and electronics engineers for use in the electrical, electronics, computer science, and computer programming fields.
49–50, 116–17; professional organization, 312

Illustration: a visual representation of a physical object or concept, usually a sketch or drawing.
72

Index: a list of specific terms in a report and the page numbers where they can be found.
267

Inference: a conclusion that can be reached based on available data.
23

Instructions: a set of detailed steps that function as directions for how to complete actions successfully.
198, 202–3; best practices, 204–10; model of, 199; template, 205; versus procedures, 201

Introduction: a section of a report that describes the problem and defines the report's purpose, scope, background, and method of analysis.
263; for proposals, 232; for short reports, 240; model of, 274

J

Jargon: words and phrases, technical or otherwise, that are unfamiliar to a general audience.
43, 184; example of, 16

Judgment: opinion-based, reasonable actions based on available facts, inferences, and values.
23

K

Keyword: a specific word or phrase that relates directly to a specific topic.
146

Known-new Contract: the principle of communication where the creator begins with what their audience knows before introducing new information.
195

L

Ladder of Abstraction: a visualization of the need to move from abstract to concrete language to be precise.
21

Left Alignment: a consistent connection in vertical text along a straight line at the left margin, creating a ragged right margin. *See alignment.*

Legality: the observance of laws and regulations; one of the six ethical principles embraced by the society for technical communicators. See also ethics.
35

Letter of Transmittal: a brief document that precedes a report, informing the audience of the report's delivery.
260; model of, 261, 269

Levels of evidence: a continuum on which each piece of evidence falls, with specialized knowledge at one end and general knowledge at the other end.
256

Line Graph: a visual representation of data as points that are connected by a through line. *See graph.*

M

Main Body: the sections of a report that contain the collected data, analyses, or results.
263; in short report, 240

Medium, Media: a means of transmission to store or deliver information.
9–10, 79, 81

Memo: a printed sheet of information to be distributed or displayed internally within a workplace.
164; model of, 165

Message: the content of a document or deliverable. *See also text message.*
6, 238; illustration of, 85.

Methodology: an explanation of how data is gathered and what research strategies, tools, and sources will be used in a report.
263; model of, 264, 275

Minutes: a document that records the outcomes of an in-person meeting.
167; model of, 168

MLA Style: a style of writing and documentation defined by the modern language association for use in literature, languages, and the humanities.
48–49, 114

Mode: a style or manner in which communication occurs or is experienced, expressed, or done.
9–10, 79–80, 81

Multimedia Communication: a process involving the use of more than one means of information transmission.
10, 79

Multimodal Communication: a process involving the use of more than one method of generating content.
10, 79, 81–83

N

Name: the specific word for a term, thing, or concept.
188–89

Negation: an explanation of what a term does not mean, used to help clarify meaning.
191

O

Obfuscation: the intentional act of hiding or obscuring something's true meaning. *See also jargon.*
38

Objectivity: the use of external evidence and verifiable facts to support a conclusion.
256; in tone, 243

P

Page Design: the deliberate organization of text and images on a page. *See also design.*
55–6

Parallelism: a technique where elements in a group or list all take the same form, creating a pattern.
204; *faulty,* 189–90, 192, 262; *in instructions,* 68; *in lists,* 68, 268

Paraphrase: a restatement of information in your own words.
112

Parenthetical Definition: an explanation of a term immediately after its first use, typically enclosed in parentheses. *See definition.*

Precision: the use of clear and recognizable words to express exact meaning.
21–22, 182–83

Primary Research: new data that has not been collected before.
106, 254–55; *versus secondary,* 107

Problem-solution Framework: a flowchart that illustrates how technical communication moves from problem to solution by considering the needs of audience, purpose, and message.
ix, 5–6; *for definitions/descriptions,* 180; *for design,* 53–54; *for ethics,* 29–30; *for formal reports,* 247; *for instructions,* 202–3; *for job materials,* 126–27; *for multimodal communication,* 82–83; *for procedures,* 211; *for proposals,* 226; *for research,* 97–98; *for short reports,* 236; *for workplace communication,* 157

Problem-solution Organization: a two-part structure that describes an issue and suggests a response or resolution.
68

Procedures: an overview of the best methods required to complete a process.
198, 209–11; *best practices,* 213–15; *models of,* 200, 216; *versus instructions,* 201

Professionalism: characteristics or behaviors associated with respectful workplace conduct; one of the six ethical principles embraced by the society for technical communicators. *See also ethics.*
37

Proposal: a form of business writing that persuades someone to approve a service or course of action.
224, 242–44; *template for,* 225; *types of,* 229–30

Proposal, External: a persuasive form of business writing intended for audiences outside an organization.
229–30

Proposal, Internal: a persuasive form of business writing intended for audiences inside an organization.
229–30

Proposal, Planning: a persuasive form of business writing that suggests a method for dealing with a task. *See also proposal.*
229

Proposal, Research: a persuasive form of business writing that suggests a rationale for gathering data about a specific topic. *See also proposal.*
229

Proposal, Sales: a persuasive form of business writing suggesting that the audience purchase a particular product or service to meet their needs. *See also proposal.*
229

Proposal, Solicited: a persuasive form of business writing that has been specifically requested by its audience.
230

Proposal, Unsolicited: a persuasive form of business writing that has not been specifically requested by its audience.
230

Proximity: the spatial distance between two or more elements in a document that can create meaning.
65

Public Domain: the designation for content that is not under any form of legal copyright.
47, 119

Purpose: the reason behind a report's creation.
5, 7; for formal reports, 252; for procedures, 212; for proposals, 237; for short reports, 228; illustration of, 85; model of, 216; organization by, 128

Q

Qualitative Research: information interpreted using subjective forms of reasoning, usually involving opinions, interviews, or case studies.
255

Quantitative Research: information interpreted using objective forms of reasoning, usually involving countable data such as survey results and numerical information.
255

Quality: the measurement or degree of excellence; one of the six ethical principles embraced by the society for technical communicators. *See also ethics.*
36

R

Redundancy: the unnecessary repetition of words, phrases, or ideas.
21; example of, 20

Report, Formal: a long document that presents solutions to complex issues involving research, analysis, methodology, results, and recommendations.
246–47; model for, 262, 264–66, 269–96; outline for, 259; types of, 248–51

Report, Progress: a short document that updates an authority on the status of a project. *See status report.*

Report, Recommendation: a document that presents a suggested course of action based on research.
69

Report, Research: a short document that presents data about a specific topic.
238

Report, Sales: a short document that presents data about product sales.
239

Report, Short: a brief document that informs others about a specific objective, event, or ongoing issue.
235; elements of, 240; principles of, 242–44

Report, Status: a short document that provides an update about an ongoing situation.
238

Research: the act of search for, collecting, and evaluating information on a specific topic.
96, 99–106; advanced, 120–21; evaluating, 107–9; for job materials, 134; methodology, 279; narrowing topic of, 102; preliminary, 101; primary, 106, 258–59; qualitative, 255; quantitative, 255; secondary, 107, 255–56

Rhetoric: the artful use of language to persuade an audience.
84

Rhetorical Awareness: the act of thinking critically about the choices involved in the creation of a persuasive appeal.
84

Right Alignment: a consistent connection in vertical text along a straight line at the right margin, creating a ragged left margin. *See alignment.*

S

Sans Serif Font: typography that is simplistic and uses more separation between characters to provide a cleaner appearance. *See font.*

Scanning: looking for a specific piece of information in a document.
24; design for, 145, 207

Scope: the boundaries of what a report will and will not include.
253; for proposals, 233, 257

Secondary Research: existing data extracted from interpretations by other creators. *See research.*

Secondary User: any additional people who may access a creator's content by chance. *See user.*

Sentence Definition: an explanation of a term within a complete sentence. *See definition.*

Sequential Pattern: a method of organizing information along a logical, step-by-step progression.
68

Serif Font: typography that is decorative and contains connective flourishes that aid in faster reading. *See font.*

Short Report: a brief document that informs others about a specific objective, event, or ongoing issue. *See report, short.*

Size: a visual element of large or small items that creates emphasis through contrast.
63–64

Skimming: looking for the general or main ideas in a document.
24; tips for, 105

Subheading: a word or phrase that creates a secondary unit of information within a larger section of text.
65; models of, 19, 272

Subjectivity: the use of personal perception and interpretations to support a conclusion.
256

Summary: a one-paragraph description of an entire source. See also abstract.
111–12

T

Table of Contents: a list of the various sections in a report and their page numbers.
260; model of, 262, 272

Technical Communication: the act of creating and delivering content requiring precision, clarity, and accuracy.
3; characteristics of, 8–14; technical communicators, 307–12

Technical Document: a mode of communication, whether online or in print, that involves content designed to meet a specific need and produce a desired result.
3

Text Message: an electronic message sent from one cell phone to another.
159–60

Thesaurus: a reference manual used to identify synonyms.
20–21

Thread: the back-and-forth dialogue in an email exchange.
161

Title Page: a single page including basic information about a report, including the report's title, author(s), sponsoring organizations, and date of preparation.
260; model of, 271

Tone: the attitude conveyed by one's choice of words.
172, 243; examples of, 173

U

Usability Testing: an unbiased examination of the effectiveness of a document.
121, 215; best practices, 217–19

User Profile: a collection of information about potential audiences.
13

User: the audience for a given technical communication. *See also audience.*
11, 13–15

V

Verb Mood: the specific form of an action word that indicates whether the action or idea is happening in the past, present, or future.
204

Verb Tense: the specific form of an action word that shows how an idea is expressed, either as a command (imperative), statement (indicative), or hypothetical (subjunctive).
204

Virtual Reality: a computer-generated environment that creates the illusion that the user is somewhere else.
90

W

White Space: any space surrounding figures, tables, visuals, or text that is otherwise empty.
63; model of, 131

Work for Hire: a type of contract where a hired creator releases ownership of the content they create to a client.
118

Workplace Communication: the exchange of information that takes place between individuals or groups trying to complete a job or task.
157; types of 158–71

Acknowledgments

Chapter 4, figure 7. Used with permission from Tom Johnson's I'd Rather Be Writing podcast at (https://idratherbewriting.com/).

Chapter 9, figures 1, 10, and 15. Used with permission from Sauder Woodworking Co.

Chapter 8, figure 8. Student work is copyrighted and may not be used with permission from the publisher.

Chapter 9, figures 2 and 12. *Sexy Technical Communication* is licensed under a Creative Commons Attribution 4.0 International License at (http://distanceed.hss.kennesaw.edu/technicalcommunication/).

CPSIA information can be obtained
at www.ICGtesting.com
Printed in the USA
LVHW060751191119
637768LV00002B/2/P